To ELENI

3/14/18

An
Uncertain
Ally

An
Uncertain
Ally

Turkey under
Erdogan's Dictatorship

David L. Phillips

Routledge
Taylor & Francis Group

LONDON AND NEW YORK

This book is dedicated to Lawrence S. Phillips, my father who recently passed away. He devoted himself to healing the world, inspiring me, my children, and many others.

First published 2017 by Transaction Publishers

Published 2017 by Routledge
2 Park Square, Milton Park, Abingdon, Oxon OX14 4RN
711 Third Avenue, New York, NY 10017, USA

Routledge is an imprint of the Taylor & Francis Group, an informa business

ISBN-13: 978-1-4128-6538-8 (hbk)
ISBN-13: 978-1-4128-6545-6 (pbk)

Library of Congress Cataloging-in-Publication Data

Names: Phillips, David L. (Writer on Turkish politics), author.
Title: An uncertain ally : Turkey under Erdogan's dictatorship / David
    L. Phillips.
Description: New Brunswick, U.S.A. ; London U.K. : Transaction
    Publishers, [2017] | Includes bibliographical references and index.
    Identifiers: LCCN 2016055994 (print) | LCCN 2016057009 (ebook) |
    ISBN 9781412865388 (hardcover) | ISBN 9781412865456 (pbk.) | ISBN
9781412864732
Subjects: LCSH: Turkey--Politics and government--1980- | Erdofgan,
    Recep Tayyip. | North Atlantic Treaty Organization--Turkey. | Turkey--
    Foreign relations--1980-
Classification: LCC DR603 .P5 2017 (print) | LCC DR603 (ebook) |
    DDC 956.104/12--dc23
LC record available at https://lccn.loc.gov/2016055994

Contents

Introduction

The Republic of Turkey was forged in the crucible of conflict. As the Ottoman Empire collapsed at the end of the First World War, millions fled their homes in the Balkans, Caucasus, and Mesopotamia. The 1920 Treaty of Sèvres reduced Turkey to a rump state, encompassing merely a third of its territory under the Ottomans.

Many Turks experience what is called the "Sèvres Syndrome." They believe that the world is conspiring to diminish Turkey and divide the country. Turks developed a siege mentality. They feel beset by threats both real and imagined. Enemies lurk within and without.

While modernization propelled the West, Turkey was left behind. Mustafa Kemal Ataturk ("the father of all Turks") emerged during this moment of self-doubt. Ataturk launched the War of Independence, appealing to the wounded pride of Turks. The Great Powers were weary of fighting and did not oppose Ataturk's ambitions. The 1923 Treaty of Lausanne nullified Sèvres, restoring control of many Ottoman lands to Turkey. "Kemalism" enshrined Ataturk's Republican People's Party (CHP) as guardian of the state and secular rule.

After Ataturk's death in 1938, the CHP was taken over by corrupt and self-interested politicians. The so-called deep state—a web of security services, politicians, bureaucrats, and criminal gangs—emerged as a powerful shadow force. With the National Intelligence Agency (MIT) monitoring oppositionists, the Turkish General Staff (TGS) was the ultimate arbiter and the deep state its enforcer.

Turkey joined the North Atlantic Treaty Organization (NATO) in 1952. It emerged as an indispensable ally of the United States during the Cold War. Turkey was also an important strategic partner. As a secular, pro-Western democracy, it had a moderating influence on Muslims in Europe and served as a bridge to Muslim majority countries in Central Asia.

In the Cold War and decolonization context, Turkey like many countries was subject to leftist influence. The military conducted a coup in

1980, aimed at suppressing ideological divisions and violence. Turkey adopted a military constitution in 1982. The CHP ruled with an iron fist. Ethnic identity was denied. Sectarianism suppressed.

Despite the paramount position of secular institutions, Kemalism as a state ideology could not deny the pious character of many Turks. Political parties emerged, inspired by Islamist values. The Welfare Party (*Refah Partisi*) tried to operate stealthily, skirting secular rules in the constitution. However, the secular establishment viewed it as threat. The Constitutional Court banned the Welfare Party in 1997 for undermining secular principles.

Ethnic issues also polarized society. Turkey tried to deny the existence of Kurds, who comprise about 20 percent of the total population. They were called "mountain Turks." Kurdish villages were given Turkish names. Kurdish newborns were forced to accept Turkish names. Laws were adopted allowing land seizure and the deportation of Kurds on security grounds. The Kurdistan Workers' Party (PKK), a Marxist-Leninist group, emerged as the voice of Kurds, demanding political and cultural rights. The PKK was initially a separatist organization, which sought independence for "greater Kurdistan," encompassing Kurdish territories in Turkey, Syria, Iraq, and Iran. Beginning in the 1980s, a civil war between the Turkish Armed Forces (TSK) and the PKK claimed approximately forty thousand lives.

Turkey was increasingly divided. Kurds chafed under Turkish domination. Leftists opposed the military establishment. Muslims opposed secularists. Western-oriented Turks sought Euro-Atlantic integration, while others resented the West. Turks do not feel welcome in Europe. Nor are Turks a part of the Arab world. From the East, Turkey looks like a Western country. From the West, Turkey is decidedly Oriental.

Turkey's President Recep Tayyip Erdogan and his Justice and Development Party (AKP) won national elections in 2002. Erdogan is a skillful politician who tapped feelings of inadequacy, alienation, and frustration. He appealed to the pride of Turks, asserting Turkish nationalism. Erdogan presented himself as a man of the people and a pro-Western modern Muslim.

The United States was initially wary of Erdogan's pious personality. However, Erdogan sent all the right signals. He reaffirmed Turkey's commitment to joining the European Union (EU). He pledged cooperation with international mediators on Cyprus. Erdogan rescued Turkey's economy, which was reeling from unemployment and double-digit inflation. He built infrastructure, raised living standards, and expanded the delivery of basic services, such as water and electricity. He used Turkey's EU candidacy to justify reforms, bringing Turkey's military and bureaucratic establishment to heel. Under Erdogan, Turkey became a world power and a leading country in the G-20. He pursued an independent path, demanding international respect. The United States welcomed Erdogan's constructive role in foreign affairs and commitment to democracy.

Erdogan also had a positive approach to Turkey's conflict with the PKK. He initiated a political dialogue that led to a ceasefire in 2003. Erdogan was acknowledged for his efforts to end the Kurdish conflict. He was celebrated in capitals the world over and nominated for the Nobel Peace Prize. Many Turks heralded his accomplishments, putting him on a par with Ataturk. Turkish voters showed their appreciation for Erdogan's leadership by giving the AKP a mandate in four national elections—2002, 2007, 2011, and 2015.

However, the AKP's electoral success did not strengthen Turkish democracy. Erdogan became increasingly authoritarian and Islamist. He developed a Hobbesian view of the world. According to Erdogan, Turkey was threatened on all fronts by "terrorists." He took special umbrage at Fethullah Gulen, his former friend and ally, who lived in exile in the Poconos. Erdogan accused the Gulen movement of establishing a state within the state to undermine the AKP.

Erdogan is systematic assault on freedom of expression cowed Turkey's once-vibrant civil society and independent media. The Press Freedom Index of Reporters Without Borders ranked Turkey 151 out of 180 countries in 2016. Hundreds of journalists were jailed for "insulting Turkishness" and nearly two thousand detained for "insulting the president." Peaceful protesters in Gezi Park were victims of police brutality, which spread to sixty cities across the country.

Corruption was rampant. A corruption scandal in 2013 touched Erdogan, his son Bilal, and members of the inner circle. Wiretaps disclosed sordid self-enrichment scandals, forcing four cabinet members to resign. Erdogan accused Gulen of masterminding the leaks to embarrass him and overthrow the government.

Erdogan espoused a "zero problems with neighbors" policy. Yet Turkey found itself in conflict with every neighbor. Turkish F-16s downed a Russian war plane near the Turkish-Syrian border on November 24, 2015. The incident precipitated a major crisis in bilateral relations between Turkey and Russia. Turkey's role in Syria's civil war was a lightning rod for controversy with Russia, Iran, and the United

States. Turkey provided weapons and money to Islamist groups fighting to overthrow the regime of Syria's President Bashar al-Assad. ISIS oil was exported via Turkey, providing a lifeline to the Islamic State. Turkish journalists who reported on collusion between MIT and ISIS were thrown in jail.

US-Turkish relations reached a low point by 2016. Erdogan chastised the Obama administration for supporting the People's Protection Units (YPG), Syrian Kurds allied with the United States. Under the guise of fighting ISIS, Turkey invaded and occupied Syria in a bid to keep the YPG east of the Euphrates River and prevent the establishment of a contiguous Kurdish territory in Syria along the Turkish-Syrian border.

Erdogan insisted that the YPG was an extension of the PKK. He cynically re-started Turkey's civil war with the PKK to rally his nationalist base, creating a crisis and then presenting himself to voters as the only one who could solve it. The ruse worked. Following a setback in the first round of national elections on June 7, 2015, the AKP gained more than 49 percent in November 2015.

Erdogan systematically consolidated his power by eroding checks and balances. He wants to change Turkey's constitution and establish an executive presidency with himself at the helm. Erdogan used the failed coup of July 15, 2016 as an opportunity to strengthen his dictatorship, using pre-prepared lists to eliminate opponents. As of this writing, about one hundred twenty-five thousand military officers, police, judges, civil servants, and educators were arrested or forced to resign.

Erdogan accused the United States of masterminding the failed military coup. Further undermining US-Turkish relations, he castigated the Obama administration for refusing to extradite Gulen. Erdogan was increasingly out of control. When he visited Washington in March 2016, Erdogan's security guards assaulted a female journalist, calling her a "PKK whore."

The "new Turkey" is a tragedy. Turkey has so much potential. It is rich in natural and human resources. Turks are warm and hospitable. They have a positive nature and are forward-looking. However, Turkey is gripped by fear today. A knock on the door could signal arrest or dismissal from one's job. Turks are beset by violent conflict, fearing bombings by ISIS and civil war. The future is dark; Turks are uncertain.

Turkey is at a fork in the road. Down one path lies Islamic radicalization, dictatorship, and unrest. Another path leads to stability and security, on the basis of further integration with Europe and a renewed partnership with the United States. Turkey is critical to US foreign and security policy, if it upholds values of the Atlantic community. Turkey's direction has serious consequences for the Turkish people, as well as for NATO and the United States.

An Uncertain Ally is a contemporary political history. It relies on news accounts published in both English and Turkish rather than sociological or academic research in scholarly journals. An international, multilingual research team was invaluable to sourcing materials. Both AKP and government officials anonymously provided information. Drawing on inside sources, the book provides information not previously available to Western readers.

These pages describe domestic crises under Erdogan, including his crackdown on freedom of expression, chronic corruption, and warmongering against the Kurds. They offer a critique of Turkey's regional relations, terror ties, and its role in Syria's civil war. The book provides an unvarnished account of Erdogan's authoritarianism and steps to consolidate power after the failed military coup of July 15, 2016. *An Uncertain Ally* explains how Erdogan's hubris polarized Turkish society, alienating the military and secularists, emboldening them to try and remove him from power.

The final chapter offers policy recommendations aimed at improving Turkey's internal conditions and its interaction with the United States. Recommendations are offered to the US and Turkish governments as well as the international community. Admittedly, these recommendations are more hopeful than realistic with Turkey on its current course under Erdogan.

David L. Phillips
New York City
December 1, 2016

Part I

Domestic Issues

1

Erdogan

Democracy is like a streetcar. You get off
when you have reached your destination.[1]

—Recep Tayyip Erdogan

Recep Tayyip Erdogan comes from an industrious blue-collar family. He spent his teenage years in Kasimpasa, a poor neighborhood in the Beyoglu district of Istanbul. Erdogan struggled for his education, income, and to make his way in politics. He worked hard—and advanced.

Ahmet Erdogan, Tayyip Erogan's father, moved his family to Rize, on the northeast shore of Turkey's Black Sea coast, east of Trabzon, when his son was a small boy.[2] Rize was home to a strategic base of Turkey's naval forces, which monitored the Soviet Union's naval operations. Ahmet Erdogan was a member of Turkey's coast guard. Russia's Black Sea Fleet defeated the Turks in 1790 and fought the Ottomans during the First World War. Rize became an important early warning post protecting the Republic of Turkey and NATO from Soviet aggression.

Ahmet Erdogan was a strong disciplinarian who regulated all aspects of family life. "My father was very authoritarian. He was very instrumental in both our upbringing and character formation," said Erdogan. "The penalty for even opening your mouth to utter a bad word was very heavy."[3] Ahmet Erdogan sent his son to work in Rize's fields, collecting tea and nuts.

Rize is a socially and religiously conservative community, where Turkish nationalism in the model of Mustafa Kemal Ataturk blended seamlessly with religiosity. The residents of Rize are known for their patriotism as well as intolerance toward minorities such as Kurds, Armenians, and Jews.[4] Erdogan's mother, Tenzile, was a traditional housewife who never left her home without a headscarf (*hijab*). She spent her days cleaning the home, preparing traditional Turkish foods over a wood stove, and looking after the children. The Erdogan family was average size. Erdogan had three brothers and one sister. The siblings looked after one another.

Perched on a picturesque hillside, Rize's modest homes stretch to the seaside. Despite its natural beauty, Rize's economy was stagnant. Ahmet Erdogan decided to leave Rize for Istanbul when Tayyip Erdogan was thirteen years old.[5] They settled in Kasimpasa where tea stalls and fishmongers crowd the street fronts. Cluttered stores sell snacks, flowers, and hardware products.[6] Kasimpasa is teaming with day laborers, Roma, and new immigrants from Turkey's Anatolian heartland. The neighborhood never sleeps. Vendors are out at all hours, hustling to make a living. Erdogan joined them. "I was rather active in my childhood, actively engaging in community relations, knowing everybody in the neighborhood." He played street games, such as dodgeball and leapfrogging. His family was too poor to afford a bicycle.

Ahmet Erdogan provided his son with a weekly allowance of 2.5 Turkish lira, less than a dollar. With it, Erdogan bought postcards and resold them on the street. He sold bottles of water to drivers stuck in traffic. Erdogan also worked as a street vendor selling sesame bread rings called "simit." Simit is a staple breakfast food for Turks. It is made from dough covered in grape-juice molasses and sprinkled with sesame seeds. Baked until crusty, simit is a cheap and filling staple of the street. The act of preparing, selling, and consuming simit is a national ritual. Erdogan wore a white gown, selling simit from a red three-wheel cart with simit rolls stacked behind glass. Work was cyclical, yet ceaseless. The bread rings are baked twice a day, in the early morning and early afternoon. Vendor and customer alike take pride in the simit experience. Simit appeals to all Turks. It is classless.

Etiler is an upscale neighborhood in contrast to Kasimpasa. Its gleaming buildings are adorned with glass and chrome. Inside its gated residential communities live Turkey's wealthy, secular elite. Mustafa Kemal Ataturk lived in Etiler. Sakip Sabanci, one of Turkey's most wealthy industrialists, was a more recent resident. Butlers, drivers, and house cleaners who work in Etiler may originate from Kasimpasa, but they have a different status and lifestyle. Behind the veneer of cordial civility, Etiler's elite differ from the uneducated, unrefined, and religiously conservative residents of Kasimpasa. While Etiler feels like a street in Paris, Kasimpasa is like an urban slum in Damascus. Wealthy Etilers drive through Kasimpasa in luxury cars with tinted glass. They send the driver to run errands and shop, while remaining at arm's length from the street.

Etiler and Kasimpasa represent the fissures in Turkish society. Turkey is polarized between members of the wealthy and working classes, between secularists and pious, between the educated and uneducated. In state building, Mustafa Kemal Ataturk created the veneer of social harmony. He adopted a mantra: "Happy is he who can call himself a Turk." Turkishness was both a shared identity and a unifying concept. Beneath the surface, however, underclass resented the privileges and European lifestyle of the secular elite. The upper class looked down on the poor, whose religiosity was a threat to Turkey's secularity and coherence. Migrants and minorities were viewed with suspicion.

Access to education was also an important social determinant. Erdogan was hard-working, but not a brilliant student. He graduated from the Kasimpasa Piyale Primary School in 1965 and then received his high school education at Istanbul Fatih Imam Hatip School. So-called Imam Hatips were established in accordance with Ataturk's basic education law of 1924. They are parochial schools funded by the state, offering religious education and vocational training.[7] One quarter of the curriculum involves study of the Qur'an, the life of Muhammad, and the Arabic language. Social sciences are taught according to conservative values. Other subjects are math, literature, history, and science.[8]

Like his contemporaries, Erdogan studied the Qur'an at an Imam Hatip. He attended meetings of a nationalist student group called "Milli Turk Talebe Birligi." The group sought to raise a conservative cohort of young people to counter the rising movement of leftists in Turkey.

The Imam Hatip's principal, Ihsan Hoca, introduced Erdogan to Islamic studies. Erdogan recalls: "The teacher asked 'Who will pray?' I raised my hand and he called me over. He placed a newspaper on the floor. I said 'Teacher, we cannot pray on top of a newspaper. The table cloth may work.' The table cloth was spread across the floor and I prayed." Ihsan Hoca gave Tayyip a congratulatory slap on the back. Ihsan Hoca told Ahmet Erdogan, "We should send Tayyip to Prayer Leader and Preacher School." Ahmet Erdogan responded, "Whatever you see fit." According to Erdogan, "This is how the Prayer Leader and Preacher School entered my life."[9] Erdogan's classmates began calling him "hoca," which means "Muslim teacher."[10]

Erdogan was inspired by his experience at the Imam Hatip. When he became prime minister, he adopted a "pious generation" education project.[11] The project expanded the state-sponsored religious schooling system and broadened religious education in secular schools. While providing a more conservative cultural environment for students, the pious generation project also entrenched religiously conservative personnel in schools and the education bureaucracy.[12]

Girls attended Imam Hatips, but social relations between boys and girls were frowned upon. Erdogan adopted an egalitarian world view. He objected to the fact that girls were not allowed to wear the hijab at publicly funded educational institutions or to their work places in public administration. To Erdogan, wearing the hijab was a matter of privacy and personal choice. "In this country, ones covered and not covered should enjoy all the opportunities," said Erdogan. "They should all have the same rights—not one more or not one less."[13]

Erdogan was pious as a teenager, but not overly devout. In Kemalist Turkey, employment for students who graduated from Imam Hatips was limited. Even gifted students had few choices beyond becoming a preacher. Erdogan was distinguished by his oratorical skills. He developed a penchant for public speaking and excelled in front of an audience. He won first place in a poetry-reading competition organized by the Community of Turkish Technical Painters. His prize was five hundred lira, a princely sum. Subsequently, Erdogan was included in oratory competitions at the high school level. He acquired skills of critical thinking, preparing for his speeches through reading and research. According to Erdogan, "These competitions enhanced our courage to speak in front of the masses."[14]

He was also fiercely competitive. According to Erdogan, "I had a passion toward soccer," which we played in "the school garden." He joined a neighborhood team, becoming a member of the Kasimpasa soccer club and working part-time at an athletic facility. At seventeen, he transferred to the Camialti soccer club. According to Erdogan, "I equate soccer with politics." Soccer requires a "collective understanding." It necessitates "drive and belief in success." Erdogan is a proponent of collective action on the pitch, as well as in politics. According to Erdogan, "You have to believe." He proclaimed, "I accept that I was sinful for wearing shorts while playing soccer during those years." Erdogan did not have his father's permission to play soccer. "My father did not know, and when he learned he was furious, but then got used to it."[15]

Playing soccer did not distract Erdogan from his studies. He worked hard to pass a high school equivalence exam.[16] He wanted to pursue advanced studies at Mekteb-i Mulkiye, but Mulkiye only accepted students with a regular high school degree, not graduates of Imam Hatips. Mulkiye was known for its political science department, which trained many statesmen and politicians in Turkey.

Erdogan was admitted to the Eyup High School, a regular state school. He passed finals and received a high school degree, but his grades were not good enough for admission to Mulkiye. Erdogan was, however, admitted to Aksaray's Economy and Trade Faculty in 1982, which was associated with prestigious Marmara University. He went on to study at Marmara University's Faculty of Economics and Administrative Sciences, all the while playing semi-professional football. It was unusual for a street kid to attend high school and gain admission to Marmara University.

Erdogan's first foray in politics was in 1976 with the National Turkish Student Union, an anti-communist government-funded action group. He was charismatic and a natural leader. One of his peers commented: "This man would come ahead of all of us in the future."[17] He became the leader of a local youth branch of the Islamist National Salvation Party (MSP), a religious party founded in 1972 by Necmettin Erbakan. Erdogan regularly joined MSP rallies. These meetings were like an evangelical group gathering. They were attended by ultranationalist, conservative, and religious followers of the MSP. Speakers used ideological rhetoric to whip up the crowd. Erdogan was a good public speaker. He was acclaimed for his inspirational remarks when he introduced Erbakan one night at the Tepebasi Casino and Music Club.

Emine Gulbaran, a young girl from Tillo town of Siirt, in Southeast Turkey, was in the crowd that evening. She was a member of Idealist Women's Organization, a political group of conservative Muslim women. Emine was devoted to Islamic studies, especially teachings of Said-i Nursi, a contemporary Islamic theologian. Emine was immediately drawn to Erdogan. According to Emine, "I had a dream of a man dressed in a white suit, and was told that this is the man you would marry. That man was Erdogan."[18]

Erdogan noticed Emine from his position on stage. "At that meeting, my wife (Emine) was sitting at the front row and she drew my attention," recounts Erdogan. "I was electrified and fell in love there. She was with me at all the party meetings and activities."[19] Erdogan and Emine married on July 4, 1978. They had two daughters, Esra and Sumeyye, and two sons. Their first son was named Ahmet Burak, after Erdogan's father. The second son, Necmettin Bilal, was named after Necmettin Erbakan. All four children received strong religious education, graduating from Imam Hatips.[20] Erdogan extolled Emine's virtues: "From the moment we married to today, I was never questioned: why did I come home late (from party meetings)?"[21]

Later Necmettin Erbakan founded the Felicity Party. It was banned after the 1980 military coup. On April 4, 1980, four Islamic youth protesting the coup were killed by the police. Erdogan led four hundred young Islamists in a protest march. When the police stormed their picket line, Erdogan told protesters to get on their knees and start praying. Police beat the protesters with truncheons and arrested them. The front page of a leading Islamist paper had a picture of Erdogan with the caption: "The real leader of Islamic youth—Tayyip Erdogan."[22]

Erbakan's movement regrouped under the Welfare Party after Felicity was banned. Erbakan avoided the struggle between nationalists and leftists, saving his followers from recrimination after the military coup.[23] However, Erbakan was virulently anti-Western. He strongly opposed the European Union (EU) as an exclusive Christian club. He was humiliated by Turkey's subservience to the United States. He viewed Turkey's military and police as instruments of Western imperialism. Erbakan was angry that Felicity was banned, but espoused non-violent tactics to oppose the regime.[24]

The elderly Erbakan mentored Erdogan and other rising stars such as Abdullah Gul, who served as his senior foreign policy adviser. Erdogan rose in the Welfare Party ranks and gradually assumed a leadership role. Erdogan became the party's Beyoglu district chair in 1984. In 1985, he became chairman of Welfare's Istanbul city branch. Erdogan ran unsuccessfully for a parliamentary seat, representing Istanbul in 1986. He ran for mayor of Beyoglu in 1989. His inclusive campaign used the slogan "One of Us."[25]

Erdogan expected to win the election and become Beyoglu's mayor. However, hidden hands manipulated the final tally. Ballots were found in garbage bags, which led to allegations of vote rigging. Erdogan was convinced the election was stolen and accused the electoral commission, which was dominated by appointees of the Republican People's Party (CHP). He served a one-week sentence for publicly criticizing the authorities.

In 1991, Erbakan put Erdogan on the party list as a candidate to represent Istanbul's Fatih district in the national parliament, the Turkish Grand National Assembly (TGNA). Erdogan won a seat but was prevented from serving. Though Erdogan was on the party list, another candidate received more individual votes and was awarded the seat under the preferential system for counting ballots. Erdogan seethed at this electoral injustice.

Dogged and determined to succeed in politics, Erdogan competed in the local elections of 1992. His rhetoric had become radicalized by previous defeats, which he blamed on corrupt secular administrators. Erdogan's view of secularism and politics evolved and became more strident. He asserted, "You cannot be both secular and Muslim. You are either secular or Muslim."[26]

In 1994, Erdogan was elected mayor of Istanbul. Erdogan's victory was propelled by Erbakan who joined him in many joint public appearances. Less inclusive, Erdogan targeted Islamist voters. He promised to build a mega-mosque in Taksim Square. He pledged to open Ayasofya for public worship. He announced plans to close brothels and to ban the sale of contraceptives and alcohol. Erdogan criticized his opponents for corruption and vowed a clean administration.[27]

Erdogan referred to himself as the "Imam of Istanbul" during his swearing-in ceremony and oath of office. Erdogan understood that all politics is local. He consolidated support by pro-actively expanding services for Istanbul's nearly twenty million residents, tackling pollution, water shortages, and traffic that ground the city to a virtual standstill during rush-hours.

The Welfare Part won only 21 percent of the vote in national elections of December 1995. In a fluke of coalition politics, Erbakan formed an alliance with the center-right True Path Party and became prime minister. Erbakan was Turkey's first openly Islamist head of government. In foreign affairs, Erbakan tilted toward the broader Muslim community. He visited Libya in his first overseas trip. Erbakan signed a $23 billion gas deal with Iran. He threatened to suspend security cooperation with Israel and cancel Operation Northern Watch, which allowed US war planes to use Incirlik Air Force base near Adana in Southeast Turkey as a staging ground for enforcing a no fly zone over Iraqi Kurdistan. Erbakan opposed the foreign presence at Incirlik, harshly criticizing the United States and NATO for exploiting Turkey.

On June 18, 1997, six months after Erbakan became prime minister, the military removed him from office. Many Islamists were targeted in the crackdown, charged with violating secular tenets in the 1982 constitution. Erbakan's removal was the fourth time since 1960 that the military allegedly intervened to depose an elected government. It was dubbed a "post-modern coup." Erbakan's followers urged him to confront the military, but he sought to avoid confrontation. "They are sons of this country, too."[28]

Erdogan was less conciliatory. He railed against the secular estab-lishment for removing Erbakan from office. He made a public speech in the southeastern province of Siirt, denouncing the closure of the Welfare Party. Erdogan recited lines of a poem from the Turkish War of Liberation:

"The mosques are our barracks,
the domes our helmets,
the minarets our bayonets,
and the faithful our soldiers."

In September 1998, a court sentenced Erdogan to a ten-month prison term for "inciting hatred based on religious differences."[29] He served four months. While in jail, Erdogan reflected on his strategy and political path.

After getting out of jail, Erdogan refined his political message and rhetoric. Rather than define the hijab issue on the basis of religion, he cast it as an issue of human rights and freedom of expression. According to Erdogan, "The Western man has freedom of belief. In Europe, there is respect for worship, for the headscarf. Why is there not in Turkey?"

Erdogan broke with Erbakan and other religious conservatives. Unlike Erbakan, he did not see authoritarian secularism as an extension of Western influence. Instead, Erdogan embraced Western values as a vehicle to create a more liberal Turkey. He concluded that Islamic and Western values could coexist. Erdogan highlighted liberalism and progressive positions in the Qur'an, signaling support for human rights. He also broke with Erbakan on financial and foreign policy, embracing both the free market and Turkey's EU membership.

From the remnants of the Welfare Party, Erdogan teamed up with Islamist cohorts who shared his practical approach. The coterie of young Islamists was more politically sophisticated than Erbakan. In 2001, Erdogan and Gul established the Justice and Development Party (AKP). *Ak* in Turkish means "white," suggesting clean government. The party chose a light bulb as its logo. The AKP was cast as a party of enlightenment. Erdogan asserted, "[The AKP] is not a political party with a religious axis," but a mainstream conservative party.[30] The AKP was envisioned as modern and inclusive.

The AKP focused on political liberalization and economic growth. It was strongly critical of widespread corruption in Turkey's secular par-ties, espousing clean government. The AKP built a rainbow coalition of hard-core Islamists formerly associated with the Welfare Party, Islamic modernizers, socially conservative businessmen, secular reformists, and Kurds. By casting a wide net, Erdogan led the AKP to a big victory in the general election of November 3, 2002. The AKP received 34.3 percent of the vote.

There were sixteen parties running. Many were notorious for incompetence and corruption. To keep Islamists and Kurds out of the TGNA, Turkey's generals had pushed through an electoral law requiring parties to receive 10 percent of the national vote. In November 2002, only the AKP and the CHP passed the 10 percent barrier and won seats, allowing the AKP to have a two-thirds majority in the parliament.

The election was a sea change in Turkish politics. The AKP, an Islamist party, formed a single party government. In a dramatic departure from his predecessors, Erdogan showed pronounced humility. "We did not come to be master to our 73 million citizens, but to be their servitude."[31]

Erdogan was the unquestionable leader of the AKP. However, he could not become prime minister right away. According to Turkish law, Erdogan was banned from holding elected office because of his conviction for inciting social divisions using religion. Gul became the caretaker prime minister. The Supreme Election Board found there were voting irregularities in the Siirt district and, with support from the TGNA, canceled the result. A special election for the parliamentary seat from Siirt was held on February 9, 2003. Under terms of the revised electoral law, Erdogan became a candidate and received 85 percent of the vote. Becoming a member of parliament triggered the transfer of power between him and Gul who relinquished the post of prime minister, allowing Erdogan to take over.

Secular Turks doubted Erdogan's commitment to Kemalist principles. They were alarmed by his sectarian leanings, doubting his commitment to the core principles of the Turkish republic. Erdogan pronounced: "Democracy is like a streetcar. You get off when you have reached your destination."[32]

Notes

1. "Getting Off the Train," *The Economist*, February 4, 2016, accessed May 9, 2016, http://www.economist.com/news/special-report/21689877-mr-ians-commitment-democracy-seems-be-fading-getting-train.
2. "Turkey's Charismatic Pro-Islamic Leader," *BBC News World Edition*, November 4, 2002, accessed April 27, 2016, http://news.bbc.co.uk/2/hi/europe/2270642.stm.

3. Ustanın Hikayesi Başbakan Recep Tayyip Erdogan. [Online Video], *Beyaz TV*, September 3, 2013, accessed April 27, 2016, http://www.beyaztv.com. tr/program/usta-nin-hikayesi/, accessed May 4, 2016. Also available from: https://www.youtube.com/watch?v=qKmY5bHUw08.
4. In the national elections on November 1, 2015, 75.9 percent of voters cast ballots for the Erdogan's Justice and Development Party (AKP).
5. "Turkey's charismatic Pro-Islamic Leader," November 4, 2002.
6. M. Hakan Yavuz, *Secularism and Muslim Democracy in Turkey*. 1st ed. (Cambridge: Cambridge University Press, 2009), 118.
7. Ustanın Hikayesi Başbakan Recep Tayyip Erdoğan. [Online Video].
8. Ibid.
9. "Erdoğan, çocukluk anılarını anlattı" (Erdogan Shared His Childhood Memories), July 6, 2011, Gazete5, accessed May 28, 2016, http://www.gazete5. com/haber/erdogan-cocukluk-anilarini-anlatti-121687.
10. Ibid.
11. Enrollment in Imam-Hatips increased dramatically under the AKP (2002–2015) from 65,000 to 932,000 students. The percentage of middle-school students in Imam-Hatips increased from zero to 10.5 percent. The percentage of high school students increased from 2.6 percent to 12.9 percent. See A. Makovsky, *Re-Education Turkey: AKP Efforts to Promote Religious Values in Turkish Schools* (Center for American Progress, December 14, 2015), accessed April 27, 2016, https://www.americanprogress.org/issues/security /report/2015/12/14/127089/re-educating-turkey/.
12. Makovsky, *Re-Education Turkey*.
13. Ustanın Hikayesi Başbakan Recep Tayyip Erdoğan. [Online Video].
14. Ibid.
15. Ibid.
16. "Presidency of the Republic of Turkey. Biography: Recep Tayyip Erdoğan," accessed April 27, 2016, http://www.tccb.gov.tr/en/receptayyiperdogan /biography/.
17. Recep Tayyip Erdoğan Belgeseli. [Online Video], December 29, 2011, BelgeselIzle (Watch Documentaries), accessed May 9, 2016, http://www .belgeselizle.org/belgeseller/Recep-Tayyip-Erdogan-Belgeseli-692.html.
18. "Emine Erdoğan'in Ilginç Hayati" (Emine Erdoğan's Exotic Life), December 21, 2006, AktifHaber, accessed May 5, 2016, http://www.aktifhaber.com /emine-erdoganin-ilginc-hayati-95150h.htm.
19. Recep Tayyip Erdoğan Belgeseli. [Online Video].
20. Ibid.
21. Ustanın Hikayesi Başbakan Recep Tayyip Erdoğan. [Online Video].
22. Ibid.
23. Ibid.
24. "Turkey's Islamists: Erbakan's Legacy," *The Economist*, March 3, 2011, accessed May 9, 2016, http://www.economist.com/node/18289145.
25. Recep Tayyip Erdoğan Belgeseli. [Online Video].
26. Ibid.
27. Ibid.
28. "Turkey's Islamists: Erbakan's Legacy."

29. "Erdoğan goes to prison," *Hurriyet Daily News*, March 27, 1999, accessed August 5, 2016, http://www.hurriyetdailynews.com/erdogan-goes-to-prison.aspx?pageID=438&n=erdogan-goes-to-prison-1999-03-27.
30. "AKP İslamcı Bir Parti Değil!," *Aktif Haber*, December 28, 2014, accessed August 5, 2016, http://www.aktifhaber.com/akp-islamci-bir-parti-degil-1097465h.htm.
31. Recep Tayyip Erdoğan Belgeseli. [Online Video].
32. "Getting Off the Train," *The Economist*, February 4, 2016, accessed May 9, 2016, http://www.economist.com/news/special-report/21689877-mr-erdogans-commitment-democracy-seems-be-fading-getting-train.

2

Secularism

*Those who use religion for their own benefit are
detestable. We are against such a situation and will not
allow it. Those who use religion in such a manner have
fooled our people; it is against just such people that
we have fought and will continue to fight.*[1]

—Mustafa Kemal Ataturk

Turkey is a Muslim majority country; 97.8 percent of Turks are Muslim.
Of these, 72 percent are Sunnis. Shiites and Alevites are 25 percent.
Bektasi Sufiism, a dervish branch of Sunni Islam, has deep roots in
Ottoman history. Sufiism is a moderate and mystical practice with
ties to Shiism. Turkey's secular system of governance established the
impartiality of the state towards all religious groups. Impartiality was
intended to mitigate potential conflict between religions and sects.
Though Mustafa Kemal Ataturk created a secular state from the remnants of the Ottoman Empire, the Hanefi branch of Sunni Islam was
dominant in society.

Islam's roots in Anatolia date back to the eleventh century. The con-
quest of Ottoman armies subsequently spread Islam across the Ottoman
Empire from the border with Persia in the East to the Western Balkans
and the gates of Vienna. Ottoman forces led by Sultan Mehmet II
captured Constantinople, the capital of Byzantium, in 1453. Mehmet II
converted many churches into mosques and established a caliphate in
Constantinople, which was renamed Istanbul.

Beginning in 1516, the Sultan was also the caliph. The term "caliph"
refers to the successor of Muhammad, which is used to describe the
leader of all Sunni Muslims in the world. The "caliphate" describes the
organizational body, which manages the caliph's affairs. The caliphate
was an affirmation of the sultan's imperial and spiritual power. Ottoman
sultans were omnipotent with supreme political and religious authority.

The Ottoman Empire peaked under Suleyman the Magnificent, who ruled from 1520 to 1566. It encompassed most of the Muslim world during Suleyman's reign. The far-flung Ottoman Empire was bound together by a Muslim ideology, as well as Islamic organizational and administrative structures, including Sharia law. Suleyman was widely regarded as the leader of worldwide Islam, as well as the earthly ruler of most Muslims. Religious minorities were allowed significant self-rule under the "millet system." They were granted a significant degree of autonomy, as long as they showed fealty and paid a tax to the Porte in Istanbul.

The Ottoman Empire gradually declined after Suleyman. To stem its decline, beginning in 1839, the Ottoman Empire initiated a process called "Tanzimat," which means re-organization. Tanzimat was an effort to modernize. It was a strategy to protect against nationalist movements. It also sought to address sectarianism that might divide and weaken the empire. In addition, Tanzimat was intended to deter Great Powers from contesting Ottoman rule by allowing greater rights for its subjects. In a bid to modernize, Tanzimat also sought to curtail the influence of religion. It was a defense against both internal opposition and external powers. Tanzimat reforms culminated in the First Constitution of 1876.[2]

Turkey's defeat in the First World War was the death knell of the Ottoman Empire. After the Paris Peace Conference, Great Powers imposed the Treaty of Sèvres in 1920, which effectively reduced Turkey to a rump state with just one-third of the territory it possessed prior to the First World War. Mustafa Kemal Ataturk, a Turkish army officer and revolutionary, launched the War of Independence to restore Turkish control in Anatolia. He issued the "National Oath," reasserting authority over all non-Arab territories of the former Ottoman Empire and rejecting territorial claims asserted at the Paris Peace Conference. Ataturk founded the Republic of Turkey in 1923, and became its first president.[3]

Ataturk's reforms put Turkey on the path to becoming a truly modern state on a par with its European neighbors. He embraced science and secularism, realigning Turkey with the West. He abolished the caliphate, banishing members of the Ottoman house from Turkish territory. The last caliph, Abdulmecit Effendi, was deported together with the other members of his family. As part of Ataturk's social engineering, he decreed that the Arabic call to prayer (*Ezan*) be recited in modern

Turkish. Ataturk secularized academic curricula, and replaced Turkey's Ottoman script with the Latin alphabet. He disbanded religious courts, banned Sharia law, and implemented a westernized legal system. He gave women suffrage and equal rights. Turkey's founding constitution enshrined secularism and republicanism.[4]

The constitution reflected Ataturk's core ideology called "The Six Arrows of Kemalism."[5]

1. "Republicanism" was the founding principle of the Republic of Turkey. Secular administrators and technocrats replaced the Ottoman social order, which upheld power of the sultan. The modern concept of republicanism defined Turkey's national identity, giving coherence to the country and serving the interest of its citizens.

2. "Populism" was the clarion call of Ataturk's revolution. He rejected class privileges, embracing individual rights and promoting peasant, worker, and women's rights in his vision of a classless society. Sovereignty and independence were sacrosanct. The concept of citizenship was glorified as the core of national identity.

3. "Reformism" was a top-down project of radical modernization. It emerged alongside Marxism in Russia, which was conceptually different as a bottom-up revolution of the proletariat. Both Kemalism and Marxism represented a revolutionary ideology designed to advance individual and communal rights. Both rejected incremental change in favor of dramatic reforms, revolutionary in their scope and vision.

4. "Nationalism" was the bedrock of Ataturk's movement. Ataturk rejected colonialism and imperialism, rallying supporters behind his nationalist cause. Ataturk emphasized the importance of a common Turkish identity as the basis for a modern Turkish state.[6] His mantra was: "Peace at home, peace abroad."[7]

5. "Statism" invested supreme authority in public institutions as the guarantor of social order. Economic and technological development was entrusted to the state, whose primary mission was protecting Turkey's independence. To Ataturk, the state was more than governing institutions. It was supranational, symbolizing Turkey's territory and its people. Statism started as a concept but became a sprawling bureaucracy. Absent adequate checks and balances, the bureaucracy evolved into a conglomerate of special interests bent on preserving powers and privileges under the auspices of state authority.

6. "Secularism" redefined the role of religion in affairs of the state, strictly separating religion and government. Secularism went far beyond reform and lifestyle. Turkey's identity was defined not by

religion but by cultural values shared with Europe. Secularism was a worldview, which gave primacy to reason over faith and heralded individualism over the divine. Religion received no privileges from the state, nor could it influence laws and policies. The state was not partial towards any religious groups. Nor could it interfere in religious affairs.[8]

Ataturk's six arrows were enshrined in the constitution of 1921. He established a system for preserving and protecting these principles through the rule of law. He reshaped all aspects of the state and society. Turkey was well ahead of other countries in the Muslim world by giving women the right to vote in the 1930s. Today, Turkey is the only one of fifty-seven majority Muslim countries where secularism is enshrined in the constitution.

Ataturk's devotion to secularism did not mean he opposed religion. He viewed Islam as a system of social justice, which defined the character of Turkey. However, he did not believe Islamism and democracy were compatible. Islamism rejects constitutional democracy. Islamists maintain that Sharia Law, which is God-given, transcends constitutions, which are man-made. To Ataturk, Islamism is a system of beliefs, which aims to reverse the process of cultural modernization.

Ataturk's Republican People's Party (CHP) was the country's leading force to achieve cultural modernization. Declaring the republic, Ataturk established the Turkish Grand National Assembly (TGNA), which abolished the constitutional monarchy on November 1, 1922. Although the 1924 constitution maintained Islam as the official religion of the republic, the caliphate was abolished formally that year and its powers transferred to the TGNA. Other laws closed down private religious schools and religious courts.[9] In 1928, the TGNA adopted a constitutional amendment that removed the provision stating, "Religion of the State is Islam." The 1937 constitution formally enshrined secularism.[10]

Today's current constitution was adopted in 1982, after the 1980 military coup. It makes no mention of an official religion. Although the constitution protects religious freedom, such freedoms are derogated by other laws preserving secular authority. The constitution states that the Turkish Republic is a "secular state".[11] Amending the secular state is prohibited in Article 4 of the constitution.[12]

Ataturk saw Islamic expression as an attempt to undermine the state and took steps to guard against creeping Islamization. Religious expression in government offices and publicly funded universities was restricted. Wearing the hijab, an overt expression of piety, was prohibited in state institutions.

Ataturk was a social engineer who focused on future generations. In the name of the republic, he called on teachers to "raise generations with free ideas, free consciences, free knowledge."[13] Ataturk established a network of world-class public universities across Turkey. He espoused a Western curriculum, emphasizing a mix of hard science and the social sciences. He believed that freedom of thought was derived from the study of these disciplines. Ataturk co-authored a textbook on civics in 1929."[14]

Ataturk's social engineering had a major flaw. He imposed Europeanization of the elite without adequately cultivating European values at the grassroots. His efforts focused on urban centers, neglecting less developed and more remote rural areas. Istanbul, Ankara, and Izmir were urbane and European. But people in the countryside maintained their Anatolian habits and strong Islamic identity. Ataturk allowed religious education at Imam Hatips in recognition of grass-roots religiosity.[15] He permitted some degree of instruction in the Qur'an and Arabic as a nod to the Muslim masses.[16]

The Directorate of Religious Affairs was charged with preventing antisecularist movements. Organs of the judiciary were the primary enforcers of secularism. The justice minister is the most senior official, followed by the high council of judges and prosecutors. Then comes the Constitutional Court and military courts, with jurisdiction over military personnel. Judges were subject to special examinations to determine their commitment to Kemalist ideals. The rule of law was designed to protect the state and to safeguard Kemalism. The system was not concerned with protecting individual rights or preventing the abuse of authority.

Ataturk was a general before he became a politician and an administrator. He relied extensively on security structures to defend Kemalism. Every branch of the country's expansive security system had a role protecting Ataturk's ideals, forming a web of institutions to uphold the six arrows.

The founding constitution tasked the Turkish Armed Forces (TSK) with defending against both external and internal threats.[17] The Ministry of National Defense and the Turkish General Staff (TGS) are the institutions primarily responsible for national security. The TGS assumed great powers as the CHP's security surrogate, interpreting and enforcing legislative intent. The TGS directs the land, naval and air forces. It is also responsible for the General Command of the Gendarmerie, a branch of the national police with extraordinary powers. The National Security Council (NSC) was dominated by military officers. It reported to the Council of Ministers, which was nominally under control of the prime minister. The NSC complemented the Constitutional Court and judiciary, identifying challenges to the basic principles of the constitution, as well as threats to national unity and territorial integrity.

Internal security and public order were maintained by the Gendarmerie, which was established in 1923. Powers of the national police were expanded by law 3201 in 1937. The Directorate of National Security and the Coast Guard Command were also assigned internal security and public order functions. The National Intelligence Agency (MIT) was established as a suprabody on July 22, 1965. It was an essential part of Turkey's security structure, designed to monitor society.

Even after his death in 1938, Ataturk was omnipresent in Turkish political and social life. His bright blue penetrating eyes were everywhere in photos and posters. Statues and busts of Ataturk were displayed in government offices, banks, businesses, and people's homes. In the collective memory of Turks, Ataturk personifies the Turkish Revolution. His cult of personality is enduring.

Ataturk's reforms tried to secularize society, but Islam remained a strong influence over Turkey's Muslim majority. Post-Ataturk, leaders lacked his popular appeal. Polarization became pronounced in 1980s, as leftists emerged.

In addition to Islamism and leftism, Kurdish separatism also threatened national unity. Draconian legislation targeted the Kurdish community. When the Kurds rebelled, the military was deployed to suppress their national and political aspirations. Human rights abuses were widespread.[18]

The CHP tolerated Islamic leaders as a bulwark against leftists. It also supported Turkish Hezbollah to counter Kurdish aspirations. Pious local leaders increasingly challenged the country's secular elite. In the 1990s, Islamists presented religion as a cure for Turkey's economic woes and were elected to local government posts. Erdogan was part of this wave, becoming mayor of Istanbul in 1994.

In response, the Constitutional Court banned Islamist parties that openly challenged secular institutions. To the Court, a party cannot be secular and Islamist at the same time. The military intervened in

1960, 1971, 1980, and 1997 to restore Kemalist order against leftist, conservative, and Islamist parties.[19] The National Order Party was founded in 1970, and banned by the Constitutional Court a year later. The National Salvation Party was established in 1972. It received 12 percent of the popular vote in elections of 1973, and then was banned after the 1980 military coup. A 1998 Court decision banned the Welfare Party. The Virtue Party, founded in 1997 by Necmettin Erbakan, was formally banned in 2001.

Erdogan rose to prominence in this climate of crackdown. Erdogan was a devoted political Islamist, under Erbakan's tutelage. However, Erdogan learned to moderate his Islamist views to avoid confrontation with the secular authorities. Erdogan rejected Islamist labels. He maintained, "We are not an Islamic party. We refuse labels such as Muslim-democrat." Some European opinion leaders praised the AKP as "moderate Islamic." Others cautioned that the only difference between moderate and radical Islamists is the use of the ballot box instead of violence to seize power.[20]

The AKP's rise was propelled by a Muslim community—based movement called Hizmet, which means "service." Founded by Fethullah Gulen, Hizmet is a transnational religious and social movement, which advocates a tolerant Islam based on the principles of altruism, hard work, and education. Hizmet has no formal structure, no central organization, and no official hierarchy or membership, but it grew into the world's largest Muslim network. It was also well financed. Members of the Hizmet community gave up to 20 percent of their income to the organization. Erdogan found common cause with Gulen, who provided resources and infrastructure to support the AKP. Gulenists were virtuous and devoted. They helped the AKP's crusade to restore integrity and Muslim virtue in the Turkish government. Gulenists were rewarded with ministerial and other high ranking positions when the AKP came to power.

Gulen and Erdogan collaborated to erode the secular bureaucracy. Gulen instructed his followers to infiltrate mainstream structures: "You must move within the arteries of the system, without noticing your existence, until you reach all the power centers."[21] In accordance with Gulen's instruction, many followers rose to senior positions in the police, judiciary, and intelligence services. Gulen also faced the prosecutor's rancor. In 1999, he was charged with undermining secularism and fled to Pennsylvania. As of this writing, he lives in self-imposed exile in the Poconos.

Erdogan pursued a double game, disassociating himself from political Islam, while embracing Islamic identity politics. For Erdogan, democracy and human rights were vehicles to advance Islamic expression. The AKP presented itself as an agent of change; Erdogan promised to transform Turkey's calcified and corrupt politics. He appealed to broader segments of the electorate, expanding the AKP's base of support.

Turkey's secular elite believed the AKP was merely masquerading as a mainstream conservative party. They suspected Erdogan of having a hidden agenda to Islamicize society. Erdogan rhetorically embraced the rule of law, while working towards the establishment of Sharia law. In a moment of candor, Erdogan admitted: "We have only one concern. It is Islam, Islam and Islam."[22]

The EU invited Turkey to start accession talks in 2005, in recognition of the AKP's commitment to economic and political reform. The AKP's willingness to stand up against the military ingratiated it with politicians and bureaucrats in Brussels. The AKP was the first governing party since 1960 to oppose the military's interference in politics and denounce its heavy-handed tactics. Brussels viewed the military as the antagonist to realizing European values of human rights, minority rights, and basic freedoms in Turkey.[23] For EU officials, the AKP was new, modern, and reformist.

Pursuit of EU membership was a Trojan horse for the AKP's Islamic agenda.[24] Democracy was a code word for greater Islamic rights. Erdogan presented himself as a European, but his commitment to Europe and democracy were instrumental. Reforms served a dual purpose. They reduced the military's institutional involvement in government. Under the guise of reforms, the AKP would gradually find ways of reducing the military's hold on power. In addition, the AKP and the Gulen movement systematically and stealthily developed a plan to undermine other institutions that guaranteed secular governance, such as the judiciary.

The AKP adopted a long-term approach, focusing on education. The school system was a primary instrument to enhance Islamist identity politics, inculcate Islamic values, and de-Westernize society. Hizmet founded over a thousand private schools across Turkey. Hizmet members also infiltrated the formal education system. In December 2014, Turkey's Higher Education Council called for mandatory courses on Sunni Islam at publicly funded schools for all students, starting at age six. Imam Hatip schools prepared a new generation of pious devotees, who became followers of the AKP. Alongside Hizmet, Imam Hatip graduates worked as educators and infiltrated the Ministry of Education.

Society was increasingly Islamized through daily rituals of observance. More and more people displayed a dark callous on their forehead from touching the ground five times each day in prayer. AKP members infiltrated business and the civil service. State positions in the civil service were awarded almost exclusively to Islamists. Work was suspended during prayer times in offices and government agencies. Bus drivers were instructed to pull their vehicles to the side of the road so passengers could pray.[25] With the AKP's coming to power, the social design of the Turkish society reversed. Before the AKP, secular lifestyle was dominant. With the AKP's rise, conservatism became normal. Women without the hijab were targeted. Teenage girls were disparaged and sometimes spat upon for not dressing "properly."[26]

The Turkish presidency is a prestigious but largely ceremonial post. Tensions between the AKP and the military escalated when Erdogan nominated Foreign Minister Abdullah Gul to replace Ahmet Necdet Sezer as president in 2007. The AKP provided no advance notice to the TGS or the NSC. It made no attempt to build consensus behind Gul's nomination by consulting with opposition parties, the CHP and the National Action Party (MHP). The AKP's decision to nominate Gul further polarized Turkish society. At CHP rallies, hundreds of thousands protested Gul's nomination. The CHP initiated a legal challenge to block Gul.[27]

Gul's nomination also roiled the state and military establishment. Security officials were appalled that Gul, a devout Muslim, would occupy the office once held by Mustafa Kemal Ataturk. However, the generals chose not to escalate the dispute with Erdogan. National elections were scheduled for November 2007. They worried that the AKP would go for early elections in a bid to increase its power. Unprecedented economic prosperity shielded the AKP from an outright putsch.

Instead the generals staged an "e-coup." On April 27, 2007. General Yasar Buyukanit, TGS chairman, posted a statement on the military's website warning against "furtive plans that aim to undo modern advances and ruin the Turkish republic's secular and democratic structure." He warned, "If necessary, the Turkish Armed Forces will not hesitate to make their position and stance abundantly clear as the absolute defenders of secularism."[28] Given Turkey's history of military interventions, the message was a thinly veiled threat. A more conventional coup might be in the offing.

Erdogan did not back down. Exuding self-confidence and contempt for the military, Erdogan defied the generals and called early elections. It was a bold move, which paid off. On July 22, 2007, The AKP won 46.6 percent of the vote, which equated to 341 of the 550 seats in parliament. The tally represented a significant increase from the 34 percent it received in 2002. Gul said, "It was a vote on my candidacy."[29] Moreover, the tally was a public rebuke to the generals who boasted about their power but were unwilling to exercise it. The TGS was chastened. According to Nejat Eslen, a retired brigadier general and an ardent supporter of secularism, "In Turkey, a new period has started."[30]

The AKP crowned its victory when parliament finally elected Gul to the presidency. Gul failed in the first two rounds of voting, when a two-thirds majority was needed. He was, however, elected in the third round with a simple majority. The top brass stayed away from the inauguration at the Cankaya Palace. Buyukanit boycotted the occasion. Gul's wife, Hayrunnisa, a modest Muslim woman, was also absent. Turkish law forbids wearing the hijab in public buildings. According to the respected columnist, Mehmet Ali Birand, "With a first lady in a head scarf, a taboo is finished in Turkey."[31]

Gul struck a conciliatory note in his address to the TGNA after taking the oath of office. "Turkey is a secular democracy," he said. "These are basic values of our republic, and I will defend and strengthen these values."[32] Although Kurdish members of Parliament abstained from the vote on Gul's nomination, Gul visited Diyarbakir soon after his election. He pledged support for Kurdish rights and confirmed Turkey's openness to dialogue with the PKK.

The AKP's sweeping victory was derived in part by inroads with Kurdish voters. The AKP appealed to Kurds through its conservatism and by expanding social services, building roads, schools and hospitals in predominantly Kurdish areas of the Southeast. Erdogan publicly acknowledged the Kurdish issue, promising an end to civil war. Kurds were tired of conflict. They hoped that the AKP would pursue a peace process with the PKK, resulting in disarmament and demobilization.

Kurds also hoped that the AKP would amend the constitution, recognizing Kurds as an official minority in Turkey. They expected the government would reform articles in the penal code that were used to repress freedom of expression. Many Kurds had been prosecuted under Article 8 of the Anti-Terror Act and Article 301 of the Penal Code for merely demanding greater rights.

But instead of withdrawing regressive legislation or dealing with the Kurdish issue, Erdogan focused the AKP human rights agenda on religion freedom, including the removal of restrictions on the hijab. To Islamists, the hijab is not just an article of clothing but a tangible civilizational difference between Islam and the West. Wearing the hijab is not only divisive in Turkey. An appeal was filed with the European Court for Human Rights by a Muslim woman in France who claimed that denial of a woman's right to wear the hijab was a violation of her basic human rights. In a 2004 ruling, however, the European Court of Human Rights found the right to a head scarf was not a basic human right and dismissed the complaint. In the summer of 2016, France's "burkini" debate demonstrated the enduring disagreement over the hijab.

The AKP-dominated TGNA passed legislation allowing female university students to wear the hijab at public universities and in the workplace. The Turkish Supreme Court deemed the law unconstitutional on June 5, 2008. The battle lines were drawn between Erdogan and the secular judiciary. Erdogan was quoted in *Al-Hayat:* "We are going to shut down the Constitutional Court." A confrontation between the AKP and the Constitutional Court was looming.[33]

The chief prosecutor charged the AKP with trying to undermine secularism. The prosecutor initiated proceedings to ban the party and seventy-one of its leaders, including Erdogan and Gul. The AKP called it a "judicial coup."

A majority of justices found that the AKP was advancing an Islamist agenda. However, the AKP was not banned. The court voted against closure by one vote. A decision to ban the AKP required support from seven of the eleven judges. However, only six judges voted for closure. Short of an outright ban, the Court restricted the AKP's activities and cut its state subsidy.

This punishment was a mere slap on the wrist. Justices reasoned that dissolving the party would have precipitated a serious political crisis. Banning the AKP would get rid of the party, but it would merely reconstitute under a new name, emerging as a more powerful Islamist movement than before. This shell game is familiar in Turkish politics. For example, the AKP reincarnated from the Virtue Party when it was banned in 1997.

Having survived the Court's action, Erdogan launched a campaign to discredit antagonists in the judiciary and the military. The AKP sponsored a resolution challenging the authority of the Supreme Council of Judges and Prosecutors to make judicial appointments. Another resolution changed Article 918 of the Penal Code, allowing military personnel to be tried in civilian courts and preventing the prosecution of civilians in military courts.

The battle shifted to the ballot when the AKP put forth a referendum on constitutional reform. The referendum gave President Gul and the AKP-controlled parliament greater influence over the appointments of senior judges and prosecutors. It expanded the size of the Constitutional Court from 11 to 17 members, diluting the influence of its core group. It also granted the TGNA greater power to make judicial appointments. The referendum imposed curbs on military courts, and abolished immunity for leaders of the 1980 coup. Other measures guaranteed greater gender equality and put in place measures to protect children, elderly, and the disabled.

The referendum was held on September 12, 2010. It passed with 58 percent. Most Kurds in the restive Southeast complied with instructions from the pro-Kurdish party, Peace and Democracy (BDP), to boycott the referendum. Kurds stayed home because the referendum did not address their demands for greater political and cultural rights, nor did it recognize the Kurds as an official minority. The referendum highlighted differences between the Islamists and secularists. It also showed the alienation of Kurdish voters.

The EU welcomed the referendum for enhancing accountability and making it possible for coup plotters to be tried in civilian courts. Brussels chose to ignore Erdogan's incendiary language during the campaign. Erdogan had accused referendum opponents of being "in favor of army coups." He warned they would be "eliminated."[34] After the vote, Erdogan and Gul attended the world basketball championship final in Istanbul—Turkey versus the United States. There was a chorus of boos when they entered the arena.[35]

The referendum set the stage for national elections on June 12, 2011. The AKP's support in the Anatolian heartland was strong. Voters handed the AKP a big win with 49.8 percent of the vote. This represented an increase of 3.2 percent since the 2007 general elections and an 11.4 percent increase over 2009 local elections. Turkish voters rewarded the AKP for sustaining steady growth during the global economic downturn.

In the name of democratic reforms, Erdogan intensified pressure on the military. *Taraf,* a progressive Turkish media outlet, broke a series of stories about retired military officers and members of the deep state allegedly plotting a coup to overthrow the AKP government. One of its articles reported that a cache of weapons was discovered in the hands of coup-plotters. In July 2008, twenty people were arrested including two former generals and a senior journalist for "planning political disturbances and trying to organize a coup." In October 2008, eighty-six people went on trial for plotting to overthrow the government. In June 2009, police found a document detailing military plans to undermine the AKP and eradicate the influence of Fethullah Gulen. The document implicated Chief of the General Staff Ilker Basbug. Fifty-six more former officers were charged in July 2009.[36]

The plot thickened with *Taraf*'s report on "Operation Sledgehammer," describing plans by active and retired members of the armed forces to foment unrest, which they would use to justify a coup aimed at restoring peace and stability. The fantastic plot included bombing two major mosques in Istanbul's Fatih and Beyazit districts, an assault on a military museum by people disguised as religious extremists, and raising tensions with Greece by downing a Turkish plane over Greek air space. Assassinations of major political and intellectual figures, including Nobel-winning novelist Orhan Pamuk, were also alleged.

The most prominent defendants—former army commander Cetin Dogan, former navy chief Ozden Ornek, and former air force chief Ibrahim Firtina—received twenty-year sentences. The Ankara Supreme Court of Appeals upheld the convictions of another 237 retired officers.[37] Hundreds of other officers were also put on trial, along with journalists and secular politicians. The commanders of Turkey's army, navy and air force resigned in protest. They objected to trumped-up charges, intended to silence political opponents.[38] Legal action against members of Turkey's security and bureaucratic establishment was unheard of. In Erdogan's Turkey, however, no person was untouchable.

The witch-hunt continued. In 2013, seventeen officers were jailed and given life sentences. They were convicted of plotting to overthrow the AKP in another fantastic case known as "Ergenekon." According to legend, Ergenekon is a mythical kingdom located in the inaccessible valleys of the Altay Mountains. Ancient Turks hid in the Altay Valley after a military defeat until a blacksmith melted rock, enabling Asena, the great gray wolf, to lead them to safety.

Erdogan was unabashed about his desire to amend the constitution to create an executive presidency. But he was opaque about how Turkey's new constitution would treat secularism. The military believed that the AKP would amend Turkey's constitution, voiding references to secularism.

On April 25, 2016, Parliament Speaker Ismail Kahraman suggested that Turkey's new constitution delete mention of "secularism." He proposed a "religious constitution," referencing Allah as the source of divine and worldly authority. Kahraman is a close associate of Erdogan's. It was widely believed that Kahraman was not just speaking for himself. His statement was testing the limits of religiosity. Kahraman's remarks led to protests in a number of cities and a call by CHP leader, Kemal Kilicdaroglu, for him to resign. According to Kilicdaroglu, Kahraman's remarks revealed the AKP's "true face" and "real intentions."

Erdogan abruptly removed Ahmet Davutoglu, who served as his prime minister from August 2014 until April 2016. Davutoglu resisted Erdogan's efforts to concentrate power in the presidency, fearing it would erode Turkey's democracy. They also disagreed on Islam's role in governance. Just prior to his dismissal, Davutoglu asserted: "In the new constitution that we are preparing, the principle of secularism will be included." He explained it would be a "liberal interpretation" of secularism, not an "authoritarian" version.[39] Davutoglu wanted the AKP to address the aspirations of "conservative" voters who appreciated the reference to religion, but preferred to live under a secular administration. A public opinion survey by the Pew Research Center in 2013 found that only 12 percent of Turks support "making Sharia the official law in their country."[40]

A proposal to restore the caliphate was floated. Hizb ut-Tahrir, an Islamist organization, convened the "International Caliphate Symposium." The conference was held on March 3, 2016, on the ninety-second anniversary of the caliphate's abolition. Three days later, five thousand people gathered in Ankara at the Ataturk Sports Hall for an "International Caliphate" rally. Mahmut Kar delivered the keynote address: "Caliphate: An Imagination or a Reality that will be Realized Soon."[41] Kar adopted the fiery rhetoric of Abu Bakr al-Baghdadi, the ISIS head. "Infidels who were enemies of Islam thought they buried Islam in the depths of history when they abolished the caliphate on March 3, 1924." Today, "[w]e are shouting here, right next to the parliament.[42] We will re-establish the caliphate." Erdogan refused to repudiate Kar's remarks.

In seeking to lead the Muslim world, Erdogan systematically undermined Ataturk's six arrows and sought to weaken institutions that preserved his legacy. At a meeting of the Directorate of Religious Affairs, Erdogan proposed mandatory Ottoman-language instruction at Imam Hatips and as an elective at other high schools. The proposal was interpreted as an effort to undermine one of Ataturk's core reforms, while imposing the AKP's version of history and values on Turkey's youth.

Erdogan views the AKP as a model for other Muslim countries, who are caught between traditional values, secularism, and modernity. He also sees himself as leader of the Broader Muslim Community. He greeted a crowd from the balcony of the AKP headquarters after elections on June 12, 2011. "Sarajevo won today as much as Istanbul. Beirut won as much as Izmir. Damascus won as much as Ankara. Ramallah, Nablus, Jenin, the West Bank, [and] Jerusalem won as much as Diyarbakir."[43]

Notes

1. https://www.goodreads.com/author/quotes/2793859.Mustafa_Kemal_Atat_rk.

2. B. Eryılmaz, "Tanzimat ve yönetimde modernleşme" (Tanzimat and Modernization in Administartion), *İşaret* Page 16 (1992).

3. E. J. Zürcher, "The Qttoman Legacy of the Turkish Republic: An Attempt at a New Periodization," *Die Welt des Islams* 2 (1992): 237–53.

4. D. L. Phillips, "Turkey's Dreams of Accession," *Foreign Affairs* 83, no. 1 (2004): 86–97.

5. "'Six Arrows:' The Tenets of Kemalism," *Los Angeles Times*, January 15, 1991, accessed May 19, 2016, http://articles.latimes.com/1991-01-15/news/wr-324_1_mustafa-kemal-ataturk.

6. M. K. Atatürk (1927). "Nutuk (Great Speech)." Atatürk's Nutuk (Great Speech) provides lengthy rhetorical references to his vision of a modern Turkish nation. Nutuk was instrumental in constructing a Turkish national identity and a modern Turkish nation. See for instance, A. Morin, "Crafting a Nation: The Mythic Construction of the New Turkish National Identity in Ataturk's 'Nutuk,'" UMI Diss. Services, 2007 and A. Morin and R. Lee, "Constitutive Discourse of Turkish Nationalism: Atatürk's Nutuk and the Rhetorical Construction of the 'Turkish People,'" *Communication Studies* 61, no. 5 (2010): 485–506.

7. C. Candar and G. E. Fuller, "Grand Geopolitics for a New Turkey," *Mediterranean Quarterly* 12, no. 1 (2001): 22–38.

8. S. Aksin, "The Nature of Kemalist Revolution," pages of UNA Turkey, accessed May 22, 2016, from http://www.unaturkey.org/dergiler-bulletins/38-say-02-number-02-october-1999-/58-the-nature-of-the-kemalist-revolution-.html.

9. H. Yılmaz, H. (2008).

10. Ibid.

11. The Grand National Assembly of Turkey, Constitution of the Republic of Turkey (As amended on July 23, 1995; Act No. 4121). See Article 3, accessed May19, 2016, For English: http://global.tbmm.gov.tr/docs/constitution_en.pdf.

12. See Article 4. Ibid.

13. Aksin, "The Nature of Kemalist Revolution."

14. Ibid.

15. Bekir S. Gür, "Report: What Erdogan Really Wants for Education in Turkey: Islamization or Pluralization?," *Al Jazeera Studies*, March 17, 2016, accessed May 1, 2016 http://studies.aljazeera.net/mritems/Documents/2016/3/17/c2a0ade5d313404ab8500c9ebb0375d3_100.pdf.

16. B. Akşit, . "Islamic Education in Turkey: Medrese Reform in Late Ottoman Times and imam-hatip Schools in the Republic, in *Islam in Modern Turkey*, ed. Richard Tapper (London: I.B. Tauris, 1991), 145–70.

17. M. Heper, M. "Civil-Military Relations in Turkey: Toward a Liberal Model," *Turkish Studies* 12, no. 2 (2011): 241–52.

18. For a detailed account on Human rights violations in Turkey conducted by Turkish state, see Human Rights Watch Turkey, Amnesty International Turkey, Human Rights Association, so on. They have extensive reports on the State violations in Kurdish regions. For more scholarly works: H. Bozarslan, "Human Rights and the Kurdish Issue in Turkey: 1984–1999," *Human Rights Review* 3, no. 1 (2001): 45–54; A. Roberts, "Humanitarian War: Military Intervention and Human Rights," *International Affairs* (Royal Institute of International Affairs 1944-) 69 (1993): 429–49, and H. J. Barkey, "Turkey's Kurdish Dilemma," *Survival* 35, no. 4 (1993): 51–70.

19. For a detailed account on Turkish military interventions, see: G. Jenkins, *Context and Circumstance: the Turkish Military and Politics (No. 337)* (London: Taylor & Francis, 2001); T. Maniruzzaman, "Arms Transfers, Military Coups, and Military Rule in Developing States," *Journal of Conflict Resolution* 36, no. 4 (1992): 733–55; and Ü. C. Sakallioğlu, "The Anatomy of the Turkish Military's Political Autonomy," *Comparative Politics* 29 (1997): 151–66.

20. Basbakan: Asla Islamci Parti Degiliz (Prime Minister Erdogan: We are not an Islamic party, never!), December 9, 2009, Haber5, accessed May 25, 2016, http://www.haber5.com/siyaset/basbakan-asla-islamci-parti-degiliz.

21. Christopher Torchia and Erol Israfil, "Turkey Says Failed Coup Was Decades in the Making," *Chicago Tribune*, August 16, 2016, accessed August 16, 2016, http://www.chicagotribune.com/news/nationworld/sns-bc-eu--turkey-the-long-game-20160815-story.html.

22. Turkey's Erdogan says his only concern is Islam, takes jab at atheists, *Hurriyet Daily News*, July 31, 2015, accessed May 26,2016, http://www.hurriyetdailynews.com/turkeys-erdogan-says-his-only-concern-is-islam-takes-jab-at-atheists.aspx?PageID=238&NID=86228&NewsCatID=338.

23. D. Lepeska, "'Turkey's Long Game: How 12 Years of AKP Rule Has Eroded the Secular State," *The National*, November 20, 2014, accessed May 18, 2016, http://www.thenational.ae/arts-lifestyle/the-review/turkeys-long-game-how-12-years-of-akp-rule-has-eroded-the-secular-state.

24. M. Cinar, "Turkey's Transformation under the AKP Rule," *The Muslim World* 96, no. 3 (2006): 469–86.

25. M. Somer, "Moderate Islam and Secularist Opposition in Turkey: Implications for the World, Muslims and Secular Democracy," *Third World Quarterly* 28, no. 7 (2007): 1271–89.

26. Zulal Kocer, "'Neden açık giyindin, darbecisin' diyerek saldırdılar," *Umut Gazetesi.* August 3, 2016, accessed August 8, 2016, http://umutgazetesi2.org/acik-giyindin-darbecisin-diyerek-saldirdilar/.
27. E. Knickmeyer, "Gul Elected to Turkey's Presidency," *The Washington Post,* August 29, 2007, accessed May 24, 2016, http://www.washingtonpost.com/wp-dyn/content/article/2007/08/28/AR2007082800223.html.
28. Ibid.
29. M. Tran, "Gul Elected as Turkish President," *The Guardian,* accessed May 24, 2016, http://www.theguardian.com/world/2007/aug/28/turkey.marktran1.
30. Knickmeyer, "Gul Elected to Turkey's Presidency."
31. Ibid.
32. Ibid.
33. Bassam Tibi, "Islamists Approach Europe: Turkey's Islamist Danger," *The Middle East Quarterly,* 2009, accessed August 16, 2016, http://www.meforum.org/2047/islamists-approach-europe.
34. "Turkey's Erdogan Hails Constitutional Referendum Win," *CNN,* September 12, 2010, accessed May 26, 2016, http://www.cnn.com/2010/WORLD/europe/09/12/turkey.referendum/.
35. "Turkey's Constitutional Referendum: Erdogan Pulls It Off," *The Economist,* September 13, 2010, accessed May 26, 2016, http://www.economist.com/blogs/newsbook/2010/09/turkeys_constitutional_referendum.
36. E. P. Licursi, "The Ergenekon Case and Turkey's Democratic Aspirations," *Freedom House,* February 7, 2012, accessed on May 26, 2016, https://freedomhouse.org/blog/ergenekon-case-and-turkey's-democratic-aspirations#.U1WLWFdPr3A.
37. "Turkey Sledgehammer Trial: Key Coup Sentences Upheld," *BBC,* October 9, 2013, accessed May 26, 2016, http://www.bbc.com/news/world-europe-24457491.
38. "Recep Tayyip Erdogan: Turkey's Ruthless President," *BBC,* May 5, 2016, accessed May 26, 2016, http://www.bbc.com/news/world-europe-13746679.
39. M. Akyol, "Does Erdogan Want His Own Islamic State?," *Al-Monitor: Turkey's Pulse,* April 29, 2016, accessed May 18, 2016, http://www.al-monitor.com/pulse/originals/2016/04/turkey-does-erdogan-aim-islamic-state.html#ixzz496hbLoYx.
40. Ibid.
41. "Ankara'da Hizb-ut Tahrir konferansında toplanan 5 bin kişi hilafet istedi" (In Ankara 5 thousand people called for caliphate in Ankara at Hizb-ut Tahrir's Conference), March 8, 2016, T24, accessed May 30, 2016, http://t24.com.tr/haber/ankarada-hizb-ut-tahrir-konferansinda-toplanan-5-bin-kisi-hilafet-istedi,331180.
42. Ibid.
43. "Başbakan'dan üçüncü balkon konuşması (Prime minister's third balcony speech)," *Hürriyet,* June 13, 2011, accessed May 30, 2016, http://www.hurriyet.com.tr/basbakandan-ucuncu-balkon-konusmasi-18015912.

3

Human Rights

It's not only the person who pulls the trigger, but those who made that possible who should also be defined as terrorists. There was no difference between a terrorist holding a gun or a bomb and those who use their position and pen to serve the aims.[1]

—Recep Tayyip Erdogan

Turkey became an European Union (EU) candidate country at the EU Helsinki Summit in December 1999. Its candidacy was subject to the understanding that actual negotiations would not start until Turkey met the "Copenhagen criteria," which enshrine human rights. The EU is more than a geographic area. It is a zone where "European values" and human rights are paramount. According to the Copenhagen criteria, EU candidate countries must meet economic and institutional requirements. They must also have "stable institutions guaranteeing democracy, the rule of law, human rights and respect for and protection of minorities."[2]

The prospect of EU membership is a powerful driver of reforms. The United States lobbied intensely on Turkey's behalf. It believed that human-rights improvements and a settlement of the Cyprus issue, divided since 1975, could be catalyzed by Turkey's European integration. The EU agreed at the December 2002 Copenhagen summit to start accession talks with Ankara as soon as Turkey satisfied the Copenhagen criteria.

The United States and EU Member States did not know what to expect when the Justice and Development Party (AKP) won elections in 2002. Erdogan's Islamism cast doubt on Turkey's readiness for further integration into Euro-Atlantic institutions. The AKP's ideological conflict with Turkey's secular elite also raised red flags in the West.

Erdogan inherited a legacy of widespread human rights violations from previous governments. Abuses occurred in plain sight. They were amply documented by international organizations—the United

Nations and the Council of Europe—as well as international and indigenous non-governmental organizations, such as Human Rights Watch, Amnesty International, and the Turkish Human Rights Association. Ankara strongly objected to the 1978 film, *Midnight Express*, which included scenes of torture and prison rape. Other widespread abuses included the torture and killing Kurds. Kurdish civilians were targeted in the name of fighting terrorism, sanctioned by the 1991 Law on the Fight against Terrorism. Journalists and civil society were also charged with breaches of national security for merely exercising their right to free expression.

Erdogan took bold steps after becoming prime minister in 2003. Using the AKP's parliamentary majority, Erdogan limited the powers of the National Security Council (NSC), abolished the death penalty, barred torture, and allowed greater cultural rights for Kurds in the fields of education and media. The AKP adopted a broad platform of human rights reforms by overhauling its penal code for the first time in seventy-eight years. It also amended the Turkish constitution, bringing it more in line with European standards. Erdogan was rewarded for his reforms by realizing a major foreign policy objective. The European Commission issued its 2002 "Regular report from the European Commission on progress towards accession," which recommended a date for Turkey to begin negotiations.

EU membership was potentially a counterweight to Turkey's partnership with the United States, which dominated Turkish foreign policy since Turkey joined NATO in 1952. Turkey found common ground with many European countries in its opposition to the United States–led invasion of Iraq. Turkey championed Palestinian human rights, broadening common ground with Europe. Erdogan was praised for criticizing Israel's targeted killing of Hamas leaders and lauded for calling the killing of Hamas' Sheikh Yassin a "terrorist act."

Erdogan forged an unlikely coalition with secular progressives in Turkey, despite their different conceptions of human rights. Erdogan did not support liberal democracy, as established by the Universal Declaration of Human Rights, the International Covenant on Economic Social and Cultural Rights, and the International Covenant on Civil and Political Rights. For Erdogan, human rights are Islamic rights. Women's rights are about wearing the hijab. It was expedient for Erdogan to espouse human rights in Western terms. Not because he believed in them, but because it advanced his political agenda. Compliance with the Copenhagen criteria justified measures to subordinate the military.

Developing affinities with the EU was also a way to distance Turkey from the United States, whom he blamed for chaos in Iraq. He criticized Washington for incubating a nascent state in Iraqi Kurdistan and failing to take action against the PKK in Qandil mountains of Northern Iraq.

In his role as foreign minister, Abdullah Gul was Turkey's primary envoy to Brussels. He was temperamentally well suited for the task of building relations with the EU. Gul is more liberal than Erdogan. He is statesmanlike, whereas Erdogan is confrontational at his core. Gul genuinely believes in EU values. For Erdogan, pursuit of EU membership was transactional. Having succeeded in taming the military, Erdogan tired of human rights hectoring by the Europeans and allowed Gul to become the face of Turkey in Brussels so he could focus on the domestic agenda.

Erdogan revealed his human rights preferences after the AKP won its second mandate on July 22, 2007. Though the AKP solidified its majority by gaining votes from Kurds, Erdogan did not focus on minority rights or negotiating peace with the PKK. Instead, he catered to the AKP base. Forgotten was the pledge to produce a national human rights program that mirrored milestones in the EU Accession Partnership. To the dismay of Kurdish supporters, progressives, and secularists, he used his political capital to push forward legislation allowing women to wear the hijab at universities and public institutions.

Turkey's relations with the EU started to sour when Erdogan focused almost exclusively on the hijab. The downturn in Turkey-EU relations was accelerated by France's recognition of the Armenian Genocide, as well as genocide recognition by the parliaments of other European countries. The European Commission did not make recognition of the Armenian Genocide a prerequisite for starting accession talks. However, the European Parliament adopted a resolution calling on Turkey to address its history as a condition for EU membership. When Gul became president in 2008, he focused on normalizing relations with Armenia and opening the Turkey-Armenia border gate. From 2008 to 2010, Armenia was a priority for Turkey's policy espousing "Zero Problems with Neighbors." After that, beginning in 2011, Turkey was pre-occupied with tumultuous transitions associated with the Arab Spring.

While Erdogan identified with strong leaders who were being overthrown, he also supported Islamists who rejected secular rule in favor of Sharia Law. Events in Egypt highlighted these competing goals. Mohammed Morsi of the Muslim Brotherhood led a popular movement to overthrow President Hosni Mubarak. In turn, Morsi was removed by General Abdel Fattah el-Sisi who arrested Morsi and his Muslim brothers. Morsi was convicted in a show trial and sentenced to death.

Concurrent with Morsi's overthrow in Egypt, Turks were taking to the streets to protest plans for a shopping center in Gezi Park. A rainbow coalition gathered in Gezi to demand protection of Istanbul's green areas. The movement, called "Taksim solidarity," included environmentalists, secular Turkish nationalists, Kurdish groups, hardline leftists, nonpolitical middle-class professionals, anti-capitalist Muslims and LGBT activists. Gezi was a love-fest with young people playing guitar, singing, and reading poetry.

Gezi protesters camped in the park for seventeen days. They were acting within their constitutional right guaranteeing freedom of assembly. Article 34 of the Turkish Constitution allows Turks to demonstrate peacefully without obtaining prior permission. However, the right to freedom of assembly is derogated by "national security, public order, public health, hooliganism, and actions that infringe on the rights of others."[3] Erdogan warned protesters to end their occupation. "If our brothers are still there, I am telling them in goodwill to please leave the area, because it belongs to all Istanbulites and it is not to be occupied by illegal groups."[4] Taksim solidarity members ignored his appeal, demanding a change in the zoning plan. Erdogan responded, "We've made our decision, and we will do as we have decided."[5]

Some twenty-five thousand police surrounded Istanbul's Taksim Square, then riot police attacked on May 30, 2013. In the name of "public order," they used tear gas and water cannons to crack down and disperse the crowd. The tent camp was burned; protesters fled in all directions to escape the tear gas. According to a local shopkeeper, "They have declared war on us. This is out of all proportion."[6]

Police brutality sparked a spiral of violence. On Istiklal Caddesi, the pedestrian street leading from Taksim, a fifteen-year-old boy was hit in the head by a gas canister; he later died. In the melee, Gezi protesters burned property and hurled concrete slabs at police vehicles. They defaced buildings with graffiti. Pitched battles left four people dead and more than five thousand injured. In the aftermath, Erdogan added insult to injury by pledging to build a mosque in the square that would further encroach on green space.

While Gezi was the epicenter of protests, antigovernment demonstrations occurred in sixty cities across Turkey. The contagion of violence spread from Istanbul to Ankara, Izmir, and Bodrum. The police crackdown further fueled protests. Erdogan delivered an ominous warning. He threatened to summon AKP supporters to the streets. "If you use provocative words, our people will never forgive you," Erdogan said. "If you gather 100,000 people, I can gather a million."[7] It was a familiar refrain, which Erdogan actualized during the failed coup of July 2016.

Plans to build a shopping mall galvanized protests. However, malaise was much deeper. Erdogan's authoritarianism was the real problem. "We are fed up," said a student in Gezi. "They don't give us any breathing space anymore."[8] Turks were upset by Erdogan's intrusion into their private lives. For example, Erdogan publicly called on women to bear at least three children. He made comments about their make-up, lip stick color, and what clothes they should wear. The Gezi protests occurred in the wake of a bill that restricted alcohol sales.

International condemnation was swift. The US State Department spokeswoman said, "We are concerned about the number of people who were injured when police dispersed protesters in Istanbul's Gezi Park. We believe that Turkey's long-term stability, security and prosperity is best guaranteed by upholding the fundamental freedoms of expression, assembly and association, which is what it seems these individuals were doing."[9] The State Department added, "We certainly support universally peaceful protests."[10] Amnesty International condemned the "use of excessive force" by police. It called the police action "brutal denial of the right to peaceful assembly in Turkey."[11]

EU Enlargement Commissioner Stefan Fuele added, "Peaceful demonstrations constitute a legitimate way for groups to express their views in a democratic society. Excessive use of force by police against these demonstrations has no place in such a democracy." Erdogan responded angrily to Fuele's comments. He accused the EU of double standards, maintaining that European governments would respond much more harshly under similar circumstances. Erdogan insisted he was open to "democratic demands," but would not tolerate "terrorism, violence, and vandalism." He blasted the EU enlargement process for "unjust obstructions." Criticizing the EU played to growing discontent among Turks towards the enlargement process. Whereas more than 70 percent of Turks supported Turkey's bid to join the EU in 2005, support was down to 30 percent by 2013.[12]

There was scant media coverage of the Gezi protests. During the height of street battles, state media showed a documentary about penguins. The protest in Gezi, and subsequent crackdown, signified a turning point in Erdogan's approach to human rights and freedom of expression. Turkey increasingly limited press freedom.[13]

Gezi also marked a new phase in Turkey's crackdown on social media. As many as five million social-media messages were sent during the protests to share information on the events and mobilize protests across the country. According to Erdogan, "Social media is the worst menace to society. The best example of lies can be found [on Twitter].[14] The government launched an investigation to track down tweets during the protest and expose "provocateurs."[15]

Rounding up activists was a direct violation of laws to protect freedom of expression. Article 26 of Turkey's constitution guarantees freedom of expression and dissemination of thought. "Everyone has the right to express and disseminate his/her thoughts and opinions by speech, in writing or in pictures or through other media, individually or collectively. This freedom includes the liberty of receiving or imparting information or ideas without interference by official authorities. The provision shall not preclude subjecting transmission by radio, television, cinema, or similar means to a system of licensing."

However, Article 26 is derogated by provisions in the penal code and the criminal procedure code. The broadly worded antiterrorism law effectively leaves punishment of normal journalistic activity to the discretion of prosecutors and judges. The government restricted Internet, Facebook, and Twitter. According to Amnesty International, "Criminal investigations have been started against commentators who documented the [Gezi] protests. They were followed by random prosecutions of people posting opinions on social media during the protests."[16]

In violation of Article 26, forty-six journalists were arrested for working in the "press wing" of the Kurdish Communities Union (KCK). They were charged under the antiterrorism law for membership in an illegal group, but released pending trial.

Reforms were uneven. The Fourth Judicial Reform package was adopted by the TGNA in April 2013, at a time when the government was trying to restart negotiations with the PKK. Articles 6/2 and 7/2 of the Antiterrorism Law made the publication of statements by illegal groups less restrictive. To be a crime, the statement must involve coercion, incite violence, or represent a genuine threat. The impact of reforms was limited by preexisting provisions such as Article 125 on criminal defamation, Article 301 and 314 of the Penal Code.

A Fifth Judicial Reform package was passed in February 2014. It reduced the maximum period of pretrial detention from ten to five years. As a result, several journalists pending trial were released from jail. The TGNA passed amendments to the penal and criminal procedure codes in December 2014, which lowered the threshold of evidence required for searching individuals or premises from "strong suspicion based on concrete evidence" to "reasonable suspicion."

Within a year, the government assumed increased powers to shut down websites.[17] The Internet Law No. 5651 of February 2015 empowered Turkey's Telecommunication Directorate (TIB) to block websites without court approval. As a form of protection, the court was required to uphold TIB's order within two days for the block to stay in effect. In September 2015, the law was strengthened to allow the government to block websites in the interest of "national security, the restoration of public order, and the prevention of crimes." A month later, however, the Constitutional Court overturned these powers.

Adopted in April 2015, the Law Amending the Law on State Intelligence Services and the National Intelligence Organization allowed the National Intelligence Agency (MIT) to access personal data without a court order. It provided immunity to MIT personnel from legal violations committed in the course of their work. It also criminalized reporting on MIT's activities. A new law allowed sentences of up to nine years for publishing information from leaked intelligence material.[18]

On July 1, 2016, TIB blocked access to the websites of news sources including *Yeni Hayat Gazatesi, Yarina Bakis Daily, Subuo Haber*, and *On Yedi Yirmi Bes*.[19] TIB said it was acting under authority of Article 8 of Law 5651. But TIB quickly retracted; Article 8 only allows for blockage of publications that promote drug use, prostitution, sexual abuse, suicide and gambling. While disassociating itself from acting under authority provided by Article 8, TIB continued to block some web sites.[20]

Article 301 of Turkey's Penal Code makes it a crime to denigrate "the Turkish Nation, the State of the Turkish Republic or the organs and institutions of the State."[21] The TGNA adopted a set of largely cosmetic amendments to Article 301 in 2008. For example, the maximum prison sentence was reduced from three years to two. The Ministry of Justice was required to approve prosecutions using Article 301 on a case-by-case basis, which significantly curbed its application in practice. While very few of those prosecuted under Article 301 were actually convicted, the trials are time-consuming and expensive. Nonetheless, Article 301 exerts a chilling effect on speech. Between 2003 and 2014, sixty-three journalists were sentenced to prison for violating Article 301.[22]

Article 216 of the Penal Code, which bans incitement of hatred or violence based on ethnicity, class, or religion carries a prison term of up to three years. It is used against journalists and other commentators. Kurds and those associated with the political left were prosecuted under Article 216 and Article 314.

Article 299 of the Penal Code established criminal liability for insulting the President. Between August 2014 and March 2016, the prosecutor opened 1,845 cases based on Article 299.[23] Scholars were prosecuted for merely retweeting messages.[24] Even schoolchildren were arrested for insulting the President.[25] Pending cases were dismissed in July 2016.

The German satirist and comedian, Jan Boehmermann, read a poem about Erdogan, sarcastically accusing him of "beating girls" and having sex with goats and sheep.[26] The poem also asserted that Erdogan likes to "repress minorities, kick Kurds and beat Christians while watching child porn."[27] Turkish authorities issued an official demarche to the German government demanding it prosecute Boehmermann. Germany was in the middle of sensitive negotiations with Turkey over the refugee and migrant crisis. Chancellor Angela Merkel acceded to Erdogan's demands. The German prosecutor brought charges against Boehmermann for "insulting organs and representatives of foreign states."[28]

The Gulen movement was a lightning rod. On December 14, 2014, security forces conducted raids across the country against outlets suspected of affiliation with Gulen. Leading media groups affiliated with the Gulen movement—Zaman, Koza Ipek Media group, and Samanyolu Broadcasting Group—were effected. Several journalists were arrested, including Ekrem Dumanli, *Zaman's* editor in chief, under suspicion of "establishing and managing an armed terror organization" to seize state power. While Dumanli and other prominent detainees from *Zaman* were released pending trial, Hidayet Karaca, general manager of the Samanyolu Broadcasting Group, remained in pre-trial detention for more than a year. The editor of *Cumhuriyet*, a secular opposition newspaper, was detained on October 31, 2016. Arrest warrants were issued for 13 other of the paper's journalists and executive. Turkish courts ordered a ban on reporting of the detentions.

Turkish courts and regulators issued gag-orders on coverage of specific topics. A ban on allegations of MIT involvement in weapons shipments to Syria was imposed in February 2014. Another was issued in March 2014, restricting dissemination of leaked audio recordings of a national security meeting at the Foreign Ministry. In May 2014, a mining disaster near the town of Soma killed 301 miners. News articles raised concern about safety regulations and collusion between the AKP and the Soma mining company. The Supreme Council of Radio and Television (RTUK), Turkey's broadcast regulator, instructed media to refrain from airing material that may be "disrespectful to feelings of the families of victims." In June 2014, an Ankara court imposed a ban on reporting about the humiliating kidnap of forty-nine Turkish citizens from the Turkish consulate in Mosul, Iraq. In November 2014, another court in Ankara banned covering a parliamentary inquiry into corruption allegations concerning four former ministers implicated in a financial scandal the previous year.

Minority rights remained a concern, not only for the international community, but for peace-loving Turks tired of civil war. In January 2016, more than fourteen hundred academics signed a "peace petition" calling for an end to Turkey's "deliberate massacre and deportation of Kurdish people." The petition, entitled "We will not be party to this crime", also called for peace talks with the PKK.

The government responded with a broadside on academic freedom and freedom of expression. Erdogan pronounced: "We are not in the position to seek permission from the so-called academics. These [people] should know their place." Erdogan referred to the peace petition as a "betrayal." He called its signatories "darkest of the dark" and "a fifth column" for terrorists. Signatories were harassed and targeted with various forms of recrimination. Some received death threats on their university voice mail and social media. According to Erdogan. "They commit the same crime as those who carry out massacres."[29]

The European Parliament (EP) issued its bi-yearly progress report on April 14, 2016. The 52-page report was harshly critical of Turkey on a number of fronts. "Turkey still has one of the highest number of imprisoned journalists in the world" and, "according to the ranking made by Freedom House for freedom of the press and media, Turkey is still ranked as not having a free press and its Internet freedom [is] only partly free." By November 2016, Turkey had more journalists in jail than any country in the world. It noted "serious backsliding," over the past two years, on freedom of speech, expression and opinion. The report condemned "statements by the president of Turkey against the Constitutional Court. It called for the immediate release of all jailed journalists and encouraged European diplomats to closely monitor criminal cases against journalists." The report deplored "the increasingly authoritarian tendencies of the Turkish leadership." It expressed concern about "rapidly deteriorating" security situation in the country, especially in the southeast where Kurdish civilians were targeted. While the report acknowledged "Turkey's legitimate right to fight against terrorism, subject to international law," it insisted that that "all operations by security forces must be proportional and not take the form of collective punishment." According to the EP, "The Turkish government has a responsibility to protect all people living on its territory, irrespective of their cultural or religious origins."

The report was repeatedly delayed so as not to upset negotiations between the EU and Turkey on curtailing refugee flows to Europe. The EP was self-critical for delaying the report's release. Many Members of the European Parliament (MEPs) believed that Europe's coddling of Erdogan signaled a preference for realpolitik over a principled position on human rights. The delay also gave Erdogan time to coerce the EU into greater concessions as part of the refugee deal. "The EP believes that the postponement of the Commission's 2015 report until after the November 2015 Turkish elections was a wrong decision, as it gave the impression that the EU is willing to go silent on violations of fundamental rights in return for the Turkish government's cooperation on refugees." The EP also called on the European Commission and the European Council "not to ignore internal developments in Turkey and to clearly stand up for respect for the rule of law and fundamental rights in Turkey, as stipulated in the Copenhagen criteria, and irrespective of other interests."

The report did not use diplomatic language such as "call attention to" or "express concern" about human rights. It used much stronger language, setting aside diplomatic niceties. The term "condemn" was used more than a dozen times. In a blow to Turkey's EU candidacy, the report explicitly stated, "There has been a regression moving increasingly away from meeting the Copenhagen criteria to which candidate countries must adhere." Turkey's human rights record was worse in 2015 than it was in 2004, when Turkey started accession negotiations.

Ankara was offended by repeated condemnations. It was livid at reference to the "Armenian Genocide" in the EP report, which was released just ten days prior to the centennial and worldwide remembrance activities of the Armenian Genocide. Turkey's EU Minister Volkan Bozkir angrily rejected the report, declaring it "null and void."[30]

Kemalism gave rise to institutions and laws that routinely violated human rights in supposed service of territorial integrity and secularism. The machinery and legal basis for abusing human rights was expanded in response to the leftist movement of the 1970s and 1980s. Security measures intensified during the period of martial law in southeastern provinces during the 1980s and 1990s when fighting terrorism was used to justify gross human right abuses. Erdogan's egregious human rights abuses sought to silence dissent by civil society and independent media. Turkey was condemned by free-speech advocates for its wholesale arrest and dismissal of journalists and other so-called oppositionists after the coup of July 2016.

Notes

1. Gianluca Mezzofiore, "Turkey Protests: Terror Squads Lead Government Crackdown on Protesters and Social Media." *International Business Times*, June 18, 2013, accessed on July 28, 2016, http://blog.amnestyusa.org/europe/scholars-jailed-in-turkeys-on-going-war-against-freedom-of-action-how-you-can-take-action/.
2. "Accession Criteria (Copenhagen Criteria)," accessed July 28, 2016, http://eur-lex.europa.eu/summary/ glossary/accession_criteria_copenhague.html.
3. "The Constitution of the Republic of Turkey," accessed July 31, 2016, http://www.allaboutturkey.com/constitution.htm.
4. Emre Peker and Joe Parkinson, "Police Launch Crackdown to Clear Istanbul Park," *The Wall Street Journal*, June 16, 2013, accessed July 28, 2016, http://www.wsj.com/articles/SB100014241278873237343045785468205079313 96.
5. Constanze Letsch, "Turkey Protests Spread after Violence in Istanbul over Park Demolition," *The Guardian*, May 31, 2013, accessed July 29, 2016, https://www.theguardian.com/world/2013/may/31/istanbul-protesters-violent-clashes-police.
6. Ibid.
7. Jacob Resneck and Clare Morgana Gillis, "Anti-government Protests Spread Across Turkey," *USA Today*, June 3, 2013, accessed July 29, 2016, http://www.usatoday.com/story/news/world/2013/06/02/turkey-protests/2381911/.
8. Letsch, "Turkey Protests Spread after Violence in Istanbul over Park Demolition."
9. Resneck and Gillis, "Anti-government Protests Spread Across Turkey."
10. Letsch, "Turkey Protests Spread after Violence in Istanbul over Park Demolition."
11. "Gezi Park Protests: Brutal Denial of the Right to Peaceful Assembly in Turkey," *Amnesty International*, October 2012, accessed July 28, 2016, https://www.amnestyusa.org/sites/default/files/ eur440222013en.pdf.
12. Chris Morris, "Turkey Protests: Erdogan Rejects EU Criticism," *BBC News*, June 8, 2013, accessed July 29, 2016, http://www.bbc.com/news/world-europe-22817460.

13. Mark Lowen, "The Problem with Insulting Turkey's President Erdogan," *BBC News*, April 16, 2015, accessed July 16, 2016, http://www.bbc.com /news/world-europe-32302697.

14. Mezzofiore, "Turkey Protests."

15. Ibid.

16. "After Gezi: Amnesty Issues Major New Report," *Human Rights Turkey*, June 10, 2014, accessed July 29, 2016, https://humanrightsturkey.org/2014/06/10 /after-gezi-amnesty-issues-major-new-report/.

17. Ibid.

18. "Turkey," *Freedom House*, Accessed July 28, 2016, https://freedomhouse. org/report/freedom-press/2015/turkey.

19. "Independent Daily Defies Censor: 'We Are Under Attack over Voicing Gov't's Failure to Fight ISIS," *Turkish Minute*, June 2016, accessed July 28, 2016, https://www.turkishminute.com/2016/07/01/independent-daily -defies-censor-attack-voicing-govts-failure-fight-isis/.

20. Ibid.

21. Veronika Bílková, et al., "European Commission for Democracy through Law (Venice Commission)," *Council of Europe*, March 15, 2016, accessed July 28, 2016, http://www.venice.coe.int/webforms/documents/default. aspx?pdffile=CDL-AD(2016)002-e.

22. Lowen, "The Problem with Insulting Turkey's President Erdogan."

23. Associated Press in Ankara, "1,845 Erdogan Insult Cases Opened in Turkey since 2014," *The Guardian*, March 2, 2016, accessed July 28, 2016, https:// www.theguardian.com/world/2016/mar/02/turkeys-justice-minister -defends-allowing-1845-insult-cases-to-go-ahead.

24. Erdogan announced that all charges brought under Article 299 would be dropped on July 30, 2016.

25. "Lise öğrencisi Erdogan'a hakaretten tutuklandı!," *Evrensel*, December 24, 2014, accessed July 16, 2016, https://www.evrensel.net/haber/100567/ lise-ogrencisi-erdogana-hakaretten-tutuklandi.

26. "German Prosecutors Open Case against Comedian Jan Böhmermann," *Deutsche Welle*, July 4, 2016, accessed July 16, 2016, http://www.dw.com /en/german-prosecutors-open-case-against-comedian-jan-böhmermann /a-19170468.

27. Adam Taylor, "A German Comedian Read a Lewd Poem about Turkey's Erdogan. Now He Could Face Jail Time," *The Washington Post*, April 7, 2016, accessed July 16, 2016, https://www.washingtonpost.com/news/worldviews /wp/2016/04/07/a-german-comedian-read-a-lewd-poem-about-turkeys -erdogan-now-he-could-face-jail-time/.

28. "German Prosecutors Open Case against Comedian Jan Böhmermann."

29. Ari Khalidi, "Turkish President Slams Academics Calling for Peace," *Kurdistan 24*, January 12, 2016, accessed July 30, 2016, http://www.kurdistan24.net/en /news/1a7b68b6-9b83-459e-82a9-813843aa6b27/Turkish-President -slams-academics-calling-for-peace.

30. Cengiz Candar, "EU Report Ruffles Turkey's Feathers," *Al-Monitor*, April 15, 2016, accessed July 30, 2016, http://www.al-monitor.com/pulse/originals /2016/04/turkey-european-union-progress-report.html.

4

Corruption

*All the dirty laundry will come out. Many people
won't sleep a wink tonight.*[1]

—Kemal Kilicdaroglu, chairman of the
Republican People's Party (CHP)

Erdogan touted principles of honesty, ethics, and virtue in his 1994
race for mayor of Istanbul. He defeated an incumbent of the "Republican People's Party (CHP) incumbent who was mired in allegations
of corruption. In 2002, the AKP ran on a platform of clean and honest
government. The AKP rose in response to Turkey's legacy of corruption.
Erdogan appealed to voters by declaring war on the Three Ys: *Yolsuzluk*
(corruption), *Yasaklar* (prohibitions), and *Yoksulluk* (poverty). The
concept of clean and effective government was new in Turkish politics.

Corruption was widespread among Turkey's political elites, as in other
countries. The urbanization process, which started in the 1950s, helped
ingrain corruption. Urbanization involved illegal construction in the
inner cities across Turkey. These houses were called *Gecekondu*, which
means "built at night." Once a house was built, laws protected the house
from being torn down. Construction firms bribed local officials so they
could turn these slum shanties into apartment complexes. Fortunes were
made by the developers and local officials with whom they conspired.

After the military coup of 1980, corruption discredited center-right
political parties such as the Motherland Party and the True Path Party.[2]
Turgut Ozal presented himself as a paragon of nationalist virtue.
However, he had a seamy side. Ozal opposed foreign investment in lieu
of a state-run economy, which gave rise to widespread patronage and a
pervasive underground, unreported, and unregulated economy. Nepotism was rampant in his administration. Ozal's brothers, sons, nephews,
and other relatives rose in government and business circles. His son,
Ahmet, fled the country under a cloud of corruption allegations.[3]

Tansu Ciller served as prime minister from 1993 to 1996. She and her husband, Ozer, were notorious for self-dealing. Ozer was a manager at Istanbul Bankasi, which financed eight companies owned by the Cillers. When the bank failed, the Turkish government assumed its debts. Prime Minister Ciller tampered with the privatization of Tedas, an electric company, and Tofas, an automobile manufacturer, generating fees for Ozer. Six million dollars from her prime minister's discretionary fund went missing. The prime minister's discretionary fund was often used for special intelligence and other dark operations. The so-called Susurluk incident occurred in 1996 during Ciller's administration. A traffic accident in Susurluk killed three people. Contents of the vehicle led to credible accusations of state-mafia connections and state-sponsored assassinations.

Erdogan also used his political posts for self-dealing. Upon embarking on a political path, Erdogan said: "I have only this ring as an asset. If you hear that I have assets more than this, you can call me a thief." During his term as Istanbul's mayor, Erdogan's net worth increased thirteenfold.[4]

Beyond personal enrichment, Erdogan's corruption benefitted Turkish officials, their family members, and financial supporters of the AKP. He also used financial levers to silence dissent. A new class of wealth holders emerged in Turkey's conservative Anatolian heartland through Erdogan's patronage. The AKP brought Turkey out of economic recession by borrowing money to spend on construction and infrastructure, propelling an economic boom and making Turkey a powerhouse in the G-20. At the same time, there was a commensurate increase in contributions to the AKP. The so-called pooling system required businessmen who received government contracts to donate 10 percent of a contract's value to the AKP.[5] The Ministry of Transport, Maritime Affairs, and Communications, headed by Binali Yildirim who is currently prime minister, became a cash cow for the AKP.

Those who refused to play by Erdogan's rules paid a steep price. Large construction and engineering companies with historic ties to the CHP, such as Enka, all but stopped bidding on government contracts. Conglomerates with media holdings self-censored their news reporting, lest the government reject their bids on public tenders. The Turkish government targeted Dogan Holdings in 2008, a multibillion-dollar industrial conglomerate owning properties and media outlets such as *Hurriyet, Posta*, and *CNN Turk*. Dogan's news organizations reported corrupt practices in the development of commercial properties involving AKP local officials and their business cronies in

Istanbul, Gaziantep, and Batman. Erdogan accused Aydin Dogan of using his media outlets to target the government. In reprisal, Dogan Holdings was denied permission to renovate its Istanbul Hilton property. Its request to upgrade the broadcast license for *CNN Turk* was also rejected. Turkey's Capital Markets Board, under AKP control, fined Dogan $3.22 billion for tax evasion.

As part of the EU accession process, Turkey was required to implement laws against corruption. The government adopted an anticorruption action plan in 2010. It upgraded the penal code to criminalize corrupt activities such as bribery, extortion, money laundering, and abuse of office. These reforms were merely window dressing. In practice, anticorruption authorities were ineffective. Rules were lackadaisically enforced. After the AKP won elections in 2011, earning a third mandate, officials became increasingly bold in their self-dealing. Impunity fostered a culture of corruption that touched the highest levels of government, as well as the Erdogan family.

Police officers raided several homes and detained fifty-two people with ties to the AKP on December 17, 2013. During the raids, police seized $17.5 million in cash, including $4.5 million from Suleyman Aslan, the director of state-owned Halkbank, and $750,000 at the home of Baris Guler, son of the interior minister. Prosecutors accused fourteen people of bribery, corruption, fraud, and money laundering. Reza Zarrab, a dual Iranian-Turkish national was charged with gold smuggling and bribing cabinet ministers.

As the crackdown unfolded, implicating the off-spring of three cabinet ministers, Erdogan allegedly called Bilal, his son, instructing him to dispose of cash at several family homes. Wiretaps of the conversation were released on YouTube. At eight in the morning on December 17, 2013, Erogan called Bilal: "Now I'm telling you, whatever you have in the house, get rid of it, OK?" Father and son spoke several times during the day. In their fourth conversation just before midnight, Bilal indicated that he still had "30 million euros ($39 million) that we could not yet get rid of" and suggested they give the money to a businessman "or buy a flat." Erdogan assured Bilal, "Whatever, we will deal with it." Bilal asked, "Do you want all of it to disappear, or do you want to keep some money for yourself, father?" Erdogan replied, "No, it can't stay, son."[6] Bilal also asked, "Berat has an idea to buy villas from Sehrizar Apartments. What did you think?" The real estate registry confirmed that Berat Albayrak, Erdogan's son-in-law and current minister of energy, purchased two villas in Sehrizar.[7]

Erdogan did not dispute the contents or authenticity of the voices on the recordings. However, he called the phone tapping a "despicable and treacherous act" and an "immoral montage."[8] He confirmed that branches of the Turkish government have been wiretapping him and other top politicians, calling it the "biggest eavesdropping scandal in Turkish history."[9] Erdogan said: "They have been eavesdropping on our ministers, our MPs, and all of their families . . . for years. They even eavesdropped on the state's encrypted lines. A president cannot speak with a prime minister without being wiretapped."[10]

Erdogan blamed Fethullah Gulen, whom he accused of an "attempted coup." He accused Gulen's "parallel state" of permeating the judiciary, police, and the media. Erdogan complained about Gulen's "interference" in a phone call with Obama, demanding his extradition. "The person who is disrupting our internal affairs is a guest in your country."[11]

Turkish officials charged Gulenists with treason and called them "terrorists." Erdogan called actions by prosecutors and police a "coup attempt." The government filed a complaint charging Gulen and sixty-nine co-defendants with plotting to overthrow the Turkish government and with membership in a terrorist organization. If convicted, Gulen and the other defendants would face jail terms of up to 330 years.[12]

The conspiracy mentality fueled a witch hunt, leading to the dismissal of police officers, prosecutors, and judges across the country. "We knew we would be taken off duty within hours," said Yasin Topcu, the former deputy head of Istanbul's financial crimes unit. "In fact, Ankara's response was slower than we thought."[13] Erdogan tightened the reins, taking control over the future appointment of judges and prosecutors. Rules were also adopted imposing more scrutiny over communications and the Internet. Twitter and YouTube were banned.

Erdogan insinuated that foreign ambassadors were behind the corruption investigation, including US Ambassador to Turkey Francis J. Ricciardone. When Ricciardone criticized the rule of law in Turkey and defended Gulen from accusations of terrorism, Erdogan blasted him for "provocative actions" and threatened to throw him out of the country. The State Department issued a written statement: "The United States is in no way involved in the ongoing corruption and bribery operation. Nobody should put Turkey-US relations in danger with unfounded claims."[14] Other foreign envoys were also scapegoated. Interior Minister Efkan Ala accused Israel of involvement.

Ahmet Davutoglu declared, "[We will] break the arm of anyone involved in graft, even if it's our own brother."[15] Four ministers were implicated and took the fall. Economy Minister Zafer Caglayan, Interior Minister Muammer Guler, European Union Affairs Minister Egemen Bagis, and Environment and Urban Planning Minister Erdogan Bayraktar were forced to resign. By throwing them under the bus, Erdogan successfully deflected accusations that he and his family were involved.

Turkey's stock market fell after the revelations, as did the Turkish lira. However, markets quickly rebounded. With Turkey's economy humming along, Turks wanted to put the incident behind them. Erdogan successfully managed to sweep the scandal under the rug. There was no lasting impact. A majority of Turks believed the corruption allegations were credible, but they bought the AKP's line about Gulen's role.

In May 2014, the Public Prosecutor's Office announced it was closing the case, dropping all charges against fifty-three suspects implicated in the corruption scandal. As part of the cover-up, the Parliamentary Corruption Investigation Commission announced it would not refer cases against ex-ministers to the Supreme Council, which is responsible for prosecuting senior officials. The commission announced it would destroy recordings of the accused ex-ministers and their sons, essentially destroying the evidence. Though Aslan and Guler maintained that the cash found at their homes on December was planted by the police, the prosecutor's office returned the money with interest.

When the AKP took over in 2003, the Turkish Anti-Smuggling and Organized Crime Department offered to prepare a new anti-corruption law. However, it was rejected by the government. Instead the AKP amended the Public Procurement Law 163 times between 2003 and 2015, creating conditions more favorable to corrupt practices.[16] According to Transparency International's Corruption Perceptions Index (CPI), corruption in Turkey was getting worse. Transparency International ranks countries on a scale of 0 to 100. Zero is "very corrupt" and hundred "very clean." In the CPI of 2014, Turkey experienced the sharpest drop of any of the 175 countries surveyed, falling five points to a CPI score of 45. It slid from fifty-third to seventy-fourth in the overall rankings.[17] Erdogan insisted there was no corruption in his country during remarks in Brussels in January 2013. According to Transparency International, "If the government really wants to lift Turkey into the ranks of the top 10 economies in the world by 2023, as it has so often said, then sooner or later Ankara will have to face up to its own sleaze problem."[18]

The EU published its progress report for Turkey as a candidate country in October 2013. The report highlighted corruption in Turkey.

The word "concern" was mentioned 39 times in the 80-page report.[19] According to the report, "The government's response to allegations of corruption targeting high-level personalities, including members of the government and their families, raised serious concerns over the independence of judiciary and the rule of law".[20] The EU demanded a fully transparent and impartial investigation. Questioning Erdogan's claim that Turkey was free of corruption, EU officials asked why four ministers had to resign if there was no corruption.[21]

Erdogan made special efforts to shield Reza Zarrab. He vouched for Zarrab's character, calling him a "philanthropist" whose work had "contributed to the country". Zarrab made donations to a charity established by Emine Erdogan called the Social Development Center for Education and Social Solidarity. Before he and prosecutors involved in the case were forced to resign, Deputy Police Chief Yasin Topcu compiled a dossier on bribery and other lavish gifts provided by Zarrab to ministers and the CEO of HalkBank, which included a $37,000 grand piano, a $350,000 watch, and millions of dollars in cash.

Zarrab required reciprocity for his largess. He called in favors, including release of his impounded plane and police escorts through Istanbul's heavy traffic jams. Zarrab owned many companies in Turkey, such as the Mapna Group, Royal Holding, Durak Foreign Currency Exchange, Al Nafees Exchange, Royal Emerald Investments, Asi Precious Metals, ECH Jewelry, and Gunes General Trading. These enterprises were favored by Turkish regulators. Topcu's 309-page file detailed Zarrab's gold trade, which Zarrab publicly acknowledged to be worth $12 billion.[22]

Selling Iranian gold and laundering the proceeds through Turkish banks violated US sanctions. US investigators started quietly investigating Zarrab and building a case against him for sanctions-busting, fraud, and money laundering. On March 19, 2016, Zarrab arrived at Miami International Airport for a holiday in the United States with his pop-star wife and daughter. He was taken out of the queue while going through customs, handcuffed, and arrested. Why Zarrab acted so recklessly is unknown. Zarrab may have believed he was acting legally, exploiting a perceived loophole in US sanctions on Iran to buy oil and gas in exchange for gold. Or Zarrab could have concluded he was untouchable after Erdogan intervened personally to squash the charges against him in 2013.

A former senior AKP official, who wishes to remain anonymous, alleges that Erdogan sanctioned a scheme to launder tens of billions of dollars. Zarrab managed the transactions. Officials were skimming 15 percent with revenue to be divided between Erdogan and Gulenists in the customs agency and police. Erdogan refused to hand over Gulen's share. Furious, Gulen approached Bulent Arinc and proposed to dump Erdogan, make Arinc prime minister and Abdullah Gul president. Erdogan was outraged when he learned of Gulen's proposal. Erdogan swore Gulen a mortal enemy.[23]

Preet Bharara, the US Attorney for the Southern District of New York, was in charge of the Zarrab case. Bharara has a reputation for tenacity, integrity, and splashy media-grabbing prosecutions. Known as the "top cop" on Wall Street, Bharara has prosecuted white-collar criminals, New York politicians, gang members, and crooked foreign nationals. Bharara orchestrated the arrest in Thailand of the Russian arms merchant, Viktor Bout. In response, Bharara was banned from traveling to Russia. He indicted the Jamaican drug lord, Christopher 'Dudus' Coke. He charged seven Iranians with cyberattacks against US banks and trying to take over control of a dam in Westchester near New York City. Bharara was familiar with international controversy. Under Bharara, the Southern District had a tradition of independence. Bharara was known to resist direction, leading to tensions with the Justice Department and the US Department of State.

Zarrab's indictment was unsealed in the Southern District of New York. It could put Zarrab behind bars for a very long time. Zarrab could be sent to jail for five years if convicted of defrauding the United States, twenty years for violating the International Emergency Powers Act, which regulates Iran sanctions, thirty years for bank fraud, and twenty years for money laundering. Bharara tweeted: "[Zarrab will] soon face American justice in a Manhattan courtroom."[24]

Zarrab's legal counsel at the prestigious international law firm of Baker & McKenzie maintained his innocence, insisting that Zarrab was not a flight risk. They petitioned for Zarrab to be released on his own recognizance and be allowed to reside in a luxury apartment with an electronic ankle bracelet to monitor his movements. Bharara took a hard line, opposing bail for Zarrab and threatened to freeze his assets.

The indictment of Zarrab revealed a sordid picture. When Iran was denied access to the SWIFT international money transfer system as a result of US sanctions, the Iranian government developed a strategy for by-passing SWIFT using Turkey's Halkbank. Zarrab was allegedly the bag man. He sent money to front companies in China, identifying the transfers as export reimbursements. Funds were moved from the

Chinese companies to companies in Turkey, also identified as export reimbursements. Then the funds were used to buy gold, which was transported to Iran via middlemen in Dubai. Zarrab was careless with his e-mail. On December 3, 2011, he wrote the governor of Iran's Central Bank expressing his readiness for "economic jihad against sanctions."

Zarrab paid bribes to Turkish officials to look the other way. The Minister of Economy, Zafer Caglayan, received between 0.3 and 0.4 percent on each deal. His total take was $35 million. Zarrab also paid $5.67 million to HalkBank's CEO, Arslan. HalkBank had experience with gold transactions involving Iran. It was already purchasing Iranian oil and gas using gold as the method of payment. The US banned gold exports to Iran in July 2013.

Conspiracy theories abound. Former AKP Deputy Fevzi Isbaran speculated that Zarrab feared the AKP would kill him for knowing too much about the involvement of senior AKP officials. Isbaran believes that Zarrab told the FBI of his visit to Miami, with the purpose of being arrested. Zarrab agreed to rat out Turkish officials in exchange for a light sentence and an agreement to retain part of his wealth.[25]

It is unlikely that Zarrab gave himself up to the FBI. He filed an elaborate bail motion. The prosecutors would have told him at the outset not to file difficult motions if he wanted to get credit as a cooperator. Zarrab spent a fortune on legal fees with Baker & McKenzie, suggesting he was really fighting the prosecutors.

Other speculation includes Zarrab's complicity with MIT to arm ISIS. In 2013, MIT needed funds to arm Islamists and move them from Turkey to Syria. A portion of Zarrab's profits from illicit gold sales may have been skimmed to cover the Turkish government's costs. Zarrab was Erdogan's agent. Hakan Fidan implemented the scheme.

Such theories are notional. However, Zarrab has incentive to tell Bharara what he knows in exchange for more lenient treatment. Ankara issued no official response when Zarrab was arrested. The CHP's Kemal Kilicdaroglu predicted, "All the dirty laundry will come out. Many people won't sleep a wink tonight."[26]

Bharara was hailed as a hero in Turkey, and became a sensation on social media. He gained nearly three hundred thousand Twitter followers, many of them Turkish. One twitter user in Turkey asked Bharara, "You want anything from Turkey? Turkish raki, shish kebab, lokuum, Turkish carpet? Just ask. We are at your service."[27]

Erdogan's spin doctors launched a campaign to defame Bharara, making absurd allegations. Bharara was accused of joining an international conspiracy against Turkey. *Sabah*, a pro-government newspaper, accused him of being a part of the "Fethullah Gulen terror organization." *Sabah* also published a doctored photo of Bharara accepting a prize from Hizmet, the Gulen organization.

Bilal Erdogan was one of the Turks nervous about Zarrab's arrest. Bilal was routinely the center of controversy. He and Zarrab were both implicated in the corruption scandal of 2013. On December 25, 2013, the Turkish Anti-Smuggling and Organized Crime Department opened an investigation into Bilal's insider trading on government contracts. The department alleged that Bilal set up a company to receive government contracts, which he would resell for a huge profit. For example, Bosphorus 360 was awarded a government tender to build a police training school for $550 million. The company resold the contract for $1.1 billion. Bilal's partner, Yasin El-Kadi, was allegedly involved in terrorist financing. El-Kadi was a major target of the investigation launched on December 25, 2013, which included pay-to-play kickbacks provided to then Prime Minister Erdogan.[28]

Complying with Bilal's request, "Ankara blocked websites detailing alleged criminal connections between him and a businessman recently arrested in the United States." It blocked twenty-one news websites.[29] Bilal Erdogan's London lawyers, Simons Muirhead & Burton, sent letters to news outlets who published articles critical of Bilal Erdogan which accused them of defamation. The letters from his lawyers were identified as a "[p]re-action letter of claim written in accordance with the pre-action protocol for defamation." They called for the "[i]mmediate removal or retraction of the allegations. A full and unequivocal retraction and apology to Mr. Erdogan to be published in a manner and in terms with prominence agreeable to us. The payment to our client of substantial damages to demonstrate the baseless nature of the allegations."[30] Britain's permissive libel laws are sympathetic to the accuser, allowing opportunity for legal action.

An Italian investigation of money laundering added to Bilal's woes. Murat Hakan Uzan, brother of Cem Uzan who founded an opposition party in Turkey, filed a criminal complaint against Bilal with the Bologna Public Prosecutor, accusing Bilal of violating both European and Italian financial laws when he moved to Italy in October 2015. Prosecutor Manuela Cavallo investigated claims that Bilal came to Italy for the purpose of laundering roughly $1 billion. Bilal refuted the claim, saying he and his wife entered Italy so he could resume his Ph.D. studies at the Bologna campus of Johns Hopkins University, which he began in 2007 but never finished. It was also alleged that Bilal arrived in Bologna with armed bodyguards who were barred from entering the country. A few hours later, they were issued Turkish diplomatic passports and allowed entry.[31]

Corruption for Tayyip Erdogan was a way to reward family and friends, undermine opponents, and consolidate his power. His concentration of power is another form of corruption. Erdogan is adamant about retaining a parliamentary majority in order to avoid a parliamentary commission that could investigate his corrupt practices. Constitutional reform establishing an executive presidency with Erdogan in charge would protect him and consolidate his gains. Erdogan was also motivated by the prestige of staying in office through 2023 when the Republic of Turkey would celebrate the centenary of its founding.

Notes

1. L. Pitel, "Turkey Corruption: Gold Trader's Arrest in Miami Could Put President Erdogan in the Spotlight Once Again," *Independent*, March 22, 2016, accessed June 28, 2016, http://www.independent.co.uk/news/world /middle-east/turkey-corruption-gold-trader-s-arrest-in-miami-could-put -president-erdogan-in-the-spotlight-once-a6946901.html.

2. M. K. Kaya, "Turkish Political Corruption: The AKP, Too?," *The Turkey Analyst* 1, no 14 (2008), accessed June 27, 2016, http://www.turkeyanalyst.org /publications/turkey-analyst-articles/item/136-turkish-political-corruption -the-akp-too?.html.

3. "Turgut Özal Facts," *Biography*, accessed July 1, 2016, http://biography. yourdictionary.com/turgut-ozal#26v4Gx4uycWt8eyR.99.

4. A. Donmez, *Yuzde 10 Adil Duzenden Havuz Duzenine* (Istanbul: Klas Kitaplar, 2014).

5. Ibid.

6. "Erdogan Overheard Telling Son to Get Rid of Cash as Turkey Corruption Probe Takes New Twist," *McClatchyDC*, February 25, 2014, accessed June 25, 2016, http://www.mcclatchydc.com/news/nation-world/world/article24764239.html.

7. https://www.youtube.com/watch?v=Cvf4aeRLu0E.

8. "Erdogan Overheard Telling Son to Get Rid of Cash as Turkey Corruption Probe Takes New Twist," *McClatchyDC*, February 25, 2014, accessed June 25, 2016, http://www.mcclatchydc.com/news/nation-world/world/article24764239.html.

9. Ibid.

10. Ibid.

11. G. Solaker, "Turkey's Erdogan Calls on U.S. to Extradite Rival Gulen," *Reuters*, April 29, 2014, accessed June 26, 2016, http://www.reuters.com/article/ us-turkey-erdogan-idUSBREA3S0A120140429.

12. "Erdogan Critic and Ex-police Chiefs Go on Trial Over Corruption Inquiries," *The Guardian*, January 6, 2016, accessed June 27, 2016, https://www.theguardian.com/world/2016/jan/06/recep-tayyip-erdogan-critic-fethullah-gulen-turkey-police-chiefs-corruption-trial.

13. O. Ant, "Turkey's Corruption Probe Turns into Plot and Power for Erdogan," *Bloomberg*, January 8, 2015, accessed June 28, 2016, http://www.bloomberg.com/news/articles/2015-01-08/turkey-s-corruption-probe-turns-into-plot-and-power-for-erdogan.

14. "Ricciardone Refutes Claims US 'Behind Turkey Graft Probe'," *Hürriyet Daily News*, December 21, 2013, accessed June 30, 2016, http://www.hurriyetdailynews.com/ricciardone-refutes-claims-us-behind-turkey-graft-probe-.aspx?pageID=238&nID=59938&NewsCatID=315.

15. As cited in B. Orucoglu, "Why Turkey's Mother of All Corruption Scandals Refuses to Go Away," *Foreign Policy*, January 6, 2015, accessed June 29, 2016, http://foreignpolicy.com/2015/01/06/why-turkeys-mother-of-all-corruption-scandals-refuses-to-go-away/.

16. http://www.cumhuriyet.com.tr/haber/turkiye/305183/Degistirilen_yasalar_yolsuzluklara_zemin_oldu.html, accessed August 22, 2016.

17. "Corruption Perceptions Index 2014: Clean Growth at Risk," *Transparency International: The Global Coalition against Corruption*, December 3, 2014, accessed July 3, 2016, https://www.transparency.org/cpi2014/press.

18. Orucoglu, "Why Turkey's Mother of All Corruption Scandals Refuses to Go Away."

19. S. Gultasli, "In the 'New' Turkey, Corruption is a Thing of the Past!," *EUObserver*, October 31, 2014, accessed June 27, 2016, https://euobserver.com/opinion/126311.

20. Ibid.

21. Ibid.

22. Ant, "Turkey's Corruption Probe Turns into Plot and Power for Erdogan."

23. Anonymous senior AKP official.

24. J. Toobin, "The Showman: How U.S. Attorney Preet Bharara Struck Fear into Wall Street and Albany," *New Yorker*, May 9, 2016, accessed June 30, 2016, http://www.newyorker.com/magazine/2016/05/09/the-man-who-terrifies-wall-street.

25. F. Tastekin, "Is Corruption Suspect's US Arrest Bad News for Erdogan?," *Al Monitor: Turkey Pulse*, March 23, 2016, accessed July 2, 2016, http://www.al-monitor.com/pulse/originals/2016/03/turkey-iran-usa-arrest-of-zarrab-bad-news-for-erdogan.html.

26. L. Pitel, "Turkey Corruption: Gold Trader's Arrest in Miami Could Put President Erdogan in the Spotlight Once Again," *Independent*, March 22, 2016, accessed June 28, 2016, http://www.independent.co.uk/news/world/middle-east/turkey-corruption-gold-trader-s-arrest-in-miami-could-put-president-erdogan-in-the-spotlight-once-a6946901.html.

27. As cited in Fehim Tastekin, "Is Corruption Suspect's US Arrest Bad News for Erdogan?"

28. Anonymous source within the Turkish Anti-Smuggling and Organized Crime Department. Information provided on August 24, 2016.

29. "Erdogan's Son Blocks Access to Websites Detailing His Criminal Connections," *Sputniknews*, April 1, 2016, accessed July 1, 2016, http://sputniknews. com/middleeast/20160401/1037330209/erdogan-bilal-crime-website.html.

30. Drawn from a Letter Written by Simons, Muirhead & Burton to a Major US News Organization in 2014.

31. M. Day, "Bilal Erdogan: Italy Names Turkish President's Son in Money Laundering Investigation Allegedly Connected to Political Corruption," February 17, 2016, *Independent*, accessed July 4, 2016, http://www.independent. co.uk/news/world/europe/bilal-erdogan-italy-investigates-turkish-presidents-son-over-money-laundering-allegedly-connected-to-a6879871.html.

5

The Kurdish Question

Kurds have no friends but the mountains.

—Kurdish Proverb

Kurds have a history of betrayal and abuse. There are about forty million Kurds living in Turkey, Iraq, Iran, Syria, and Armenia. Kurds are the world's largest population without a state of their own. About half, twenty million, live in Turkey where they represent approximately 20 percent of the population. Kurds in Turkey are predominant in the Southeast. However, they are scattered across the country. After Diyarbakir, the largest number of Kurds in Turkey live in Istanbul.

Though Kurds have been present in Mesopotamia for more than two thousand years, they are Neither Arab, Persian, or Ottoman. Kurds have a distinct language, culture, and history. Kurds in Turkey (North Kurdistan) and Kurds in Syria (West Kurdistan), also known as "Rojava," have strong tribal and cultural affinities. Both speak the Kurmanji Kurdish dialect. Extended Kurdish families live on either side of the Turkey-Syria border. For sure, differences exist among Kurds. Rivalries have been exploited and exacerbated by the states where Kurds reside. But Kurds come together under duress. They are unified by their pursuit of greater cultural and political rights, which can be secured through independence, federation, or autonomy.

At the end of the First World War, Kurds sent a delegation to the Paris Peace Conference to petition for independence. The Kurdish question bedeviled negotiators. The Great Powers agreed to partition the Ottoman Empire. However, they punted on the status of Kurdistan. The 1920 Treaty of Sèvres, which memorialized agreements at Versailles, promised the Kurds an internationally supervised referendum within one year to determine their national status. The referendum was never held.

Mustafa Kemal Ataturk rejected Sèvres and declared the National Oath, asserting Turkish control over all non-Arab territories of the Ottoman Empire. He launched a war of independence. Weary from the First World War, Great Powers acceded to Ataturk's demands. The Treaty of Sèvres was replaced by the Lausanne Treaty in 1923. The words "Kurd" or "Kurdistan" were not mentioned in the Lausanne text.

Lausanne created captive Kurdish nations. Kurds in Iraq were subjected to King Faysal's pan-Arab rule. Kurds in Iran became an afflicted minority. Kurds in Syria were abandoned to French colonialism and subsequent subjugation by Arab Baathists. The Republic of Turkey sought to assimilate, repress, and contain the Kurds.[1] It violently suppressed Kurdish national aspirations and Kurdish cultural identity, which led to a series of uprisings.

Kurds launched the Kocgiri Rebellion (1920–21), Seyh Said Rebellion (1925), Ararat Rebellion (1927–30), and the Dersim Rebellion (1937–38). Thousands of Kurds were killed in the Dersim uprising, which occurred just prior to Ataturk's death.[2] Turkish leaders adopted draconian security measures, denying the very existence of Kurds in Turkey. They banned the Kurdish language. Celebrating cultural festivals such as "Newroz," the Kurdish new year, was outlawed. Use of Kurdish for personal and geographic place names was prohibited. The very existence of Kurds was denied. They were called "Mountain Turks." Billboards across the country echoed Ataturk's credo: "Happy is he who can call himself a Turk."[3] Assimilation sought to relieve Kurds from their backward identity and imbue pride in their Turkishness. Repression worsened after the military coup of September 12, 1980.

The Kurdistan Worker's Party (PKK) emerged in response to Turkey's repression of leftists and its crackdown against the Kurds. Founded by Abdullah Ocalan in 1978, the PKK was established as a Marxist-Leninist group, which sought a proletarian revolution. The founding charter envisioned the PKK as a "worker-peasant alliance," acting as "the vanguard of the global socialist movement."[4] The charter condemned the "repressive exploitation of Kurds" and called for the creation of an autonomous Kurdistan on all the territories where Kurds reside. It espoused democracy, human and women's rights, as well as environmental sustainability.[5] Ocalan and other PKK founders were influenced by the worldwide anticolonial movement at the time, as well as the leftist movement in Turkey. Armed struggle was envisioned as a way to bring the Turkish state to the negotiating table. According to one of the PKK's founding commanders, "Negotiation and diplomacy are the only means for ending the fight with the PKK, but democratization is the sole means to resolve the Kurdish problems. Democratization not only for the Kurds, but for every group in Turkey, for Turkey's peoples." He warned, "When words end, guns talk."[6] The civil war between Turkey and the PKK cost up to forty thousand lives over four decades.

In 1984, the government put several southeastern provinces under martial law in response to PKK attacks and escalating violence. It declared a sweeping state of emergency in the late 1980s. The government established a legal basis for fighting the PKK by invoking Article 14 of the constitution, which criminalized any activity that threatened the "indivisibility of the state." Article 125 of the Penal Code stipulated that "[a]ny person who carries out any action intended to destroy the unity of the Turkish state or separate any part of the territory shall be punishable by death." Article 8 of the Law for Fighting against Terrorism defined terrorism so broadly it criminalized any discussion about Kurdish issues.

Turgut Ozal, who served as president from 1989 to 1993, tried confidence-building measures to create conditions for a ceasefire and political talks. After elections in October 1991, independent deputies associated with the pro-Kurdish People's Labor Party (HEP) entered the Turkish Grand National Assembly (TGNA) with twenty-two seats. It was the first time that a Kurdish party gained legal representation in the parliament. Kurds were allowed to publish two newspapers, *Yeni Ulke* (New Country) and *Ozgur Halk* (Free People). Ozal lifted the ban on Kurdish music in February of 1991, and Kurds were allowed to celebrate Newroz. Ozal and Ocalan exchanged letters, giving hope for peace. However, the peace process came to an abrupt ending when Ozal mysteriously passed away on April 17, 1993.[7]

The military's pursuit of a security solution to the Kurdish question was unrelenting. It launched major military operations in 1989 and 1992. These operations did not defeat the PKK. Rather, they fueled the insurgency and expanded popular support for the organization. PKK activities peaked in 1993. By 1995, as many as one hundred and fifty thousand Turkish troops were deployed in the Southeast. Between 1989 and 1996, approximately fifteen hundred Kurds were victims of unidentified killings, which included political assassination, killing by government-backed death squads, disappearances, and death from torture while in police custody. Inestimable numbers of villages were razed to the ground. Up to four million Kurds were displaced by Turkey's scorched earth policy.

Abuses were committed by both sides. Under Ocalan, the PKK exercised Stalin-like discipline. It dispensed swift punishment to Kurds it believed were collaborating with the state, including members of local militias called "village guards." It collected funds from Kurds in Turkey as well as the diaspora. Extortion and protection rackets were widespread. Smuggling was also rampant. After 9/11, Ankara successfully petitioned the US Government to list the PKK as a foreign terrorist organization (FTO). The United Kingdom, Canada, and the EU followed, listing the PKK as an FTO in 2001.

Turkey and Syria signed the Adana Agreement on October 20, 1998. The Adana Agreement required Syria to list the PKK as an FTO and evict Abdullah Ocalan. Ocalan fled Syria and began a global odyssey to Moscow, Rome, Amsterdam, Athens, and Nairobi, where he was captured by Turkish Special Forces working in conjunction with US Intelligence. Ocalan was brought to Turkey. Hooded, drugged, and humiliated, he appeared on television appealing for peace. Kurds across Europe stormed embassies and self-immolated in protest. Ocalan called for calm and offered to end the armed struggle. "The democratic option is the alternative to solving the Kurdish question. Separation is neither possible nor necessary. We want peace, dialogue, and free political action within the framework of a democratic Turkish state."[8] Ocalan declared a ceasefire from the Imrali Island prison on August 2, 1999.

The Kurdish conflict was in a lull when Erdogan became prime minister in March 2003. Kurds welcomed the AKP's rise. During the 2002 campaign, Erdogan criticized previous governments for failing to address the Kurdish question. He accused his predecessor of missing an opportunity for peace after Ocalan's arrest in 1999. Erdogan's promises for greater democracy, freedom, and human rights inspired hope in many segments of society, including among the Kurds.

The alternative was unsavory. The Republican People's Party (CHP), associated with Ataturk and the military, had waged war on the Kurds for decades. The National Action Party (MHP) comprised right-wing extremists. Paramilitaries acting in consort with the MHP, so-called gray wolves, were responsible for assassinations and disappearances of Kurdish politicians and community leaders. Erdogan represented change and a prospect for peace.

The PKK tried to reinvent itself in parallel with the national elections of 2002. It formally renounced armed struggle in April 2002, renaming itself the Kurdistan Freedom and Democracy Congress (KADEK). Turkey's secular establishment rejected KADEK's peace overtures. Turkey's Supreme Court banned KADEK's political wing, the Peoples' Democratic Party (HADEP) on March 13, 2003. Erdogan did not condone the ban, but he chose not to challenge the judiciary so soon after becoming prime minister.

Erdogan inherited the Kurdish question. As an Islamist leader already under scrutiny by the Kemalist judiciary and military, any conciliatory attempt on Kurdish issues risked charges of treason. If Erdogan crossed the line, the AKP could be shut down like the Welfare Party. The Turkish state, the security establishment, the bureaucracy, and secular judiciary strongly opposed the idea of negotiations with the PKK. Erdogan had to balance the demands of domestic hardliners and pressure for peace talks from the United States and EU. For their part, Kurds supported closer ties between Turkey and EU. They believed their goals could be realized via Turkey's Euro-Atlantic integration rather than through the independence of a rump state called "Kurdistan."

Erdogan was caught between competing forces. His body of work on Kurdish issues was erratic. He allowed dialogue when doing so cultivated a progressive domestic constituency he needed for other goals. Conversely, he attacked the Kurds when confrontation was in his political interest. His approach was unprincipled and unpredictable. Kurds hoped that Erdogan would bring peace. He disappointed.

The US invasion of Iraq in March 2003 roiled Turkish politics. Erdogan feared that the emergence of a de facto independent Iraqi Kurdistan under protection of the United States would inspire Kurds in Turkey to demand the same or, at a minimum, democratic autonomy. To Erdogan, autonomy was a pit-stop on the path to independence. No Turkish leader could countenance federalism, lest it lead to fragmentation and the ultimate breakup of Turkey. After Sèvres, democratic autonomy was a radioactive concept. Autonomy was a code word for independence.

A debate emerged between Kurds about their goals and methods. Some KADEK leaders supported a peaceful path to secure more democratic rights, while others advocated a return to armed struggle for independence. The peace crowd prevailed; KADEK was renamed the Kurdistan People's Congress (KONGRA-GEL) in October 2003. KONGRA-GEL presented itself as a political organization and renewed its appeal for negotiations between the Turkish state and Ocalan. Erdogan's government did not respond to calls for political talks. Rather, the military intensified attacks in the southeast and across the border.

These events occurred in the context of Turkey's discussions with the EU about its candidacy. Minority rights and Kurdish issues were chief among the European Commission's concerns. In a clever political move, Erdogan used the EU prospect to justify cultural concessions to the Kurds. In June 2004, he granted limited Kurdish-language broadcasts on TRT 3, a state channel. The AKP also allowed the limited use of Kurdish names and Kurdish language. It permitted Kurdish mayors and local government officials to use Kurdish when interacting with their Kurdish constituencies. Restrictions on Kurdish cultural celebrations were relaxed. Though reforms were limited, Kurds welcomed the positive trend. Osman Baydemir, the former Peoples' Democratic Party (HDP) parliamentarian and long-serving mayor of Diyarbakir reflected on TRT 3 broadcasts in Kurdish. "This first Kurdish broadcast brought down an 80-year old taboo."[9]

Again, Erdogan was caught between competing interests. Cultural concessions were not sufficient to mollify Kurdish hardliners who rejected the pacifist approach of KONGRA-GEL and the PKK's People's Defense Forces. The ceasefire collapsed on June 1, 2004. Erdogan did not try to patch things up with political negotiations. Nor did he restrain the military from going on the offensive. KONGRA-GEL abandoned the name change in April 2005, calling itself the PKK once again. Hardliners regrouped under the banner of the Kurdistan Freedom Falcons (TAK).

Erdogan understood the power of words. When Erdogan visited Diyarbakir on August 12, 2005, he affirmed his commitment to peace and acknowledged past mistakes of the Turkish state. He pronounced, "The Kurdish question is my question."[10] He rejected the failed policies of official denial, forced assimilation and collective punishment. He maintained that the Kurdish question could not be solved through military actions alone.[11] He affirmed that more democracy, not more repression, was the answer to the long-standing grievances of Kurds.[12] Erdogan's strategy for peace focused on economic development. He adopted an agenda aimed at bridging the development gap between the eastern and western parts of the country. He pledged to invest billions of dollars in public projects in the Kurdish-populated areas. He also encouraged private sector investment.

Ibrahim Kalin, Erdogan's spokesman, presented a bold vision. "It is not possible. However, to solve the Kurdish issue in isolation from the conditions that produced it in the first place. This entails a major revisiting of such fundamental notions as the role of the state, national security perceptions, democracy and political representation in Turkey. What is certain is that solving the Kurdish issue will liberate Turkey from decades of misplaced statism, petty nationalism, and societal antagonism. While seeking to solve the Kurdish issue, Turkey is also rebuilding her identity."[13]

Kurdish voters rewarded the AKP for providing services to the Kurdish community on July 22, 2007. The AKP gained 46.6 percent of the national vote. Its margin was fueled by support from Kurds in the South and Southeast. The AKP won some municipal governments formerly held by pro-Kurdish parties, and became the second party in the Southeast after the Democratic Society Party (DTP). When it came to ratifying Gul's nomination for president, Kurdish deputies mostly abstained. Kurds hoped that the AKP would use its electoral mandate to focus on human rights and minority rights. However, Erdogan made lifting the ban on women wearing the hijab in public institutions his signature issue.

The PKK reverted to political violence. When Special Forces were ambushed in Sirnak, Turkish public opinion demanded a response. Turkey intensified its military operations against the PKK. It finalized an intelligence-sharing agreement with the United States, expanding attacks on the PKK headquarters in Qandil, the PKK's remote mountain headquarters in Iraqi Kurdistan near the Iranian border. Likewise, Turkey cooperated more closely with the government in Syria and Iran to attack PKK affiliates in those countries. Erdogan declared: "Our security forces will do whatever is necessary regardless of whether it involves women and children. There is no Kurdish question if you do not think about it."[14]

Erdogan's erratic policy vacillated between threats and confidence building measures. In January 2009, he allowed more Kurdish-language broadcasts on state television. He inaugurated the broadcast by speaking in Kurdish. This was unheard of in a country that for decades had prohibited the Kurdish language and all forms of Kurdish cultural expression. TRT 6 would later become Turkey's first and only Kurdish language channel. Erdogan maintained, "Whatever political risk, political gain or cost, we cannot have any other goal but to resolve the Kurdish issue. [Peace is in] Turkey's interest, for the sake of our seventy-one and half million citizens, and for our future."[15]

Confidence-building measures were intended to create conditions for negotiations. Gul intimated that "good things" were in the works on March 11, 2009. The PKK announced a ceasefire the following month. In response, the government announced its peace initiative. It used different names—"The Kurdish Initiative", "The Democracy Initiative", "The Unity and Fraternity Project", and the "Resolution Process." It finally settled on the "National Unity and Brotherhood Project." At the core of the initiative was recognition that democracy and economic development were the most effective ways to end PKK violence. Erdogan declared in July 2009: "By means of raising basic rights and freedom standards, and enlarging democratization we aim to open a pluralist and free space where every perspective is expressed peacefully, where resolution proposals are discussed in mutual tolerance."[16]

The AKP published a fifty-five-page peace plan highlighting political participation, justice, and amnesty arrangements. The plan also focused on human rights in the fields of language, education, and media. Interior Minister Besir Atalay maintained, "These developments will align our domestic policies with the European Convention on Human Rights."[17] Erdogan affirmed, "We will issue circulars in the short term, pass laws in the medium term, make constitutional amendments in the long term, and take required steps."[18]

Erdogan simultaneously cultivated civil society to gain their support for his National Unity and Brotherhood Project. He convened sixty-two of the country's leading singers and musicians, asking for their help to create an ambience for peace through performance and visual arts.[19] "Your songs have the power to transcend deaf walls. You are the heartfelt voice of this country. I ask you to help this movement of change with your artistic sensitivity."[20]

Working with artists was part of a broader strategy to gain popular support for peace. Erdogan said, "[This Initiative] aims to bravely resolve the issues that have not been resolved for years, and for which there has been no effort to resolve."[21] Erdogan always paid special attention to domestic politics. The AKP was reaching out to Kurdish communities in local elections. Erdogan thought he could gain their support by appealing to the grassroots. Erdogan sought to include DTP deputies in his coalition for changing the constitution. Erdogan needed their support to win the 2011 referendum on constitutional reform. Direct election of the president was part of Erdogan's plan to put Turkey on the path to an executive presidency.

In a setback to Erdogan's plan, the Constitutional Court banned the DTP on December 11, 2009. The Court accused the DTP of acting as "a center of activities against the unity of the state and the nation." DTP members were "in contact and solidarity" with the PKK, and supported "armed attacks." The DTP co-chairs, Ahmet Turk and Aysel Tugluk, were stripped of their parliamentary immunity. In addition, thirty-six other DTP members were barred from politics for five years. More than three thousand members of the KCK were arrested and charged with terrorism.[22] The Court's decision to ban the DTP revealed the deep state's continued opposition to accommodating the Kurds. It also highlighted the extent of opposition to Erdogan in secular and opposition circles.

The Court's action did not end the participation of Kurdish groups in politics and the peace process. The DTP renamed itself the Peace and Democracy Party (BDP). Some of its members, including Ocalan's lawyers, were flown to Imrali Island in military helicopters to meet "the boss." At the same time, MIT representatives were secretly meeting PKK representatives in Oslo, Norway. The Oslo channel was disclosed when a recording of their fifth meeting was leaked to the Dicle News Service. An uproar ensued. Fethullah Gulen and others called for an investigation. Gulen demanded that Erdogan fire MIT's Hakan Fidan.

Meetings between MIT and the PKK's representatives, Mustafa Karasu, Sabri Ok, and Zubeyir Aydar, had started in 2009 and continued until September 2011 when the recording was leaked.[23] Erdogan denied knowledge of the back channel negotiation in an effort to mitigate the political fallout from secret talks with the PKK. He denied that the talks were setting an agenda for more formal negotiations between the Turkish government and Ocalan. All along, the PKK participants in the Oslo process were angling for Ocalan's participation. After the recording leaked, they increased their demands, seeking Ocalan's release from Imrali as a precondition for continuing negotiations. Erdogan refused. In the face of fierce domestic political opposition, the Oslo process collapsed.

Meanwhile Ocalan was working on a roadmap for peace from his prison cell at Imrali. The roadmap identified issues to be resolved and ten basic principles for resolving them. Though the roadmap was pre-sented to MIT on August 15, 2009, its existence was not made public until the following year.[24] Part of the roadmap included the phased return of PKK members from Iraqi Kurdistan, and amnesty options for fighters who would lay down their arms. The Active Repentance Law, established via Article 221 of the Penal Code, created the legal basis for repatriating PKK members.

Eight PKK members and twenty-six Kurds from the Makhmour refugee camp crossed the Habur Border Gate from Iraqi Kurdistan into Turkey as a test case on October 19, 2009.[25] Instead of a discreet process and positive precedent, the PKK arrived at the border in flashy military uniforms. Thousands showed up to greet the "peace caravan," waving PKK flags and bearing posters of Ocalan. Turkish public opinion was fundamentally against amnesty. For decades, Turkish media and politicians demonized the PKK. Reintegrating PKK members was a bitter pill to swallow. By making their return a victory lap, the PKK further alienated Turkish society and turned them against reconciliation. Emotional protests from mothers who had lost their sons in the conflict poisoned the process, stopped the returns, and turned public opinion against the National Unity and Brotherhood Project. A second group of ex-combatants was supposed to return from Europe, but plans were canceled.

Erdogan was vilified for mismanaging the return and reintegration of ex-combatants. Opposition parties went so far as to accuse Erdogan of treason. The CHP accused the AKP of "separatism, [bowing] to the goals of the terrorist PKK, violating the constitution, causing fratricide and/or ethnic polarization between Kurds and Turks, being an agent of foreign states, and even betraying the country." The MHP "declared the AKP to be dangerous and accused it of treason and weakness."[26]

Ultrasensitive to criticism, Erdogan maintained that peace was not a concession to the PKK. He asserted unwavering support for Turkey as a unitary state. Erdogan walked a fine line between seeking Kurdish votes and preserving relations with Kemalist institutions. He was prepared to weather criticism from opposition parties, but was careful not to antagonize the security establishment. In deference to opposition from the deep state, Erdogan halted the process. He turned a blind eye to the judiciary's banning of the DTP. He also looked the other way as the security services arrested KCK members.[27]

Ocalan ignored hardline commanders, calling on them to extend the ceasefire. He said, "Dialogue still goes on here. We have come to set out some practical terms."[28] According to Ocalan, 2011 would be the year to resolve the Kurdish question.[29] Like Ocalan, Erdogan was determined to carry on the process. On June 15, 2012, PKK Commander Murat Karayilan said, "The solution was very close in Oslo". Karayilan urged that talks continue.[30] Norway was a good channel. It is too remote to have a vested interest in the outcome. Third-party facilitation proved effective. Both Ankara and the PKK needed the political cover of a facilitator. Diyarbakir Deputy Leyla Zana met with Erdogan on July 1, 2012. She spent ten years in Ankara's maximum-security prison for saying her oath of office in Kurdish, and was a symbol of non-violent resistance. She declared, "Erdogan could solve Kurdish issue." Leyla Zana demanded a resumption of talks with the government.[31]

Erdogan convened a conference of civil-society leaders to launch the "Wise People Group." They met at the Dolmabahce Palace, an ornate former administrative center of the Ottoman Empire in Istanbul, on April 4, 2013. The Wise People Group consisted of sixty-three renowned writers, journalists, singers, actors, unionists, lawyers, businessmen.[32] They were tasked with outreach to different segments of society, directly affected communities, local nongovernmental organizations, and governors. Consultations were intended to gauge public opinion and create a groundswell of support for peace.[33] The Wise People Group languished soon after it was launched. Though it assigned Deputy Prime Minister Bulent Arinc as the point of contact, there was no follow-through or deeper commitment by the government.

The on-again, off-again peace process was driven by domestic politics and Turkey's election cycle. In advance of national elections, Erdogan arranged an historic gathering with Iraqi Kurdistan President Masoud Barzani in Diyarbakir on November 16, 2013. For years, Barzani was demonized by Ankara for his pro-independence stance. Turkish officials would not utter the words "Iraqi Kurdistan's," lest it imply political recognition. In his public remarks, Erdogan spoke of "Kurdistan." He addressed Barzani as "President of Iraqi Kurdistan." Barzani was elated by the reception. He endorsed the AKP's policies on Kurdish issues and declared: "Long live Turkish-Kurdish Brotherhood."[34]

Kurds in the audience were gratified by Erdogan's pledge, [PKK members] "would see the return from mountains to home." To them, this represented an endorsement of their reintegration into society. He also spoke about emptying prisons, which was seen as support for a general amnesty to end the PKK conflict.[35] Barzani's visit appeared as a threshold, creating the possibility to address Kurdish issues in both Turkey and Iraq.

The Barzani appearance included an emotional moment. Barzani was accompanied by Sivan Perver, the famous Kurdish singer from Sanliurfa who had lived in exile for thirty-seven years. Sivan Perver and Ibrahim Tatlises, another well-known singer of Kurdish origin, sang Perver's anthem, "Daye Megri," which means "Do not cry mother." Perver and Tatlises held hands as they sang, swaying to the music. Perver expressed his hope that Erdogan could end the tears of many mothers who had lost their children on both sides of the conflict. The audience was very emotional. Erdogan and Emine were visibly moved.[36]

HDP deputies made regular visits to Imrali, facilitating dialogue between Ocalan and the Turkish government. Kurdish and government representatives met on February 28, 2015 at the Dolmabahce Palace. Kurdish delegates, Pervin Buldan, Idris Baluken and Sirri Sureyya Onder issued a joint statement with Deputy Prime Minister Yalcin Akdogan and Interior Minister Efkan Ala on February 28, 2015. The statement is known as the Dolmabahce Consensus.

At the event releasing the Dolmabahce Consensus, Onder offered Ocalan's ten-point action plan for resolving the conflict. He read a statement: "We are on the verge of an historic decision. Since the beginning, the problem has concerned the transformation of the state. The existing dominant state mentality has been about maintaining power, which led to violence. Without peace and democracy, we cannot expect rights, justice and equality. Peace can be achieved when the suffering of all communities is recognized throughout the history of the republic."[37]

Yalcin Akdogan responded: "We know that the process requires sincerity, bravery and decisiveness. We consider this declaration as a step towards giving up arms and the ending armed conflict. With arms out of the equation, democratization will gain momentum. With the blessing of our people, we are determined to reach an ultimate solution. We see a new constitution as an important opportunity to resolve many chronic and long-standing problems."[38]

Ocalan also supported the Dolmabahce Consensus: "Democracy has always been our principal aim to end the thirty-year conflict and achieve lasting peace. I call on the PKK to hold an extraordinary congress in the spring months to take a strategic and historic decision to abandon the armed struggle."[39]

Millions of Kurds attended the 2015 Newroz celebration in Diyarbakir. The mood was celebratory. They waited anxiously for Ocalan's new year's message, which was read in Kurdish and Turkish: "Our struggle for democracy, freedom, fraternity and honorable peace of our country's people is now about to be realized. This struggle of our movement over forty years involved pain, but it will not be in vain [if we achieve peace]."[40]

Nationalists predictably criticized Erdogan for making concessions to the PKK. Unpredictably, however, Erdogan caved to criticism and disassociated himself from the Dolmabahce Consensus. He even denied knowledge of the Dolmabahce Consensus document, betraying his own negotiators. Erdogan said, "What is the Dolmabahce blueprint? Where did this happen? There is no such a deal. This government never had a deal with a terrorist organization."[41]

According to the HDP, not only was Erdogan informed. He was called several times during the meeting to resolve differences over the text as well as seating arrangements for the event to present the Dolmabahce Consensus to the press and public.[42] Bulent Arinc also disputed Erdogan's claim. There is much conjecture about Erdogan's about-face. It was likely in response to the HDP's refusal to endorse a presidential system. Erdogan was focused on enhancing his powers. He was prepared to make deals with those who supported his proposed constitutional reform, and he was ready to punish those who stood in his way.

Events in Syria also affected the peace process in Turkey. The battle for Kobani raged between September 2014 and January 2015. Kurds from Turkey rushed to help Kobani's defenders. However, Turkish security forces prevented them from crossing the border and joining the battle. Kurds protested, including violent demonstrations in Istanbul and across the Southeast. Scores were killed as Turkish police used water cannons and live ammunition against the protesters.

The United States asked Erdogan to play a larger role in the international coalition combatting ISIS, but Erdogan insisted on a broader strategy. He demanded that the United States make deposing Syria's President Bashar al-Assad its priority. He insisted on a no-fly zone in northern Syria and a security buffer on the Syrian side of the border, to be manned by Turkish forces. The United States rebuffed his entreaties. To Erdogan's dismay, the United States air-lifted weapons and medical supplies to Kurdish People's Protection Units (YPG) in Kobani. YPG fighters also included the PKK. The United States also launched air strikes, which finally dislodged ISIS from the city.

Erdogan disparaged Kobani's defenders, equating them with ISIS and calling them both terrorists. He strongly criticized the United States for supporting the YPG, insisting it was one and the same as the PKK. Turkey launched artillery attacks against the YPG and deployed special forces to support jihadi groups fighting the YPG. Erdogan threatened to invade Northern Syria and establish a security zone. Salih Muslim, co-chair of the pro-Kurdish Democratic Union Party (PYD), said that a Turkish invasion of northern Syria would be an act of war against the Kurds, and appealed to Washington for protection.

Kurds were deeply disturbed by what happened in Kobani, and Turkey's response. They objected to Erdogan's blackballing the PYD and his crackdown against Kurdish protesters in Turkey. Trashing the Dolmabahce Consensus raised doubts about Erdogan's sincerity and commitment to negotiations. PKK hardliners challenged Ocalan's leadership within the organization and demanded a resumption of armed struggle. Erdogan referred to Ocalan as "the man on the island," impugning his relevance. Ocalan warned Erdogan to move forward with negotiations otherwise he could do "nothing more for the peace process."[43]

Erdogan thought he could convince the HDP to support the creation of a presidential system. However, the HDP remained strongly opposed. Erdogan tried to discredit the HDP in the hope they would lose popular support and fail to cross the 10 percent barrier in national elections on June 7, 2015. But Selahattin Demirtas, HDP co-chair, proved to be a modern candidate with broad appeal. Kurds and progressives voted for the HDP giving it 13.12 percent of the vote, which equated to 80 seats in the TGNA. The HDP's strong showing effectively blocked Erdogan from realizing his presidential system.

On July 20, 2015, Kurds gathered in Suruc on the Syrian border, planning a humanitarian convoy to assist their Syrian brethren. A bomb exploded killing thirty-three people and wounding more than a hundred.[44] Many Kurds believed that MIT was behind the bombing or, at a minimum, the police turned a blind eye, allowing the bomber to pass through a series of checkpoints. In response, young hotheads with TAK killed two policemen they accused of complicity.

Murder of the policemen was the excuse Erdogan was looking for. He exploited the situation to launch an intense air campaign against the PKK in Qandil and Kurdish communities in the southeast. Hundreds of Kurdish mayors were removed from their posts. More KCK members, including local politicians, human rights defenders, and civil society were jailed. Turkey's attacks against the PKK and jailing of civil society ended the ceasefire.

Restarting the civil war was a cynical ploy by Erdogan to consolidate his nationalist base and regain support by sewing fear and division. After half-hearted efforts to form a coalition government, the AKP called for early elections. Voters went to the polls again on November 1, 2015. Elections were held during a period of spiraling violence, instability, and insecurity. The AKP received 49.5 percent of the votes. The HDP barely passed the barrier with 10.8 percent.

On May 20, 2015, the TGNA voted to strip the parliamentary immunity of 138 deputies. Fifty HDP deputies, including Selahattin Demirtas, were included. Opposition lawmakers faced the possibility of criminal prosecutions for charges that ranged from supporting the PKK to insulting Erdogan. Demirtas and the HDP leadership were arrested and charged with terrorism on November 3, 2016. Erdogan said, "My nation doesn't want to see guilty lawmakers in this parliament—especially those that the separatist terrorist organization supports."[45]

Stripping the HDP deputies of their parliamentary immunity threatened to escalate the Kurdish insurgency. It undermined the remote possibility of reviving the Dolmabahce Consensus in the TGNA. It also exacerbated tensions with western allies concerned about the rule of law. While western leaders defended Turkey's right to fight terrorism, they were increasingly concerned that Erdogan was targeting civilians in violation of international humanitarian law.

Erdogan made eradication of the PKK a national policy. He promised to "cleanse" the country of PKK elements and drain the swamp of its supporters. Turkish officials denied that civilians were affected in its counter-terrorism crackdown. However, a video captured the killing by Turkish troops of ten Kurdish civilians in Cizre on January 20, 2016. The video went viral, causing international outrage. UN High Commissioner for Human Rights, Zeid Raad al-Hussein, urged Turkey to a conduct a "thorough, independent, impartial investigation."[46] Zeid emphasized, "If State operatives commit human rights violations, they must be prosecuted."[47]

MEPs called on Turkey to establish a national commission of inquiry, citing the Rome Statute that established the International Criminal Court and enshrined the responsibility of national authorities to bring violators of international human rights and humanitarian law to justice. In issuing the appeal, MEPs knew there was little chance of an independent, transparent, and credible investigation. The commission would be investigating the government, which was allegedly responsible. If Turkey stonewalled international efforts to investigate and prosecute those responsible, MEPs proposed a UN fact-finding mission or a commission of inquiry. Citing Turkey's deteriorating human rights situation, the European Parliament voted overwhelmingly to suspend negotiations over Turkey's EU candidacy on November 24, 2016.

Kurds protested killing with impunity. The Patriotic Revolutionary Youth Movement (YDG-H) dug trenches in the streets and put up barricades "to protect themselves from the Turkish police."[48] Turkish artillery and tanks turned Cizre, Silopi, Suruc, Sirnak, Hakkari, and districts in Diyarbakir to rubble. Civilians were trapped in the basements of homes, seeking refuge from the shelling. Thirty unidentifiable bodies were dug out of a bombed-out basement in Cizre.[49]

In a spiral of deadly violence, TAK launched suicide attacks against Turkish security forces in Ankara and Istanbul. The Iraq War brought the conflict to Turkey's borders in 2003. TAK's operations brought the conflict to the heart of Turkey.

Notes

1. M. Yegen, "The Kurdish Peace Process in Turkey: Genesis, Evolution and Prospects," *Working Paper, Instituto Affari Internazionali*, May 2015, accessed July 22, 2016, http://www.iai.it/sites/default/files/gte_wp_11.pdf.
2. For a detailed account on these Kurdish rebellions against the Turkish state, see: R. Olson, "The Kurdish Rebellions of Sheikh Said (1925), Mt. Ararat (1930), and Dersim (1937–8): Their Impact on the Development of the Turkish Air Force and on Kurdish and Turkish Nationalism," *Welt des Islams* 40, no. 1 ((2000): 67–94; R. Olson and H. Rumbold, "The Kocgiri Kurdish Rebellion in 1921 and the Draft Law for a Proposed Autonomy of Kurdistan," *Oriente Moderno* 8, no. 1/6 (1989): 41–56; and M. V. Bruinessen, "Genocide in Kurdistan? The Suppression of the Dersim Rebellion in Turkey (1937–38) and the Chemical War against the Iraqi Kurds," in *Conceptual and Historical Dimensions of Genocide*, ed. George J. Book (Philadelphia, PA: University of Pennsylvania Press, 1998), 141–70.
3. This chapter draws on the author's report, "Disarming, Demobilizing, and Reintegrating the Kurdistan Worker's Party." National Committee on American Foreign Policy, October 15, 2007.
4. As cited in D. L. Phillips, *From Bullets to Ballots: Violent Muslim Movements in Transition* (Vol. 1). (Piscataway, NJ: Transaction Publishers, 2011), 109.
5. For the PKK Charter see the link: https://pirtukxane.org/2013/12/02/pkk-tuzugu-ve-programi/.
6. Anonymous. (August 12, 2010; Ankara). Personal Interview. [This was part of my interview that took place in Ankara in the Summer of 2010 for a research study at Middle East Technical University to understand the role of political violence in the PKK movement, and whether violence is used selectively or non-selectively.]
7. "Babami Öldürdüler," *Sabah TV*, April 17, 2016, accessed July 30, 2016, http://www.sabah.com.tr/webtv/turkiye/babami-oldurduler.
8. Abdullah Ocalan, *Declaration on Democratic Solution of the Kurdish Question* (London: Kurdistan Information Centre, Mesopotamian Publishers, 1999), 85.
9. "İlk Kürtçe yayın yapıldı," *NTV*, June 9, 2004, accessed July 25, 2016, http://arsiv.ntv.com.tr/news/273398.asp.
10. T. Yilmaz, "Kürt sorunu benim sorunumdur," *Hürriyet*, August 13, 2005, accessed July 23, 2016, http://www.hurriyet.com.tr/kurt-sorunu-benim-sorunum-342020.
11. Ibid.

12. "Turkey and the Kurds: Peace be unto Uou," *The Economist*, August 18, 2005, accessed July 24, 2016, http://www.economist.com/node/4300168.

13. I. Kalin, "The Kurdish Question: Erdogan's 2+1 Strategy," *AlJazeera*, April 8, 2013, accessed July 25, 2016, http://www.aljazeera.com/indepth/opinion/2013/04/ 20134712530554912.html.

14. "Çocuk da olsa geregi yapilacak," *Evrensel*, March 21, 2006, accessed July 27, 2016, https://www.evrensel.net/haber/169942/cocuk-da-olsa-geregi-yapilacak.

15. "Sorularıve Cevaplarıyla Demokratik Açılım Süreci," *Tanitim ve Medya Baskanligi*, January 2010, accessed July 25, 2016, https://www.google.com/url?sa= t&rct=-j&q=&esrc=s&source=web&cd=4&cad=rja&uact=8&ved=0ahUKEwjjx8K-B6ZPOAhXHoD4KHb_FD3YQFgg_MAM&url=https%3A%2F%2Fwww.akparti.org.tr%2Fupload%2Fdocuments%2Facilim220110.pdf&usg=AFQjCNGYX6OK2YU3WL4s7JDbaoZH4fMb2w.

16. Author's translation of the Turkish as "Milli Birlik ve Kardeşlik Projesi ile temel hak ve özgürlüklerin standardını yükselterek demokratikleşme alanını genişletmek suretiyle her türlü görüşün barışçıl bir şekilde ifade edilebildiği, çözüm önerilerinin karşılıklı hoşgörü içinde tartışılabildiği, çoğulcu ve özgürlükçü bir ortamı sağlamayı amaçlıyoruz." In "Milli birlik ve kardeşlik projesini başlattık," *AK Party*, accessed July 24, 2016, https://www.akparti.org.tr/site/icraat/14582/milli-birlik-ve-kardeslik-projesini-baslattik.

17. Hürriyet Daily News Parliament Bureau, "Interior Minister Atalay Outlines Democratic Initiative," *Hürriyet Daily News*, November 13, 2009, accessed July 23, 2016, http://www.hurriyetdailynews.com/interior-minister-atalay-outlines-democratic-initiative.aspx?pageID=438&n=interior-minister-atalay-outlines-democratic-initiative-2009-11-13.

18. "Turkey's Government to Send Bills on Kurdish Opening to Parliament," *Today.az*, January 9, 2010, accessed July 24, 2016, http://www.today.az/news/regions/ 59156.html.

19. "Artists Pledge Support for Democratic Initiative," *Today's Zaman*, February 23, 2010, accessed July 24, 2016, http://web.archive.org/web/20100223010711/http:// www.todays zaman.com/tz-web/detaylar.do?load=detay&link=202241.

20. Ibid.

21. To inform public about the Process, AKP provided a booklet, called Democratic Openning. See: "Soruları ve Cevaplarıyla Demokratik Açılım Süreci" (January 2010), Ibid.

22. David L. Phillips, *The Kurdish Spring: A New Map for the Middle East* (Piscataway, NJ: Transaction Publishers, 2015).

23. "Chronology of Oslo Dialogues with PKK," *Hürriyet Daily News*, September 28, 2012, accessed July 24, 2016, http://www.hurriyetdailynews.com/chronology-of-oslo-dialogues-with-pkk.aspx?pageID=238&nID=31190&NewsCatID=338.

24. S. Cayan, "Öcalan'in büyük baris mücadelesi," *Özgür Gündem*, January 6, 2013, accessed July 24, 2016, http://www.ozgur-gundem.com/haber/60729/ocalanin-buyuk-baris-mucadelesi.

25. Ibid.

26. M. Gunter, "Reopening Turkey's Closed Kurdish Opening?," *Middle East Policy* 20, no. 2 (2013): 88–98.

27. For a detailed account renewed problems, see Gunter, "Reopening Turkey's Closed Kurdish Opening?

28. Cayan, "Öcalan'in büyük baris mücadelesi."

29. Ibid.

30. Ibid.

31. "Erdogan-Zana Talks Dismissed by PKK," *Hürruyet Daily News*, July 2, 2012, accessed July 24, 2016, http://www.hurriyetdailynews.com/erdogan-zana-talks-dismissed-by-pkk.aspx?pageID=238&nID=24523&NewsCatID=338.

32. K. Gürsel, "Erdogan Asks 'Wise People' to Make Case for Peace," *AlMonitor: Turkey Pulse*, April 15, 2013, accessed July 24, 2016, http://www.al-monitor.com/pulse/originals/2013/04/erdogan-wise-people-commission-peace-process.html.

33. Ibid.

34. "Diyarbakir'da Tarihi Gün," *BBC Türkce*, November 16, 2013, accessed July 24, 2016, http://www.bbc.com/turkce/haberler/2013/11/131116_erdogan_barzani.

35. For full speech of Erdogan on November 16, 2013, see: "Başbakan erdoğanın diyarbakır konuşması full . . . başbakan diyarbakırda," *Youtube*, accessed July 24, 2016, https://www.youtube.com/watch?v=cjRy2y__cRU.

36. For a full video, see: "Ibrahim Tatlises, Sivan Perver," *Youtube*, accessed July 24, 2016, https://www.youtube.com/watch?v=hEBDw2g6h1k.

37. "The Peace Process in Turkey-Kurdistan Has Reached a Serious Stage," *Kurdistan National Congress*, March 23, 2015, accessed July 24, 2016, http://www.icor.info/2015/the-peace-process-in-turkey-kurdistan-has-reached-a-serious-stage.

38. Ibid.

39. Ibid.

40. For the full English translation of Ocalan's letter, see: BIA Haber Merkezi, "Öcalan's Newroz Message," *Bianet English*, March 21, 2015, accessed July 24, 2016, http://bianet.org/english/diger/163204-ocalan-s-newroz-message.

41. "Erdogan Dolmabahçe mutabakatı diye bir şey tanımadığını söyledi," *Evrensel*, July 17, 2015, accessed July 24, 2016, https://www.evrensel.net/haber/256181/ erdogan-dolmabahce-mutabakati-diye-bir-sey-tanimadigini-soyledi.

42. "Erdogan's Denial of 'Dolmabahçe Agreement' Sparks Row," *Hürriyet*, July 20, 2015, accessed July 27, 2016, http://www.hurriyetdailynews.com/erdogans-denial-of-dolmabahce-agreement-sparks-row.aspx?pageID=238&nID=85656&NewsCatID=338.

43. V. Sirin, "The Kurds in Turkey and the Fight for Kobani," *Gatestone Institute International Policy Institute*, October 26, 2014, accessed July 27, 2016, http://www.gatestoneinstitute.org/4816/kurds-turkey-kobani.

44. "Suruç'ta katliam: 31 ölü, 104 yaralı," *BBC Türkce*, July 21, 2015, accessed July 24, 2016, http://www.bbc.com/turkce/haberler/2015/07/150720_suruc_saldiri.

45. E. Peker, "Turkish Parliament Votes to Strip Lawmakers' Immunity," *The Wall Street Journal*, May 20, 2016, accessed July 27, 2016, http://www.wsj.

com/articles/turkish-parliament-votes-on-bill-that-would-strip-lawmakers-immunity-1463735376.

46. "Turkey: Zeid Concerned by Actions of Security Forces and Clampdown on Media," *UN Human Rights, Office of the High Commissioner*, February 1, 2016, accessed July 28, 2016, http://ohchr.org/EN/NewsEvents/Pages/DisplayNews.aspx?NewsID= 17002&LangID=E.

47. Ibid.

48. L. Maï Gaveriaux, "Turkey's New Dirty War," *Le Monde*, July 13, 2016, accessed July 20, 2016, http://www.alternet.org/world/turkeys-new-dirty-war.

49. Ibid.

Part II

Regional Conflicts

6

The Iraq War

*You will make your own decision based on your
own conscience. I cannot ask you to vote in favor or not.*[1]

—Abdullah Gul

Turkey and the United States have a long history of security cooperation. Beginning in 1947, the United States provided foreign aid to Turkey. Additional assistance was given through the Marshall Plan, which included the transfer of weapons. More than five thousand Turkish troops fought side by side with US forces in Korea. Turks were distinguished for their bravery and sacrifice: 741 Turkish troops were killed and 2,742 wounded in the Korean conflict. In accordance with the Truman Doctrine, Turkey was viewed as indispensable to containing the Soviet Union. Turkey joined the North Atlantic Treaty Organization (NATO) in 1952. It played a critical role as the eastern flank of NATO, serving as a staging ground for intermediate-range Jupiter missiles pointed at the Soviet Union.

The 1960s and 1970s was a problematic period in US-Turkish relations. Moscow threatened Turkey during the U-2 spy plane crisis. The U-2 shot down over the Soviet Union was based at Incirlik Air Force Base. To Ankara's consternation, the United States offered the Jupiter missiles in Turkey as a bargaining chip during the Cuban Missile Crisis. Washington opposed Turkey's invasion and occupation of northern Cyprus in 1974 and, under sway of the Greek-American lobby, imposed an embargo on arms sales to Turkey. With consideration of Turkey's geopolitical importance, President Jimmy Carter lifted the embargo three years later. After the Iranian Revolution, National Security Advisor Zbigniew Brzezinski conducted internal discussions about an American invasion of Iran, launched from bases in Turkey. Despite Carter's emphasis on human rights, Washington turned a blind eye to Turkey's military coup of 1980, and military rule.

Arms trade was a big factor in US-Turkish relations. US firms entered into joint ventures with Turkish counterparts to manufacture armored infantry vehicles and other military equipment. Turkey also became a major customer of US military equipment, buying F-15, F-16, and F-111 fighter planes, M-60A1 and M-60A3 battle tanks, and M-113 armored personnel carriers. US military assistance to Turkey reached $750 million in 1984. As of September 1997, Turkey had $3.954 billion in outstanding loans for military procurements from the United States.[2]

Washington maintained close cooperation with the Turkish General Staff (TGS) as well as Turkey's secular parties—the Republican People's Party (CHP), Motherland Party (ANAP), and the True Path Party (DYP). In the 1990s, Turkey and the United States collaborated on several international operations—Somalia, Bosnia, and Kosovo. Richard Perle, Assistant Secretary of Defense, described US-Turkish security cooperation as, "The largest, most productive and least understood program in Southeast Europe."[3]

Iraq invaded Kuwait on August 2, 1990. At the urging President George H. W. Bush and Secretary of State James A. Baker III, Turkey joined the international coalition to liberate Kuwait from forces of Saddam Hussein. There was strong domestic opposition to Turkey's participation in the Gulf War. Seventy-four percent of Turks surveyed opposed Turkey's involvement. President Turgut Ozal assured Washington that Turkey would fully participate in US-led operations. Ozal was a stalwart ally. Use of Incirlik was critical to the multinational coalition's campaign against Saddam. Incirlik was a NATO tripwire in case Turkey was attacked.[4]

After the ceasefire ending the Gulf War, Bush urged Iraqi Kurds and Iraqi Shiites to rise up and overthrow Saddam Hussein. They did rebel, but Bush abandoned them to Saddam's reprisals. More than one million Kurds fled across the border to Turkey. UN Security Council resolution 688 characterized repression against Iraqi Kurds as a threat to international peace and security. Subsequently, Turkey joined "Operation Provide Comfort," which provided humanitarian assistance to displaced Iraqi Kurds on the steep slopes between Turkey and Iraq. "Operation Northern Watch" established a no-fly zone north of the 36th parallel in Iraq, creating conditions for Kurds to return to their homes. Use of Incirlik was established through a memorandum of understanding (MoU) between Turkey and the United States, renewable every six months.

Some Turks criticized US protection of Iraqi Kurds. They viewed it as part of a broader strategy to establish a Kurdish State. Turkey was facing an insurgency by the PKK. Renewing the MoU was used by Turkey to leverage military assistance from the United States. It was also used to exact pledges of political support for Turkey's fight against the PKK.

The 1999 Golcuk earthquake in southwest Turkey killed seventeen thousand people. Not only did the earthquake exacerbate a crisis with Turkey's economy, it profoundly affected the Turkish psyche. As the earth shook on August 17, 1999, Turkish bravado was also shaken. Mounting conflict with the PKK further increased feelings of vulnerability. President Bill Clinton visited survivors in Golcuk, expressing solidarity. He elevated US-Turkey cooperation to a "strategic partnership" in his address to the Turkish Grand National Assembly (TGNA). The strategic partnership was based on a security alliance enshrined in the North Atlantic Charter, as well as shared values and interests. Turkey was a moderate, pro-western, Muslim-majority country, which served as a model to the Arab world and countries in Central Asia. As a strategic partner, the United States responded to Turkey's needs with economic, humanitarian, and security assistance. It significantly increased weapons transfers to Turkey's military, enhancing its capabilities against the PKK. With US backing, the IMF provided $10 billion to stabilize Turkey's economy.

The 9/11 terror attacks were a defining moment in US-Turkey relations. Turks strongly sympathized with the United States. Turkey's President Ahmet Necdet Sezer and Prime Minister Bulent Ecevit were quick to condemn the attacks. In a gesture of solidarity, all Turkish flags were flown at half-mast. Turkey was one of the first countries to join President George W. Bush's Global War on Terror (GWOT). Given its conflict with the PKK, Turkey saw itself on the front-line of the GWOT. It joined US-led coalition forces in Afghanistan, contributing troops and assuming overall command of the International Security Assistance Forces (ISAF). Incirlik was an important staging ground for operations in Afghanistan.

Bush made the GWOT a centerpiece of US foreign policy during his State of the Union speech on January 29, 2002. He included Iraq and Iran in his so-called axis of evil, telegraphing US plans to decapitate the leadership in Baghdad. US officials insisted that Saddam Hussein was behind 9/11, making the case for regime change.

US Undersecretary of Defense Paul D. Wolfowitz visited Ankara on July 16, 2002 to discuss Turkey's support for Operation Iraqi Freedom.

He returned to Ankara in October to brief the TGS about US war plans and to discuss the transit of US troops across Turkish territory to Iraq. The Pentagon's battle plan envisioned a two-pronged offensive, with troops entering Iraq from Turkey in the north and from Kuwait in the south. The northern front would complement the main attack, overwhelming Iraq's overstretched forces. The deployment of ground troops in northern Iraq would also deter an attack by Saddam on ethnic Kurds, stabilizing the region when Saddam was toppled. Turkey's border with Iraq is 384 kilometers. Given uncertain support from Saudi Arabia, Turkey was indispensable to the Pentagon's war plan.

Turkey's election on November 3, 2002, was a game-changer. Typically, US officials would make one call to the TGS chairman when they needed something from Turkey. Turks are famous negotiators, but would always accede to American demands. The AKP was untested. Washington did not know how the AKP would co-exist with the military. In the immediate aftermath of elections, General Hilmi Ozkok, head of the TGS, came to Washington to meet his counterpart, Chairman of the Joint Chiefs of Staff (JCS) General Richard Meyers. Military-to-military, they had a frank exchange about Iraq and Turkey's role in the war.

Wolfowitz and Undersecretary of State Marc Grossman, a former US ambassador to Turkey, visited Ankara on December 3, 2002. They met newly designated Prime Minister Gul and Erdogan, who was still AK Party head at the time. Bush administration officials appreciated Turkey's concerns, but they did not believe that Turkey would oppose the United States. At the end of the day, Wolfowitz "counted on the fact that Turkey would be with us." As a gesture of goodwill, Gul gave a green light for US technical and military experts to assess Turkish bases, ports, and surface infrastructure for transporting US forces and military equipment to the northern front. The Pentagon allocated hundreds of millions of dollars to upgrade airfields, as well as ports along Turkey's southern coast.[5] Bush and Erdogan discussed the extent of Turkey's involvement when they met the following week in Washington.

Though Erdogan had no official position in the Turkish government, he was received like a head of state by the White House on December 10, 2002. Erdogan met Bush in the Oval Office. He also met Vice President Dick Cheney, Secretary of State Colin Powell, National Security Adviser Condoleeza Rice, General Richard Meyers, and other Pentagon top brass. Less than one year before, Erdogan had visited Washington and was shunned by senior administration officials. This time, Washington rolled out the red carpet.

Erdogan was an uncertain ally, given his Islamist orientation. However, Erdogan tried to build confidence. He presented himself as a pragmatist and modernizer. He emphasized that Turkey's EU membership was his primary foreign policy goal. In turn, the Bush administration strongly supported Turkey's EU candidacy. US officials saw it as an opportunity to bring Turkey closer to the West and show it was not at odds with the Muslim world. By hosting Erdogan, Bush signaled that the US supported a new law that would allow Erdogan to become prime minister.

Erdogan made his case against attacking Iraq, urging caution. He warned that the invasion and occupation of Iraq would cause the country to fall apart. Fragmentation was an existential threat to Turkey. The emergence of an independent Iraqi Kurdistan would fuel demands by Kurds in Turkey for their own self-governing entity. Even decentralization could undermine Turkey as a unitary state, creating a spiral of deadly violence that might destabilize the country. The PKK had already established its headquarters in Iraqi Kurdistan, from where they operated an effective insurgency.

The status of Kirkuk was another contentious issue. Erdogan argued that Kirkuk should remain apart from Iraqi Kurdistan, lest revenue from its oil supplies be used for state-building. Kirkuk was included in the Mosul vilayet during the Ottoman period. The AKP envisioned restoring Turkey's influence in the Mosul region. They even floated the idea of royalty payments from the sale of oil and gas in the Kirkuk fields.

Ankara was concerned that the Kurdistan Regional Government (KRG) would infringe on the rights of Iraqi Turkmen, a minority in northern Iraq with close ethnic and historic ties to Turkish brethren in Anatolia. Turkey supported the Iraqi Turkmen Front (ITF), as representatives of the Turkmen. The ITF worked to undermine Iraqi Kurdistan's independence. Its agents were also implicated in attempted assassinations of Kurdish politicians. Ankara purported support for the ITF, but concern for Turkmen was just another wedge issue for Turkey to assert its influence.

Erdogan also played the Iran card. He warned that democracy in Iraq would empower Iraqi Shiites, acting as proxies for Iranian mullahs. The United States had already eliminated the Taliban, Iran's enemy in Afghanistan. Getting rid of Saddam would result in a Shiite-led government in Baghdad under Iran's control. It could intensify sectarian tensions and potentially lead to a civil war between Shiites and Sunnis. With its adversaries deposed, Iran would extend a Shiite crescent from Tehran, to Basra, Baghdad, Damascus, and Beirut.

Sanctions on Iraq after the Gulf War had been costly to Turkey. Erdogan wanted compensation for Turkey's economic losses, which he estimated at $300 billion. He also asked the United States to forgive Turkey's military debt, valued at $6 billion, and for other economic and trade incentives.

Erdogan explained that, according to Turkey's constitution, the TGNA would have to authorize the basing of foreign troops on Turkey's soil. Moreover, international authorization was required for foreign troops to attack a neighboring country from bases in Turkey. Erdogan maintained that UN Security Council (UNSC) Resolution 1244 did not go far enough. International legitimacy to attack Iraq could only be gained through a new UNSC resolution specifically authorizing the use of force under Chapter 7 of the UN Charter.

Having just won elections and taken office, the Turkish government was responsive to public opinion. According to the Pew Research Center, 83 percent of Turks surveyed opposed allowing the United States to use Turkish bases to wage war on Iraq. Turks thought the war was unjustified and illegal. The percentage of Turks with a favorable view of the United States also dropped from 52 percent in 2001 to 30 percent in 2002.[6]

Erdogan thought he could prevent Bush from going to war. He did not believe that the United States would attack Iraq unless Turkey was on board. Erdogan was straight forward. He told Bush that Turkey wanted to avoid the war, but in the event of war, Turkey would "cooperate fully."[7] After explaining his concerns, Erdogan expected Bush to reconsider. Erdogan tried to stir debate about the merits of going to war in the international community as well as within the United States. He gave a speech at the Center for Strategic and International Studies in Washington, DC, "Naturally Turkey's preference is for war to be the last resort. However, if Saddam's administration continued to . . . threaten world peace, then Turkey will give the necessary support for a UN resolution."[8] US and Turkish officials agreed on a continuous dialogue, going forward.

Zalmay Khalilzad was named special presidential envoy with responsibility for mediating a security agreement between Turkey and the Iraqi Kurds. Turkish officials told him that northern Iraq was directly related to Turkey's national interests and security. Khalilzad tried to accommodate. He offered to set up a joint operations headquarters in Diyarbakir. He also proposed that Ankara designate a Turkish general for assignment at US Central Command in Qatar. Without consulting the Kurds, he suggested that Kurdish Peshmerga—"those who stand before death"—would be subject to inspection by Turkish troops. In addition, the US would provide intelligence for search-and-destroy missions against the PKK. When Khalilzad visited Ankara on March 18, he proposed that up to twenty thousand Turkish troops would follow on the heels of the Fourth Infantry Division in order to establish a twenty-kilometer buffer zone across the border. He also proposed a joint commission to manage refugees in the event of a humanitarian emergency. US officials reiterated their commitment to Iraq's territorial integrity. Ankara would have a seat at the table during negotiations over Iraq's future governance. Erdogan was amenable. He reasoned, "If we stay out of the question from the start of the operation, we won't have any control over its later developments."[9]

Erdogan authorized AKP deputies to prepare a draft law that would allow sixty-two thousand US troops to use Turkey as a base for invading Iraq. If it could not stop the United States from going to war, the AKP-led government would exact a steep price. When Foreign Minister Yasar Yakis met Colin Powell on February 24, 2002, he asked for payment of $1 billion for every thousand US troops transiting through Turkey. US officials were aghast at the cost of cooperation. One characterized Turkey's demands as "extortion in the name of alliance."[10]

US-Turkey relations were never so transactional. In response to Yakis' proposal, the United States offered a $6 billion assistance package to Turkey. Some of these funds would support $24 billion in loan guarantees from international financial institutions. Until the funds were available, the United States was prepared to provide a bridge loan of $8.5 billion. Washington also offered trade benefits to Turkish business, including qualified industrial zones for Turkish textiles that would generate an additional $1 billion.[11] Turkish firms were promised reconstruction contracts for infrastructure destroyed during the US invasion.

The vote in the Turkish parliament authorizing the transit of US forces was originally scheduled for February 18. However, it was delayed so the AKP could organize its members. Turkish public opinion was vehemently opposed. Hundreds of thousands rallied in Ankara to oppose the bill. The TGS took no public position, but it felt taken for granted and did not strongly support the legislation. AKP rank and file did not rally behind the bill. Some cabinet ministers openly opposed it. The Turkish president suggested that the measure was unconstitutional.[12]

The TGNA voted in closed session on March 1, 2003. Though 264 deputies voted in favor, the tally was three votes short of the required majority. From the CHP, 178 deputies voted against. They were joined by 72 members of the AKP; 19 others abstained. The bill was defeated.

The vote was a debacle. The AKP was either inexperienced, or it willfully failed to rally supporters. The vote revealed divisions in political circles—within the AKP, between the AKP and the CHP, and between the AKP and the military. The Turkish stock market plunged 12.5 percent and the Turkish lira fell 5 percent on fears that the United States would withdraw its aid package, resulting in a schism between Turkey and the United States at a time when Washington's really needed Turkey's support.[13] It also limited Washington's influence over Turkey's domestic politics when the AKP government was new and impressionable.

Undeterred, the Bush administration immediately asked the AKP to reschedule the vote. The Pentagon kept twenty-four cargo ships with tanks and other equipment and supplies for the 4th Infantry Division off the Turkish coast. US officials also pursued a second track, seeking permission for overflight rights of US planes in Turkish air space. Without Incirlik or overflight, US warplanes would have to operate from aircraft carriers in the Persian Gulf or from bases in Saudi Arabia and Kuwait. The greater distance from targets in Iraq increased flight time, adding a logistical burden and increased costs to air operations. More time in the air also increased the risk of detection and harm to US aircraft.

"Operation Iraqi Freedom" was initiated on March 20, 2003. By that time, US officials had still not gained Turkey's approval for overflights. "It feels like the Turks have taken a hot poker and stuck it in my eye," said a US official. "Don't they watch CNN? Don't they know the war has already started?"[14]

Turkey wanted to deploy military units in northern Iraq to control refugees and monitor the activity of Kurdish groups. Intensifying the dispute with Washington, Foreign Minister Gul insisted that Turkey would make its own decision on entering northern Iraq "by itself and when needed."[15] The State Department worried about a live-fire confrontation between US and Turkish forces. As many as seventeen thousand Turkish troops were based in northern Iraq after the Gulf War, as a rapid reaction force to strike the PKK. A Turkish official explained the deployment and Turkey's demand for a buffer zone. "We encountered a great amount of refugee influx in the 1991 Gulf war, and many terrorist Kurdistan Workers' Party militants entered into Turkey with the refugees."[16] Washington worried that Turkey would try to seize Erbil or Kirkuk, which could result in a military confrontation between NATO allies. A war within a war would complicate things.

A deeply divided TGNA granted access to Turkey's airspace on March 21, 2003. Turkey was the last NATO country to approve over-flight. This time, the TGS threw its support behind the deal. The AKP could not ignore the military's influence and the long tradition of cooperation between the Turkish and American militaries. There were, however, delays in implementing the agreement. The Turkish government insisted on case-by-case approval of each US flight. Legislation also included a government plan to send two Turkish army brigades to Iraqi Kurdistan, in order to protect Turkish interests across the border. The Pentagon and State Department strongly opposed any action in Iraq that was not coordinated with coalition forces.[17]

Erdogan initially impressed US officials. He dampened fears of his radical Islamic tendencies. He earned praise from Washington for his approach to Cyprus, his pro-EU stance, and robust economic reforms. Erdogan made his case against the invasion of Iraq, but then seemed to accept the outcome when Washington went to war without Turkey.[18] While seeming to acquiesce, Turkey actively tried to undermine US interests in Iraq. Failure to deploy the 4th Infantry Division had a huge impact on stability operations, fueling the insurgency and contributing to Iraq's anguish. It also undermined Turkey's "Zero Problems with Neighbors" policy.

Notes

1. "Portre: Abdullah Gül," *Aljazeera Turk*, August 14, 2014, accessed July 5, 2016, http://www.aljazeera.com.tr/portre/portre-abdullah-gul.
2. "U.S. Military Aid and Arms Sales to Turkey: Fiscal Years 1980–1999," *Federation of American Scientists*, Accessed June 7, 2016, http://fas.org/asmp/profiles/turkey_fmschart.htm.
3. O. Karasapan, "Turkey and US Strategy in the Age of Glasnost," *Middle East Report* 160 (1989): 4–10.
4. C. Haberman, "War in the Gulf: Turkey; Turkey's Role in Air Assault Sets Off Fear of Retaliation," *The New York Times*, January 20, 1991, accessed June 3, 2016, http://www.nytimes.com/1991/01/20/world/war-in-the-gulf-turkey-turkey-s-role-in-air-assault-sets-off-fear-of-retaliation.html.
5. M. R. Gordon, "Threats and Responses: Turkey; Bush Will Meet a Leading Turk on Use of Bases," *New York Times*, December 9, 2002, accessed May 27, 2016, http://www.nytimes.com/2002/12/09/world/threats-and-responses-turkey-bush-will-meet-a-leading-turk-on-use-of-bases.html?pagewanted=all.

6. Gordon, "Threats and Responses."

7. "CSIS Statesmens Forum Hosts Recep Tayyip Erdogan," *Center for Strategic and International Studies*, December 9, 2002, accessed June 7, 2016, https://www.csis.org/events/csis-statesmens-forum-hosts-recep-tayyip-erdogan.

8. Ibid.

9. "U.S., Turks Wrangle Over Command of Troops in Northern Iraq," *Daily Times*, February 10, 2003, accessed June 7, 2016, www.dailytimescom.pk/default.asp?page+story_10-2-2003_pg4_3.

10. D. E. Sanger and D. Filkins, "U.S. Is Pessimistic Turks Will Accept Aid Deal on Iraq," February 20, 2003, accessed May 27, 2016, http://www.nytimes.com/2003/02/20/international/middleeast/20IRAQ.html? pagewanted=all.

11. C. Migdalovitz, "Report for Congress: Iraq: Turkey, the Deployment of U.S. Forces, and Related Issues," *Congressional Research*, May 2, 2003, accessed June 7, 2016, http://congressionalresearch.com/RL31794/document.php.

12. Ibid.

13. As cited in D. L. Phillips, *Losing Iraq: Inside the Postwar Reconstruction Fiasco* (Boulder, CO: Westview Books, 2005), 119.

14. As cited in Ibid.

15. "Gul: Turkey Will Decide to Enter Iraq by Itself, When Needed," *Hurriyet Daily News*, March 3, 2003, accessed June 7, 2016, http://www.hurriyetdailynews.com/gul-turkey-will-decide-to-enter-iraq-by-itself-when-needed.aspx?pageID=438&n=gul-turkey-will-decide-to-enter-iraq-by-itself-when-needed-2003-03-26.

16. Ibid.

17. R. Boudreaux, "Turkey Grants Allies Airspace Rights," *Los Angeles Times*, March 21, 2003, accessed June 7, 2016, http://articles.latimes.com/2003/mar/21/news/war-turkey21.

18. "Turkey to Cooperate with US on Iraq," *Hurriyet Daily News*, accessed June 7, 2016, http://www.hurriyetdailynews.com/turkey-to-cooperate-with-us-on-iraq.aspx?pageID=438&n=turkey-to-cooperate-with-us-on-iraq-2002-12-11.

7

Zero Problems with Neighbors

Aware that development and progress in real terms can only be achieved in a lasting peace and stability environment, Turkey places this objective at the very center of her foreign policy vision. This approach is a natural reflection of the "Peace at Home, Peace in the World" policy laid down by Great Leader Ataturk, founder of the Republic of Turkey. Besides, it is a natural consequence of a contemporary responsibility and a humanistic foreign policy vision.[1]

—Turkish Ministry of Foreign Affairs

When Foreign Minister Ahmet Davutoglu put forward the "Zero Problems with Neighbors" policy, the United States expected that Turkey would use its geographic location, economic development, and cultural influence as a force for good.[2] President Barack Obama was disappointed. According to Jeffrey Goldberg who interviewed Obama, "Early on, Obama saw Recep Tayyip Erdogan, the president of Turkey, as the sort of moderate Muslim leader who would bridge the divide between East and West—but Obama now considers him a failure and an authoritarian, one who refuses to use his enormous army to bring stability to Syria."[3]

Rather than an anchor of peace, stability, and security, Turkey's foreign policy became increasingly rash and irresponsible. Erdogan proved to be thin-skinned and impulsive. He personalized foreign policy, holding a grudge and pursuing vendettas against foreign leaders. Instead of zero problems with neighbors, Turkey found itself in dispute with almost every neighbor. Rather than projecting influence, Ankara became more isolated than ever.

Iraq

Erdogan was right about Iraq. Everything Erdogan warned George W. Bush would happen, did come to pass. After the US invasion and occupation, Iraq was torn by sectarian civil war. The Shiite-led government in Baghdad became a proxy for Iran. Iraq's 2005 constitution provided extensive self-rule to Iraqi Kurds, putting them on the path to independence. When parts of the constitution were not implemented, especially a referendum on the status of Kirkuk, the Kurdistan Regional Government (KRG) exercised *de jure* independence. Kurds in the region were inspired by Iraqi Kurdistan's progress and demanded greater self-rule.

Iraq's transition after Saddam was bound to be messy. It was, however, even more tumultuous because of Turkey's support for Sunni tribes, former Ba'athists, and Islamic extremists. Turkey's hostility towards Iraqi Kurdistan also had a destabilizing effect. Turkey was excluded from post-war arrangements because of failed negotiations with the United States over the transit of troops with the 4th Infantry Division through Turkey to northern Iraq. However, Turkey still tried to influence events through subterfuge.

A Turkish Red Crescent convoy was stopped at a checkpoint in April 2003. The contents were marked as humanitarian supplies. However, the bags contained weapons, ammunition, and flags of the Iraqi Turkmen Front (ITF). So-called humanitarian workers were actually Turkish Special Forces infiltrating northern Iraq to assist the ITF. The US military abruptly deported eleven Turkish Special Forces back to Turkey.[4]

On July 4, 2003, US troops detained thirty-two Turkish Special Forces on a mission to assassinate KRG politicians. The would-be assassins were handcuffed, hooded, and deported. Press reports of their arrest and deportation reverberated across Turkey. Turkish General Staff (TGS) Chairman Hilmi Ozkok called it the "biggest crisis" between NATO allies.[5] General Hursit Tolon said it was "disgusting." Protesters burned flags outside the US embassy in Ankara and a bomb exploded near the US consulate in Istanbul.[6]

Events in Kirkuk also exacerbated tensions. Kirkuk is a flash point of competing claims. In 1959, half of Kirkuk's population was Turkmen, with Kurds, Assyrians, Arabs, and Armenians comprising the rest. About eight hundred thousand Kurds, Turkmen, and Assyrians fled Kirkuk during the genocidal Anfal Campaign, which was launched by Saddam Hussein against the Kurds. After Saddam was toppled, Kurds rushed to reclaim homes lost during Saddam's Arabization program. Upon return, Kurds found their properties possessed. Ownership of an estimated ten billion barrels of oil in Kirkuk further polarized the situation. The failure to quickly stand-up a property claims-and-compensation process made Kirkuk even more dangerous. The Bush administration finally established a property claims-and-compensation commission, which included representatives from the Balkans and Eastern Europe.

It did not, however, include a Turkish representative or representatives of directly affected communities. Ethnic Turkmen in Turkey strongly protested the marginalization of their ethnic brethren in Iraq, prompting Ankara to more strongly demand Turkmen rights.

Iraq slipped into chaos. Insurgents targeted the international community. There were many attacks, including a bomb that exploded outside the Turkish Mission in Baghdad on October 14, 2003. Erdogan warned Bush of instability in Iraq, and sectarian conflict between Sunnis and Shiites. As sectarian strife intensified, Turkish officials blamed the United States.[7] The insurgency of former Ba'athists morphed into a civil war between Sunnis and Shiites. Sunni tribes, such as the Nuceyfi, joined the fray. Turkish intelligence provided information on tribal sheikhs to General David Petraeus, who coordinated payments and weapons transfers.

Shiite militias, called Popular Mobilization Forces, were directed by Qasim Suleimani, head of the Iranian Revolutionary Guard's Quds Force. The Popular Mobilization Forces were notorious for revenge killing and atrocities against Sunnis, which further polarized Iraqi society and made reconciliation even more difficult. Popular Mobilization Forces emerged as the preeminent power in the country, outside of Baghdad's control and answerable to Tehran.

Sectarianism worsened when Premier Nuri al-Maliki gained a second mandate in 2010. Ankara strongly encouraged the United States to drop its support for Maliki. However, US officials decided that sticking with Maliki was the best way to realize Obama's campaign pledge to withdraw from Iraq.

According to Petraeus, "What transpired after that, starting in late 2011, came about as a result of mistakes and misjudgments whose consequences were predictable."[8] He blames, "The continuing failure of Iraq's political leaders to solve longstanding political disputes, and the exploitation of these failures by extremists on both sides of the sectarian and ethnic divides for Iraq's crisis."[9] The Obama administration's half-hearted efforts to negotiate an extension of the Status of Forces Agreement (SOFA) led to the withdrawal of US troops, thereby reducing US leverage over events in Iraq. According to Petraeus, "The actions of the Iraqi prime minister undid the major accomplishment of the Surge. [They] alienated the Iraqi Sunnis and once again created in the Sunni areas fertile fields for the planting of the seeds of extremism, essentially opening the door to the takeover of the Islamic State. Whether fair or not, those in the region will also offer that our withdrawal from Iraq in late 2011 contributed to a perception that the

United States was pulling back from the Middle East. This perception has complicated our ability to shape developments in the region and thus to further our interests. These perceptions have also shaken many of our allies and, for a period at least, made it harder to persuade them to support our approaches."[10]

Al-Qaeda in Mesopotamia became al-Qaeda in Iraq, which became the Islamic State in Iraq and Syria (ISIS).[11] ISIS occupied Mosul in June 2014. Soon after Mosul's fall, Premier Heider al-Abadi started talking about liberating the city. Turkey offered logistical and military support to Sunni fighters.[12] Minister of National Defense, Ismet Yilmaz, acknowledged that Turkey was training Sunni tribe members at bases in Iraqi Kurdistan. "This training has started with the Peshmerga. We have visited the training sights, saw what is happening and the training continues . . . More training will start as soon as possible."[13] Turkey wants the KRG to provide suitable training facilities. If Sunni tribal militias say, "'Not here, but in Turkey,' we are also open to this option, however, we prefer to train them in their own lands."[14]

Ankara always wanted to establish a buzzer zone in Iraqi Kurdistan. After the withdrawal of Iraqi Security Forces (ISF) from Nineveh province, TSK Special Forces occupied Bashiqa in December 2015 and set up training facilities for ISIS opponents. Prime Minister Ahmet Davutoglu described the arrival of new troops as "a routine rotation and reinforcement." A battalion of four hundred troops came from the Siirt Third Commando Brigade, supported by armored personnel carriers and twenty-five tanks, turning the Bashiqa training camp into a permanent military base. Turkey maintained an armored battalion at Bamami in northern Iraq, elements of a tank battalion at Amadiya and Suri, and a commando battalion at Kanimasi near the Turkish border. As of May 2016, approximately three thousand Turkish personnel including Special Forces were in Iraqi Kurdistan to implement Ankara's train and equip strategy.[15] Turkey was the third-largest force of foreign soldiers in Iraq, after Iran and the United States. Baghdad strongly objected to Turkey's deployments, calling them a "violation of sovereignty." The Iraqi Foreign Ministry summoned the Turkish ambassador in Baghdad, demanding an immediate end to Turkey's "occupation." According to Abadi's office, "Turkish forces, numbering about one armored regiment with a number of tanks and artillery, entered Iraqi territory . . . without a request or authorization from Iraqi federal authorities. The Iraqi authorities call on Turkey to immediately withdraw from Iraqi territory."[16]

Turkey was surprised by Abadi's reaction. Turkish Foreign Minister Mevlut Cavusoglu said Turkish troops had gone to Iraq at the request of the Iraqi defense minister to train soldiers fighting ISIS. Davutoglu wrote Abadi to explain the role of Turkish troops in Bashiqa. Davutoglu indicated that no more Turkish troops would be sent until Baghdad agreed to the deployment. However, he did not say if and when the troops would be withdrawn.[17]

Abadi rejoined his objection on the eve of the battle for Mosul. Erdogan dismissed Abadi's concerns about Iraq's sovereignty, insisting that Turkey would participate in the liberation of Mosul, which he characterized as a Sunni city. Iraq called an emergency meeting of the UN Security Council. Erdogan responded, "You are not my interlocutor, you are not at my level, you are not my equivalent, you are not of the same quality as me," addressing Abadi. "Your screaming and shouting in Iraq is of no importance to us. You should know that we will go our own way." Erdogan admonished Abadi to "know his place."[18]

The TGS acted strategically to position Turkey as a counterweight to the anti-ISIS alliance, which was dominated by Iraqi Shiites and Iran. Focusing on security cooperation with the KRG and Sunni Arab tribes helped balance Shiite power in Iraq. Additionally, positions north and northeast of Mosul served as a buffer zone protecting Turkmen. The Turkish deployment also served as a barrier between the PKK in Iraqi Kurdistan's Qandil Mountains and the People's Protection Units (YPG) of the Democratic Union Party in Syria (PYD). They were intended to keep the PKK out of Sinjar.

Ankara's support for Iraq's territorial integrity was shallow. As Iraq slipped towards fragmentation, Ankara hedged its bets. It warmed to the idea of an autonomous region encompassing territories where Sunnis are a majority, with headquarters in Mosul, and loose ties to Baghdad. It sought to control Iraqi Kurdistan by manipulating its hydrocarbon exports and exercising a *de-facto* veto over its potential declaration of independence. Turkey used its forces to create conditions on-the-ground ensuring it a prominent seat at the table. If Iraq fell apart, Turkey wanted Nineveh Province, Mosul, and parts of Kirkuk governorate in its orbit of influence.[19]

Iran

Turkey and Iran are inheritors of great civilizations. Historically, the Ottoman and Safavid empires competed for power. Turkey and Iran still vie for influence as ideological models for the Islamic world. Turkey, with its Sunni Muslim majority, embraced secular democracy prior to the AKP's election in 2002. Shiite Iran is a theocracy, which opposes NATO and the West. According to Ayatollah Ruhollah Khomeini, Kemalism was worse than communism.[20]

Turkey shares a 560-kilometer border with Iran. Turkey's importance to the West increased after the Iranian Revolution and the Soviet invasion of Afghanistan in 1979. Khomeini expelled NATO's early warning radar systems, which were based in Iran to monitor Soviet missile and troop movements. Turkey agreed to host the radar systems. In 2010, it also agreed to host the deployment of a NATO anti-missile system. In so doing, Ankara incurred both the mullah's wrath and appreciation from Washington.

Islamist movements began flourishing in Turkey concurrent with the 1979 Islamic Revolution in Iran. Iran's theocracy inspired the so-called Turkish-Islamic synthesis. Though secular, the military sought to strengthen a broader sense of Islamic community as an alternative to leftists. General Kenan Evren recited verses of the Qur'an in public speeches.[21] He asserted, "There is no sectarianism in our religion. All of us believe in Allah, we have one Prophet, we read the same Qur'an. Then why this separation?"[22] Evren increased funds for the Religious Affairs Directorate, built mosques, introduced mandatory religious education in state schools, and promoted Imam Hatip schools.[23] Turkey's rulers deliberately opened up the social and political space for Islamist mobilization in Turkey. They sought to harness Islam and turn it into an instrument for empowering the state, complementing rather than contradicting Kemalist principles. The Turkish-Islamic synthesis became a de-facto state ideology, more benign but similar to religiosity in Iran.

Trade and economic issues are central to Turkish-Iranian relations. The Iran-Iraq War (1980–88) was a boost to the Turkish economy. Turkey traded extensively with Ba'athist Iraq and theocratic Iran. Both countries relied on Turkey as a major source of commodities. Turkey also served as the outlet for Iranian goods. Oil and gas from both Iraq and Iran were essential to Turkey's energy security.

The Kurdish issue was a major irritant in Turkish-Iranian relations. Turkey resented the haven provided by Iran to the Kurdistan Workers' Party (PKK) and its Iranian affiliate, the Free Life Party of Kurdistan (PJAK). While Iran suppressed its own Kurdish population, it supported Kurds in other countries as political leverage. Tehran believed that the United States, through Turkey, was pursuing regime change by backing the armed insurgencies of Iranian minorities. Iran's two biggest minorities are Kurds and ethnic Azeris. Iran was also suspicious of Turkish interference in its province of Azerbaijan, largely populated by Sunni Turks.

The AKP was less antagonistic to Iran than previous governments. Despite the improving trend in relations, Erdogan contested with Iran's President Mahmoud Ahmadinejad after his election in 2005. However, Erdogan and Ahmadinejad found common cause in advancing an Islamist agenda. Turkey and Iran became pragmatic collaborators. Ankara was one of the first governments to offer unqualified support for Ahmadinejad after the disputed June 2009 elections. It was silent when the Iranian regime violently suppressed peaceful pro-democracy demonstrators of the so-called Green Movement.

Erdogan's foreign policy pivoted away from the West, emphasizing new coalitions in the East and with Russia. Trade between Turkey and Iran totaled $10 billion in 2008. Despite international sanctions on Iran, bilateral trade climbed to $13.7 billion in 2014. Iran supplies about 30 percent of Turkey's oil and 20 percent of its annual natural gas imports.[24] Ankara helped Iran avoid banking sanctions. Turkish brokers deposited the proceeds from gold sales in Turkish banks, thereby providing Iran with hard currency at a time when it was blocked from international markets.

To ease the burden of international sanctions, Turkey tried to broker an agreement on Iran's nuclear activities, which would normalize economic relations to Turkey's benefit. In May 2010, Turkey and Brazil announced an agreement with Iran to ship twelve hundred kilograms of low-enriched uranium to Turkey for safekeeping. In exchange, the Iranians would receive fuel rods for the Tehran Research Reactor, which produced isotopes for medical use. The deal was a watered down version of a proposal that the United States offered eight months earlier. When the deal was first discussed, twelve hundred kilograms represented about 80 percent of Iran's uranium stocks. By the time Tehran accepted the deal, that same quantity was only half of its stock. The United States criticized Turkey for undermining international consensus among the P5 plus Germany. P5 countries with permanent seats on the UN Security Council are the United States, the United Kingdom, France, China, and Russia.

At the time, Turkey had one of the nonpermanent seats on the UN Security Council. Over Washington's objections, Turkey opposed a UN Security Council resolution to put more pressure on Iran. Ankara was against sanctions in principle. It also worried that economic sanctions would adversely affect Turkey's economy.[25] The resolution passed over Turkey's objection.

The Iran nuclear deal—"The Comprehensive Plan of Action"—was finalized on July 14, 2015. The deal was intended to normalize Iran's foreign relations by lifting sanctions in exchange for dismantling its nuclear program. Turkey welcomed implementation of the nuclear deal, hailing it as a diplomatic success that would resolve a longstanding regional problem. As a major customer of Iranian oil and gas, Turkey hoped that lifting sanctions would expedite investment by western and Turkish companies in Iran's hydrocarbon sector, speeding production.[26] However, Iranian Foreign Minister Javad Zarif was less sanguine about improving bilateral relations. According to Zarif, "Now that a nuclear agreement has been reached the relationship between Iran and Turkey will certainly further deteriorate, since Turkey benefited from sanctions against Iran, and will not be happy about Iran regaining its previous position in the region."[27] He did not visit Turkey in the aftermath of the nuclear deal.

The 2011 Arab Spring accentuated the differences between Turkey and Iran. Erdogan warned, "Iran, with its attitude that turns sectarian divisions into conflict, is seeking to light the fuse of a new and dangerous course."[28] Syria's civil war was deeply polarizing; Turkey and Iran supported different sides. The crisis in Yemen also exacerbated tensions. So did Turkey's support for the Muslim Brotherhood in Egypt. Iran accused Turkey of supporting ISIS, which was targeting Takfirs and Shiites.[29] Turkey bolstered its ties with Saudi Arabia and other countries belonging to the Gulf Cooperation Council (GCC), pledging to participate in a Riyadh-based Islamic alliance against terrorism, supporting Saudi operations in Yemen, and deepening cooperation Syrian rebels seeking to topple Assad.

Despite their regional rivalries, Turkey and Iran established a framework for cooperation. The first meeting of the Turkish-Iranian High Level Cooperation Council (HLCC) was held during the visit of President Hassan Rouhani to Ankara on June 9, 2014. Tamping down sectarianism, Rouhani said, "What matters is the unity of the Islamic world. We must tell the world: our identity is Islam, not to be Sunni or Shiite, or from another sect."[30]

The HLCC met again with Erdogan in Iran on April 7, 2015. Turkish Prime Minister Ahmet Davutoglu visited Tehran on March 4–5, 2016. He headed a major delegation consisting of five ministers and dozens of Turkish companies and businesspersons. Two weeks later, Zarif visited Turkey, affirming the importance of moving beyond regional disputes and expressing Iran's readiness to expand economic and regional cooperation.[31] The next meeting between Rouhani and Erdogan occurred in Ankara on April 16, 2016.[32] Erdogan vowed to boost bilateral trade pursuant to the lifting of most international sanctions on Tehran. He hoped bilateral trade would reach $30 billion annually. Economic relations between Turkey and Iran assumed greater importance when Russia imposed an embargo on Turkey after Turkish F-16s shot down a Russian Sukhoi-24 fighter jet near the border with Syria in November 2015.

Beyond economic cooperation, Turkey and Iran discovered shared security interests. Zarif visited Ankara on August 12, 2016. He affirmed "solidarity" and "goodwill" between Turkey and Iran based on their mutual interest in preventing the emergence of a Kurdish state. Preserving Syria's sovereignty became the basis for a transactional approach between the two countries, which included security cooperation and intelligence sharing.[33]

Russia

Turkey began deepening its ties to Russia after the AKP came to power in 2002. During a state visit to Moscow in February 2004, Foreign Minister Abdullah Gul pledged cooperation in the field of counter-terrorism as part of "a strategic partnership and cooperation against common threats."[34] Russia asked Turkey to crackdown on Chechen groups, which had established liaison offices in Istanbul. In return, Turkey sought Russia's assistance disrupting PKK finances and logistics. Putin affirmed Turkey's strategic importance to Russia during a visit to Ankara in December 2004. Erdogan did the same during a trip to Moscow in January 2005, focusing on energy issues.

Bilateral cooperation extended beyond security issues. Vladimir Putin and Gul signed two agreements on economic cooperation in the fields of energy and banking, two on military and technical cooperation, an agreement on the prevention of maritime incidents, and another establishing cooperation between strategic research centers.[35] Putin and Erdogan agreed on a role for the Russian oil pipeline operator Transneft and the Russian oil company Rosneft in the Samsun-Ceyhan oil-pipeline project. The $2.5 billion pipeline would transport 1.5 million barrels per day between Turkey's northern and southern Black Sea coasts. An agreement was finalized for a complementary pipeline called

"South Stream" in 2011, which would transport up to 63 billion cubic meters of gas annually to Bulgaria, Serbia, Hungary, Slovenia, Austria, and Italy through one leg and Croatia, Macedonia, and Greece through another.[36] Energy interdependence advanced one of Russia's strategic objectives—an outlet to the Mediterranean via Turkey.[37]

To address a trade imbalance resulting from Turkey's imports of natural gas and oil, Moscow started buying more textile and commercial goods and opening its construction sector to Turkish companies. Trade between Turkey and Russia nearly tripled between 2005 and 2010. In 2005, bilateral trade was $11 billion. By 2010, it had jumped to $30 billion. Turkish and Russian politicians optimistically projected that trade would exceed $100 billion by 2020. When Gul and President Dmitry Medvedev met in May 2010, they signed seventeen cooperation agreements, including the transfer of Russian know-how and materials to build a nuclear power plant in Mersin. Turkey was a favorite destination for Russian tourists. In June 2010, Turkey lifted visa restrictions for Russian passport holders. That year, about 5.5 million Russian tourists visited Turkey.[38]

The civil war in Syria pitted Turkey, which backed the rebels, against Russia and Iran, supporters of Syria's President Bashar al-Assad. Historically, Syria was Russia's closest ally in the Middle East. Cooperation spanned more than four decades. The Soviet Union had a long history with Hafez al-Assad, Bashar's father. In addition to weapons sales, Russian ships resupplied at the navy base in Tartus on the Mediterranean Sea. Latakia was an important Russian naval air station in northwestern Syria. Beyond strategic and commercial interests, cultural ties connected the two countries. Many Syrians studied at Moscow State University and other top schools in the Soviet Union. Marriage between Russians and Syrians was widespread.[39]

Putin had an existential concern about encirclement of Russia by NATO. He believed that humanitarian intervention was a NATO plot to project its power and negate Russia's spheres of influence. After the violent removal of Moammar al-Qhaddafi in Libya, Russian diplomacy consistently opposed military measures aimed at regime change. Four times, Russia used its veto to block resolutions aimed at ratcheting up the pressure on Assad. Its vetoes gave breathing room to the besieged government of Syria. They also undermined the credibility of the UN Security Council (UNSC), damaging its role as an international security arbiter. According to Matthew Rycroft, Britain's UN ambassador, "Syria is a stain on the conscience of the Security Council. I think it is the biggest failure in recent years, and it undoubtedly has consequences for the standing of the Security Council and indeed the United Nations as a whole."[40]

Jihadis potentially threatened Russian interests and citizens in Tartus and elsewhere along the Mediterranean. In 2014, with rebels rolling up battlefield gains, Russia launched a bombing campaign at Assad's request. According to Putin, Russia's intervention was aimed at "stabilizing the legitimate power in Syria and creating the conditions for political compromise."

Russian airpower targeted northwestern Syria, a strategic region and gateway to Assad's stronghold around Damascus. Turkmen, prevalent in the northwest, suffered the brunt of Russia's attacks. Putin said the air strikes were targeting ISIS and other jihadi groups. However, Russia's intervention was aimed primarily at propping up Assad, while diminishing the US-backed Free Syrian Army and jihadi groups supported by Turkey. Airstrikes were a show of force by Russia, challenging America as the world's sole superpower.[41] Russia's intervention also challenged Turkish interests. Just as the presence of Russian Special Forces made it impossible for the TSK to deploy troops and set up a security buffer across Turkey's border with Syria, Russia's command of the skies eliminated prospects for NATO-led no-fly zone.

Erdogan strongly condemned Russia's "very dangerous adventure" in Syria.[42] He was furious that Russia seized the strategic initiative, limiting Turkey's options. A Turkish F-16 shot down a Russian Sukhoi-24 on November 24, 2015. The plane crashed four kilometers from the Turkish-Syrian border in Latakia. The pilot, as well as a marine sent on a rescue mission, were both killed by Turkmen tribesmen. Turkey said it issued ten warnings. However, Captain Konstantin Murakhtin insisted there was no warning before being shot down by an air-to-air missile.

Putin reacted furiously, calling it "a stab in the back." Russian officials called it an "ambush."[43] Davutoglu responded defiantly, "Everyone must know that it is our international right and national duty to take any measure against whoever violates our air or land borders. Turkey will not hesitate to take all steps to protect the country's security.[44]

In the event of a confrontation between Russian and Turkish forces, Erdogan thought he could count on NATO's support. Article 5 of the Atlantic Charter states, "The Parties agree that an armed attack against one or more of them in Europe or North America shall be considered an attack against them all and consequently they agree that, if such an armed attack occurs, each of them, in exercise of the right of individual or collective self-defense recognized by Article 51 of the Charter of the United Nations, will assist the Party or Parties so attacked by taking forthwith, individually and in concert with the other Parties, such action as it deems necessary, including the use of armed force, to restore and maintain the security of the North Atlantic area."[45] Turkey immediately appealed to the North Atlantic Alliance.

The international community rhetorically supported Turkey. Obama said, "Turkey, like every country, has the right to defend its territory and its airspace."[46] NATO Secretary General Jens Stoltenberg said, "We stand in solidarity with Turkey and support the territorial integrity of our NATO ally, Turkey."[47] However, these rhetorical assertions of solidarity fell far short of mutual defense under Article 5. World leaders were more concerned with mitigating tensions than rallying to Turkey's defense. Stoltenberg called for "calm and de-escalation, and renewed contacts between Moscow and Ankara."[48] Stoltenberg added, "This highlights the importance of having and respecting arrangements to avoid such incidents in the future."[49] Members of the multinational coalition focused on ISIS. They agreed that bringing peace to Syria was the best way to avoid future incidents.

Downing the Russian plane was a strategic miscalculation, which undermined an important bilateral and commercial relationship. Russia banned construction projects in Russia with Turkish firms. It suspended work on Turk Stream, a new Black Sea gas pipeline. Russia prohibited the import of Turkish fruit and vegetables, poultry, and salt. It suspended the sale of charter vacations for Russians visiting Turkey. Canceled construction projects cost $4.5 billion. Tourist restrictions cost $3.5 billion. According to Turkey's agriculture ministry, the ban on imported agricultural products cost $764 million. Though Turkish textiles were not banned officially, Russian purchases of Turkish textiles and piece goods all but evaporated with the diminished tourist traffic.[50] French President François Hollande warned, "There is a risk of war between Turkey and Russia."[51]

Russia demanded an apology and compensation for the downed jet. Relations frayed over nine months until Erdogan relented and sent a letter of apology to the family of the downed pilot. A sign of improving relations, Putin reached out to Erdogan in the immediate aftermath of the failed coup to offer support and solidarity. Erdogan said that Putin's call was "very important from a mental perspective, this kind of psychological support."[52]

The rapprochement led to a meeting between Erdogan and Putin in St. Petersburg on August 9, 2016. They agreed to resume the Turk Stream pipeline and the construction of the Akkuyu nuclear power plant. Putin announced that Russia would lift sanctions on agricultural imports from Turkey and on Russian tourists traveling to Turkey. They failed, however, to reach agreement on Syria. Erdogan was quiet as the enormous humanitarian catastrophe unfolded in Aleppo. Erdogan and Putin papered over their differences supporting opposite sides of Syria's civil war.

Armenia

Turkey and Armenia share a common border but are divided by different perceptions of history. Armenians and most historians characterize the murder of up to 1.5 million Armenians as the "Armenian Genocide." Ankara disputes these facts, underscoring the war context in which the events occurred, calling it a "mutual tragedy" and bemoaning "shared suffering." Turks deeply resent efforts by Armenians to gain greater global recognition of the Armenian Genocide.

Erdogan sent a letter to President Robert Kocharian on April 10, 2005, proposing the establishment of a joint history commission to study archives and historical records. "We are extending an invitation to your country to establish a joint group consisting of historians and other experts from our two countries to study the developments and events of 1915 not only in the archives of Turkey and Armenia but also in the archives of all relevant third countries and to share their findings with the international public. I believe that such an initiative would shed light on a disputed period of history and also constitute a step towards contributing to the normalization of relations between our countries."[53] Kocharian was wary. He viewed it as another ploy to advance Turkey's denial and deflect support for international recognition of the Genocide.

Turkish and Armenian officials started to discuss a mechanism for addressing the issue. Armenians offered a simple text on recognition and normalization. Turkey was adamant about the establishment of a joint history commission. Switzerland played a discreet yet critical role, mediating between the two sides. Gul took the lead on Armenian issues for the Turkish government. When Gul switched from being foreign minister to president in August 2007, he was still the point man coordinating ministerial and working level meetings, facilitated by the Swiss authorities between 2007 and 2009.

Sergh Sarkissian invited Gul to Yerevan to watch the FIFA World Cup qualifying match between Turkey and Armenia on September 6, 2008. The visit was referred to as "football diplomacy." Their efforts bore fruit. In April 2009, the Turkish and Armenian foreign ministers issued a joint statement announcing the Protocol on Normalization and the Protocol on Diplomatic Relations. "The two parties have achieved tangible progress and mutual understanding in this process and they have agreed on a comprehensive framework for the normalization of their bilateral relations. Within this framework, a roadmap has been determined."[54] In a feat of constructive ambiguity, there was no mention of Nagorno-Karabakh in the agreement or its annexes. The protocols were signed in Switzerland on October 10, 2009. International mediation by the United States, specifically the involvement of Secretary of State Hillary Clinton, was indispensable.

Announcement of the protocols was controversial in both countries. Opponents in Armenia accused the government of selling out the goal of genocide recognition. Opponents in Turkey viewed the protocols as a betrayal of Azerbaijan. The process was initiated and "owned" by Gul. Erdogan did not pay much attention, nor did he ever imagine that negotiations would culminate in a deal. Erdogan traveled to Baku with newly appointed Foreign Minister Ahmet Davutoglu. Regarding de-linkage of the protocols from Azerbaijan, Erdogan called it "slander" and "disinformation." Erdogan told the press, "Azerbaijan-Turkey fraternal relations have never been the subject of discussions. The Turkey-Armenia border has been closed due to Nagorno-Karabakh's occupation and will not be solved until it is liberated." He continued, "It is impossible for us to open the border unless the occupation ends."[55]

Erdogan refused to submit the protocols to the Turkish Grand National Assembly (TGNA) for ratification. Though the protocols were never ratified, they were not formally withdrawn. Turkey demanded intensified mediation through the Minsk Group to resolve the Nagorno-Karabakh issue, with the veiled threat of violence if the situation was not addressed diplomatically.

Erdogan undermined Gul's diplomatic initiative to normalize relations with Armenia. He scuttled Clinton's mediation efforts. By going to Baku and relinking Armenian relations with a settlement of Nagorno-Karabakh, Erdogan lent tacit support to hardliners in Azerbaijan. Emboldened, they attacked Armenian positions in April 2016, risking a conflagration in the South Caucasus. Hundreds were killed in a short but intense "Four Day War." Azerbaijan's offensive was endorsed by Erdogan who pronounced, "Nagorno-Karabakh will be returned to Azerbaijan. We will support Azerbaijan until the end."[56]

Greece

Though Greece and Turkey are both members of NATO, relations were marred historically by disputes, conflict, and distrust. In 1973, Turkey made claims on Greece's continental shelf, contesting Greece's right to territorial waters 12 nautical miles from the Greek mainland as provided for in the Law of the Sea. In July 1974, Turkish armed forces occupied a third of Cyprus, displacing approximately 160,000 Greek Cypriots. In 1975, Turkish warplanes encroached on Greek national airspace. The cat-and-mouse conflict peaked in December 1996 when Turkey asserted control over so-called gray zones in the Aegean Sea. The two countries almost went to war over a disputed pile of rocks that Turkey calls "Kardiak" and Greece refers to as "Imia." Tensions remain with Greece rejecting Turkey's demands to demilitarize islands in the eastern Aegean. Beginning in 2015, the refugee and migrant crisis further complicated Greek-Turkish relations.

As an EU member state, Greece conditioned Turkey's EU accession on the peaceful resolution of disputes and respect for territorial integrity. The Greek government raised other red flags about the suitability of Turkey, noting Turkey's treatment of minorities and raising concerns about religious freedom, including restrictions on the reopening of the Halki Seminary and the rights of the Ecumenical Patriarch, who resides in Istanbul.[57]

Both Greece and Turkey were shaken by earthquakes in 1999. US Ambassador to Greece, R. Nicholas Burns observed, "I think we're in the middle of a new phenomenon that you could call seismic diplomacy or earthquake diplomacy. Images that people saw on TV had tremendous political symbolism, and there's an opportunity for both sides to build on that." Turkey's Foreign Minister Ismail Cem and his Greek counterpart, George Papandreou, negotiated a series of political, military, and economic confidence-building measures between the two countries. As a measure of the improved atmospherics, Greece reversed its position allowing accession negotiations between Turkey and the EU.[58]

Erdogan continued the process of Turkish-Greek rapprochement, focusing on economic cooperation. The AKP welcomed Greek foreign investments, which totaled $6.5 billion between 2002 and 2011. Greece became the fifth-biggest foreign investor in Turkey. Direct investments from Greece reached $6.8 billion in 2015, while Turkish investments in Greece were about $500 million. The bilateral trade volume doubled between 2010 and 2014, reaching $5.6 billion by the end of 2014. About one million Turks and Greeks visit one another's country each year. A facilitated visa procedure for visiting seven Greek islands close to Turkey went into effect in 2012, increasing the number of Turkish tourists. Commercial airline flights expanded. So did high-speed train and ferry service between Istanbul and Thessaloniki.[59]

Turkey and Greece established a High-Level Cooperation Council (HLCC) as an institutional framework for cooperation in 2010. The HLCC is chaired by the prime ministers and coordinated by the foreign ministers. The HLCC met four times as of June 2016. Business leaders convened on the margins, reaching agreements spurring travel and trade. Journalists jointly published articles and established a hot line for reporting on emergencies. Fifty-four bilateral agreements have been finalized. According to Erdogan, "We believe the constructive atmosphere between our countries, the mutual understanding and good neighborliness will strengthen our ties further" and foster stability in the eastern Mediterranean.[60]

Despite progress bilaterally, Cyprus remained a thorn in Turkish-Greek relations. Turkey based about thirty thousand troops on the island after its occupation in 1974. In subsequent years, Turkey was widely blamed for obstructing political progress aimed at reunification. In 2004, however, 65 percent of Turkish Cypriots voted to support the Annan Plan, which proposed the "United Republic of Cyprus." Only 24 percent of Greek Cypriots supported the deal. Erdogan was credited with marshaling support among the Turkish community. He wanted to resolve the Cyprus issue before the EU voted on membership for Cyprus. Erdogan asserted, "We want to bury the Cyprus problem in history."[61]

In 2014 and 2015, Nicos Anastasiades, President of the Republic of Cyprus, and his counterpart, Mustafa Akinci, met at least twenty-five times to discuss the details of an accord. According to UN Special Envoy, Espen Barth Eide, "This time, the deal will be written by Cypriots." Despite Eide's optimism, thorny issues derailed negotiations in November 2016. The two sides differed on the number of Greek Cypriots to be relocated to northern Cyprus and the redrawing of existing boundaries. Compensation for 100,000 Greek and 40,000 Turkish Cypriots who fled their homes in 1974 will cost billions.

Cyprus threatened to veto the 2015 EU-Turkey refugee and migrant deal pending the completion of reunification talks on

Cyprus. Other EU Member States also objected, raising concerns about terrorists infiltrating the refugee population and coming to Europe. Political realists said there was no alternative to the EU-Turkey deal. Absent the accord, tens of thousands of refugees and migrants would be stranded in Greece. The refugee and migrant crisis revealed deep underlying tensions. Erdogan's threat to flood Europe with refugees would have a direct, dramatic, and deleterious effect on Greece and other transit countries.[62] It was a contributing factor in the Brexit vote, whereby a majority of Britons voted to leave the EU.

The discovery of plentiful gas deposits off the coast of Cyprus is another irritant in Turkish-Greek relations. Greece wants to demarcate areas beneath the sea for gas exploration. However, wary of being cut out of the deal, Turkey has warned against unilateral moves. Israel is playing both sides, seeking to secure its offshore interests. Israeli waters could hold as much as 75 trillion cubic feet of gas. Exploiting estimated reserves would make Israel an alternative for Russian gas being exported to Turkey and European countries.

Israel

Turkey and Israel cooperated bilaterally in many areas prior to the AKP's election in 2002. They signed a free-trade agreement in 1997 and an investment treaty in 1998. Israel responded to the 1999 Golcuk earthquake with search-and-rescue efforts. It established makeshift hospitals, deploying hundreds of surgeons and paramedics. Israeli doctors worked for weeks after the earthquake, as one of the largest international assistance teams. Rescue dogs from Israel helped save many lives.

Trade and tourism were extensive. Israel imported Turkish food-stuffs, beverages, and tobacco. In turn, Turkey was an important export destination for Israeli goods and services. Turkey and Israel cooperated on technology for water conservation and dry-land farming. An average of half a million Israeli tourists visited Turkey each year, enjoying its coastline, culture, and cuisine.

Turkey and Israel also had extensive military cooperation. Agreements included air, sea, land, and intelligence cooperation; manufacturing of aircraft, armaments and missiles; and staff exchanges, training, and exercises. Since Israel has limited air space, it agreed with Turkey to use Turkish air space for training missions, including access to Turkey's Konya firing range. Israeli defense companies helped to modernize the F-4 Phantom fleet and F-5 warplanes in the Turkish air force. Turkish pilots trained at Israel's computerized firing range at the Nevatim airfield. Israel upgraded 170 of Turkey's M60A1 tanks. It provided Popeye missiles with surface-to-air capability. Turkey supplied Israel with military garb such as boots and uniforms. The two navies joined Operation Reliant Mermaid in January 1998.

Turkey and Israel also worked together on Middle East Peace. When Erdogan visited Israel in 2005, he offered Turkey as a mediator between Israel and Syria. In November 2007, Israeli President Shimon Peres visited Ankara. President Gul proposed assisting negotiations aimed at freeing Israeli soldiers held hostage in Gaza—Gilad Shalit, Ehud Goldwasser, and Eldad Regev.

The Gaza War of 2008–2009 sent Turkish-Israeli relations into a tailspin. Turkey had been facilitating negotiations between Bashar al-Assad and Israel's Prime Minister Ehud Olmert. There were five rounds of indirect talks when the Gaza War started. Erdogan was furious that Olmert did not tell him that Israel was planning an offensive against Hamas during their meeting in Ankara just a few days before the outbreak of hostilities. Olmert responded, "Why should I say to any prime minister what the military plans of the State of Israel are for defending its citizens? I don't think that it was the right thing to do. I don't think that I had to do it; I was quite unhappy with the feelings that were expressed by the Turkish prime minister."[63]

The disagreement went public when Erdogan and Peres argued during a panel on Gaza at the Davos World Economic Forum in January 2009. Despite efforts by the moderator to end the panel, Erdogan insisted on having the last word. "Mr. Peres, you are older than me. Your voice comes out in a very loud tone. And the loudness of your voice has to do with a guilty conscience." Erdogan continued, "When it comes to killing, you know well how to kill." Erdogan stormed off the stage declaring: "And so Davos is over for me from now on." Peres tried to respond by saying that Turkey would have reacted the same way had rockets been falling on Istanbul, but Erdogan was gone in a huff.[64]

Military cooperation was suspended in the aftermath of Davos. Turkey barred Israel from participating in a naval exercise with the United States called "Anatolian Eagle," scheduled for October 2009. Turkey froze defense contracts worth billions of dollars, including plans to purchase one thousand Merkava Mk-3 tanks valued at $5 billion in March 2010. It excluded Israeli Aerospace Industries from bidding on a $2 billion missile tender. In October 2010, Israel's

Tourism Ministry urged a boycott in response to Turkey's support for Hamas in Gaza.

Meanwhile, the Humanitarian Relief Foundation (IHH), an Islamist charity with close ties to the AKP, was plotting a "Gaza Freedom Convoy." Six ships sailed to Gaza, ostensibly to deliver humanitarian supplies. Israeli Defense Forces (IDF) tried to enforce Israel's blockade of Gaza. IDF naval commandos boarded the *Mavi Marmara* via helicopter in international waters after repeated warnings on May 31, 2010. They were swarmed by "humanitarians" wielding an array of knives, bats, metal pipes, and an improvised explosive device. Defense Minister Ehud Barak called the flotilla a provocation and IHH members "extremist supporters of terror."[65]

Erdogan was indignant after the *Mavi Marmara* incident. He demanded an international investigation, accountability for the IDF members involved in the operation, and compensation. Turkey initiated legal proceedings in absentia against Israeli troops involved in the raid. Turkey lodged a diplomatic protest and withdrew its ambassador to Israel, putting a deep chill on Turkish-Israeli relations.

Three years later, President Barack Obama brokered a phone conversation between Erdogan and Israeli Prime Minister Benjamin Netanyahu during which Netanyahu apologized for "operational errors." Erdogan accepted the apology on behalf of the Turkish people, but relations were still affected. Erdogan blamed Israel for masterminding the military coup in Egypt, which overthrew the Muslim Brotherhood's Mohammed Morsi. In 2013, *The Washington Post* reported that Turkey revealed to Iranian intelligence the names of Mossad agents involved in covert operations targeting Iran's nuclear program.

Turkey and Israel restored diplomatic relations on June 26, 2016. Turkey's Foreign Ministry announced that Foreign Policy Advisory Board Member Husnu Gurcan would be appointed ambassador to Jerusalem. Defense Minister Avigdor Liberman, a fierce critic of Turkey, did not oppose normalization. It was agreed that Israel would continue its blockade of Gaza, while allowing Turkey to send equipment and goods to Gaza via the port of Ashdod. Turkey was also given permission to build a power station, a desalination plant, and a hospital in Gaza. Gurcan's appointment was part of broad reshuffle of Turkish envoys, signaling Ankara's efforts to improve its international relations.[66] As a conciliatory gesture, Undersecretary Feridun Sinirlioglu, a senior and well- respected Turkish diplomat, attended the state funeral for Shimon Peres in September 2016.

The Arab Spring

The Arab Spring movement swept North Africa and Arab States between 2010 and 2012. Popular revolts demanded democracy and the removal of entrenched dictatorships. Given Turkey's reputation for harmonizing secular democracy and Islamic values, the AKP was positioned as the model for countries in North Africa and the Arab world. Erdogan envisioned himself as the movement's leader. But his response to the Arab Spring was uneven and unprincipled. He spoke in support of reforms, while preserving ties to despots with which Turkey had close political, security, and commercial relations. Turkey was caught between the status quo and the Muslim Brotherhood. Both were antidemocratic. Moreover, Turkey could hardly be a credible champion of freedoms in the region, given its own track record on human rights.

The Arab Spring started in Tunisia when an unemployed street vendor set himself on fire to protest police restrictions on his vegetable stand. His self-immolation spread like wildfire, catalyzing widespread street protests in December 2010. About three hundred people were killed before popular protests forced President Zine al-Abidine Ben Ali to resign. He stepped down in January 2011 after twenty-three years in power. Erdogan was silent on Ben Ali's fate. Parallels existed between Erdogan and Ben Ali. Erdogan feared that supporting Ben Ali's exile and conviction could boomerang, inspiring Turks to demand accountability. Stability is the highest priority in Middle East politics. Similarly, Erdogan emphasized stability in Turkey to preserve his authority.

The Ennahda Party, which originated from the Muslim Brotherhood, won Tunisia's democratic parliamentary elections in October 2011. Though Ennahda' co-founder, Rashid al-Gannouchi, pointed to the AKP as a model, President Moncef Marzouki was a more modern man who rejected Islamist rule. Tunisia ultimately adopted a liberal constitution in 2014, blending the country's Islamic heritage with progressive freedoms. The constitution established Islam as the state religion, while enshrining individual rights, group rights, equal rights for men and women, freedom of religion, and an independent judiciary. The constitution is far more progressive than Turkey's military constitution of 1982. Tunisia's penal code does not include regressive legislation, which can be used to silence freedom of expression.

Ennhada's Islamist faction advocated AKP's course for Tunisia. However, Ennhada's leadership had other ideas. Ennhada rejected the "Islamist" label, embracing an identity as "Muslim democrats." Its leaders proclaimed their commitment to politics in lieu of religious activities. Its approach was similar to the AKP's upon coming to power in 2002. Tunisia established a system of checks and balances through its constitution, as well as the National Dialogue Quartet, civil society leaders who won the Nobel Prize for Peace in 2015.[67]

After Tunisia, Libya was the next country affected by the Arab Spring. Turkey's response to events in Libya was also ambivalent. Turkey had extensive economic relations with Libya. At least thirty thousand Turkish workers were employed in Libyan government financed construction projects valued at $1.5 billion. Around $15 billion worth of future contracts would be lost if Moammar al-Qhaddafi were overthrown.[68] Erdogan and Qhaddafi also had a close personal relationship, further complicating bilateral relations. On December 1, 2010, Erdogan accepted the Qhaddafi International Human Rights Prize. The prize was bestowed at a time when Qhaddafi was intensifying pressure on his domestic political opponents. Turkish civil society groups admonished Erdogan to return the prize.

Libyan reformists were disappointed by Erdogan's support for Qhaddafi. When Erdogan endorsed an arms embargo on Libyan rebels, Benghazi revolutionaries tore down the Turkish flag and attacked the Turkish consulate. The North Atlantic Council met to consider its response to the spiral of deadly violence in Libya. Erdogan argued: "NATO's intervention in Libya is out of the question," calling it "absurd."[69] Erdogan's position was based partly on personal pique. Members of the international community met in Paris to discuss Libya's political transition, but Erdogan was not invited. Erdogan's reaction to being excluded further undermined Turkey's position as a regional superpower.

Erdogan wanted to keep his options open. But when Britain and France started bombing Libyan air defenses, Erdogan reluctantly joined a "coalition of the willing." On May 3, 2011, Erdogan ratcheted-up his rhetoric, condemning "bloodshed" and calling on Qhaddafi to step down "for the sake of the country's future."[70] Turkey sent a frigate to evacuate Turkish citizens and a hospital ship to treat wounded in Benghazi. It eventually supported NATO's command, contributing aircraft and navy ships. Turkey also joined discussions about a political transition.

Erdogan changed course as the violence in Misurata was dramatically escalating. It was a month before general elections in Turkey, and Erdogan wanted to be seen as siding with the people. Erdogan's reversal was too late to redeem Turkey's standing with Libyans. Turkey's influence in Libya post-Qhaddafi had already been marginalized. Turkey's support for Islamist factions undermined reconciliation among Libyans, prolonging the country's ongoing civil war.[71]

Unlike Libya, Erdogan was quick to support Egypt's political transition. Relations between Erdogan and President Hosni Mubarak were tense. Mubarak was wary of Erdogan's pandering to the Arab street. He also resented Turkey's encroachment of diplomatic files that had been Cairo's responsibility—Gaza and reconciliation between the Palestinian Authority and Hamas. As protests mounted in Cairo's Tahrir Square, Erdogan was the first world leader to call for Mubarak's resignation.

Mohamed Morsi, head of the Muslim Brotherhood, was elected Egypt's president in June 2012. Turkey welcomed Morsi, pledging nearly $2 billion in September 2012. Morsi was elected with only 52 percent of the vote. He failed to reconcile with Mubarak's supporters or govern effectively. Progressives and Mubarak backers believed Morsi was ultimately loyal to the Muslim Brotherhood and its Islamist ideals. Morsi tried to consolidate his executive powers, bypassing the judiciary to advocate a new constitution that enshrined Islamism. Deadly street fights forced Morsi to withdraw the draft in November 2012. From Morsi's first days in office, Egypt's military began plotting his removal from the presidency. Morsi would stay in power for just over a year.

To justify deposing Morsi, the military engineered demonstrations on June 30, 2013. General Abdel Fattah el-Sisi demanded Morsi step down on July 1. Two days later, Sisi ordered his arrest. Then he launched a systematic crackdown on the Muslim Brotherhood. Thousands of dissidents were killed and tens of thousands arrested. Morsi and more than one hundred other defendants from the Muslim Brotherhood were convicted of charges ranging from espionage to incitement. Morsi was sentenced to death.

While some heralded Morsi's removal as a triumph for democracy, Erdogan called it an "unacceptable coup."[72] Erdogan also condemned the international community: "The United Nations as well as the democratic countries have done nothing but watch events such as the overthrow of an elected president in Egypt and the killings of thousands of innocent people who tried to defend their choice. And they lend their legitimacy to the person who carried out this coup."[73] Bilateral relations between Turkey and Egypt collapsed. In a diplomatic tiff, Turkey accused the Egyptian military of atrocities. In turn, Egypt said it would recognize the Armenian Genocide.[74]

Erdogan believed that his fate was connected to Morsi's. At the same time as street protests swept Egypt, liberal and secular Turks were rallying in Gezi Park and sixty other Turkish cities demanding reform and accountability of Erdogan's administration. Erdogan conjured a Western conspiracy to get rid of both Morsi and himself. He accused Israel of plotting the coup.[75] Turkey withdrew its ambassador from Cairo. Its ambassadors in Tel Aviv and Damascus were also withdrawn.

Turkey's response to the Arab Spring was uneven. Erdogan vacillated between support for Islamists and loyalty to dictators in countries where Turkey had commercial or security interests. His approach lacked principle. It was based on narrow and shortsighted sectarian self-interest. Turkey barely reacted to events in Yemen and Bahrain, where Shiite dissidents rebelled against Saudi-backed monarchies. The absence of a consistent, principle-based approach to the Arab Spring estranged Turkey from Arab States.

Syria represented another conundrum. Turkey and Syria had good relations when Syria's revolution started on March 15, 2011. Erdogan expected that Bashar al-Assad would quickly fall, and the Muslim Brotherhood would ascend. Supporting democracy meant supporting Sunni Arabs who would advance Turkey's agenda and assist its fight with the PKK. Once again, Turkey's assumptions were wrong. Syria was a quagmire—Erdogan's Waterloo.

Notes

1. "Policy of Zero Problems with Our Neighbors," *The Ministry of Foreign Affairs, Government of Turkey*, accessed June 2, 2016, http://www.mfa.gov.tr/policy-of-zero-problems-with-our-neighbors.en.mfa.
2. Zero Problems with Neighbors policy is Ahmet Dovutoglu's doctrine to reshape Turkish foreign policy and make Turkey a leading power in the region and broader world. It is based on his book seminal book: *Strategic Depth*—which he wrote in 2001 when he was a professor of international relations. Davutoglu argued that Turkey has high historical and cultural heritage of the great Ottoman Empire, and if plays an active role through prioritizing diplomatic and peaceful relations with the neighbors, and by forming new alliances in the region and beyond, Turkey will attend a greater role in the region and beyond, and it can again lead Muslim world. See also: A. Davutoglu, "Turkey's Foreign Policy Vision: An Assessment of 2007," *Insight Turkey* 10, no. 1 (2008): 77–96; J. Walker, *The Sources of Turkish Grand Strategy–"Strategic Depth" and "Zero problems" in context (LSE Ideas)*

(London: London School of Economics, 2011); B. Aras, "The Davutoglu Era in Turkish Foreign Policy," *Insight Turkey* 11, no. 3 (2009): 127.

3. J. Goldberg, "The Obama Doctrine: The U.S. President Talks through His Hardest Decisions about America's Role in the World," *The Atlantic*, accessed June 9, 2016, http://www.theatlantic.com/magazine/archive/2016/04/the-obama-doctrine/471525/.

4. As Cited in D. Philips, *Losing Iraq: Inside the Post-War Reconstruction Fiasco* (New York: Basic Books, 2005). Ibid., 165.

5. "Policy of Zero Problems with Our Neighbors," *The Ministry of Foreign Affairs, Government of Turkey*, accessed June 2, 2016, http://www.mfa.gov.tr/policy-of-zero-problems-with-our-neighbors.en.mfa.

6. As cited in Phillips, *Losing Iraq*.

7. F. Tastekin, "Irak Bölünecekti ki Hesap Tutmadi," *Radikal*, accessed June 14, 2016, http://www.radikal.com.tr/yazarlar/fehim-tastekin/irak-bolunecek-ti-ki-hesap-tutmadi-1304836/.

8. L. Sly, "Petraeus: The Islamic State Isn't Our Biggest Problem in Iraq," *The Washington Post*, accessed June 9, 2016, https://www.washingtonpost.com/news/worldviews/wp/2015/03/20/petraeus-the-islamic-state-isnt-our-biggest-problem-in-iraq/.

9. Ibid.

10. Sly, "Petraeus."

11. ISIS or the Islamic State, was founded in 1999 by a Jordanian jihadist Abu Musab al-Zarqawi with the name of *Jamā'at al-Tawḥīd wa-al-Jihād* (the Organization of Monotheism and Jihad). Evolving over the past decade and changing its name several times, it now calls itself the Islamic State, Abu Bakr al-Baghdadi being its leader. As cited in H. Tunç, "Turkey's Kurdophobia as a Precursor to Kurdish Genocide: The Case of Kobani," *Centre for Policy and Research on Turkey (ResearchTurkey), London, Research Turkey* IV, no. 7 (2015): 69–96.

12. "Türkiye Irak'ta kendi milis gücünü yaratıyor," *SolHaberler*, March 4, 2015, accessed June 14, 2016, http://haber.sol.org.tr/turkiye/turkiye-irakta-kendi-milis-gucunu-yaratiyor-109403.

13. S. Erkus, "Turkey Extends Military Training to Local Sunni Forces and Iraqi Army," *Hürriyet Daily News*, accessed June 18, 2016, http://www.hurriyetdailynews.com/turkey-extends-military-training-to-local-sunni-forces-and-iraqi-army.aspx?pageID=238&nid=79477.

14. Ibid.

15. "Türkiye Sünni aşiretleri eğitecek," March 10, 2015, accessed June 7, 2016, http://www.aljazeera.com.tr/haber/turkiye-sunni-asiretleri-egitecek.

16. "Baghdad Calls on Ankara to 'Immediately' Withdraw Troops," *Dawn*, December 5, 2015, accessed August 16, 2016, http://www.dawn.com/news/1224377.

17. M. Gurcan, "Turkey Sticks Its Neck Out Again, This Time in Iraq," *Almonitor: Turkey's Pulse*, accessed June 6, 2016, http://www.al-monitor.com/pulse/originals/2015/12/turkey-iraq-becomes-third-largest-army.html#ixzz4ASixOB3l.

18. Susan Fraser. "Turkey's president tells Iraqi leader to 'know his place." *The Washington Post*. October 11, 2016. re https://www.washingtonpost.com/world/middle_east/turkeys-erdogan-tells-iraqi-leader-to-know-his-place/

2016/10/11/e789f530-8fa5-11e6-bc00-1a9756d4111b_story.html (accessed October 14, 2016).

19. "Türkiye Irak'ta Sünni aşiretleri silahlandıracak," *TimeTurk*, March 9, 2015, accessed June 15, 2016, http://www.timeturk.com/tr/2015/03/09/turkiye-irak-ta-sunni-asiretleri-silahlandiriyor.html.

20. H. J. Barkey, "Iran and Turkey," *United States Institute of Peace: The Iran Primer*, November 2015, accessed June 15, 2016, http://iranprimer.usip.org/resource/iran-and-turkey.

21. B. Eligür, *The Mobilization of Political Islam in Turkey* (Cambridge: Cambridge University Press, 2010), 108.

22. Ibid., 101.

23. Ibid., 108.

24. E. Peker, "Turkey Hails Iran Nuclear Deal: Turkey Calls on Iran and Six Powers to Act Responsibly," *The Wall Street Journal*, January 17, 2016, accessed June 15, 2016, http://www.wsj.com/articles/turkey-hails-iran-nuclear-deal-1453045276.

25. Barkey, "Iran and Turkey."

26. Peker, "Turkey Hails Iran Nuclear Deal."

27. Jafari, S. (September 11, 2015). Ibid.

28. Peker, "Turkey Hails Iran Nuclear Deal."

29. Takfirs means "Non-believers."

30. F. Ozerkan, "Iran and Turkey Vow to Cooperate on Terrorism, Trade," *The Times of Israel*, April 16, 2016, accessed June 15, 2016, http://www.timesofisrael.com/iran-and-turkey-vow-to-cooperate-on-terrorism-trade/.

31. H. Ahmadian, "Is Turkey Swaying Back Toward Iran?," *AlMonitor: Iran Pulse*, March 22, 2016, accessed June 14, 2016, http://www.al-monitor.com/pulse/originals/2016/03/iran-turkey-political-cooperation-davutoglu-zarif.html#ixzz4Ai2T9ug4.

32. "Turkey-Iran Relations," *Republic of Turkey Ministry of Foreign Affairs*, accessed June 5, 2016, http://www.mfa.gov.tr/turkey-iran-relations.en.mfa.

33. Cengiz Candar. "Biden's Diplomatic Triage in Ankara." *Al-Monitor*. August 28, 2016. http://www.al-monitor.com/pulse/originals/2016/08/biden-diplomatic-triage-turkey-syria-policy-iran.html?utm_source=Boomtrain&utm_medium=manual&utm_campaign=20160828&bt_email=dp2366@columbia.edu&bt_ts=1472459450539 (accessed September 5, 2016).

34. See S. McNamara, A. Cohen, and J. Phillips, "Countering Turkey's Strategic Drift," *The Heritage Foundation Backgrounder* 2442 (2010): 14 and D. B. Sezer, "Turkish-Russian Relations: The Challenges of Reconciling Geopolitical Competition with Economic Partnership," *Turkish Studies* 1, no. 1 (2000): 59–82.

35. Y. Kanli, "An Important Guest Arrives for Landmark Visit," *Hürriyet Daily News*, December 6, 2016, accessed June 14, 2016, http://www.hurriyetdailynews.com/an-important-guest-arrives-for-landmark-visit.aspx?pageID=438&n=an-important-guest-arrives-for-landmark-visit-2004-12-06.

36. "Turk-Russian Gas Deal follows Azeri Accord," *Hurriyet Daily News and Economic Review*, December 29, 2011, accessed June 16, 2016 http://www.hurriyetdailynews.com/turk-russian-gas-deal-follows-azeri-accord.aspx?pageID=238&nID=10268&NewsCatID=348.

37. Kanli, "An Important Guest Arrives for Landmark Visit."

38. S. Arsu, "Turkey's Act with Russia Will Give it Nuclear Plant," *The New York Times*, May 13, 2010, accessed June 16, 2016, p. A12.

39. "Why Russia is an Ally of Assad?," *The Economist*, September 30, 2015, accessed June 10, 2016, http://www.economist.com/blogs/economist-explains/2015/09/economist-explains-22.

40. Julian Borger and Bastien Inzaurralde, "Russian Vetoes Are Putting UN Security Council's Legitimacy at Risk, Says US," *The Guardian*, September 23, 2015, accessed June 20, 2016, https://www.theguardian.com/world/2015/sep/23/russian-vetoes-putting-un-security-council-legitimacy-at-risk-says-us.

41. J. Daunt and J. Ensor, "Why Does Russia Support Syria's Bashar al-Assad?," *The Telegraph*, February 12, 2016, accessed June 16, 2016, http://www.telegraph.co.uk/news/worldnews/middleeast/syria/11919242/Why-does-Russia-support-Syrias-Bashar-al-Assad.html.

42. Peker, "Turkey Hails Iran Nuclear Deal."

43. "Turkey's Downing of Russian Warplane – What We Know," *BBC News*, December 1, 2015, accessed June 10, 2016, http://www.bbc.com/news/world-middle-east-34912581.

44. "World Leaders React to Turkey's Downing of Russian Jet," *AlJazeera*, November 24, 2015, accessed June 10, 2016, http://www.aljazeera.com/news/2015/11/russian-jet-shot-turkey-syria-reaction-151124210400768.html.

45. "The North Atlantic Treaty," *North Atlantic Treaty Organization*, April 4, 1949, accessed June 10, 2016, http://www.nato.int/cps/en/natolive/official_texts_17120.htm.

46. "Obama: 'Turkey Has the Right to Defend Its Airspace'," *BBC News*, November 24, 2015, accessed August 16, 2016, http://www.bbc.com/news/world-us-canada-34915752.

47. "Statement by the NATO Secretary General after the Extraordinary NAC Meeting," *NATO*, November 24, 2015, accessed August 16, 2016, http://www.nato.int/cps/en/natohq/news_125052.htm.

48. Ibid.

49. Ibid.

50. S. Girit, "Turkey Faces Big Losses as Russia Sanctions Bite," *BBC News*, January 2, 2016, accessed June 10, 2016, http://www.bbc.com/news/world-europe-35209987.

51. Liz Sly, "Turkey's Increasingly Desperate Predicament Poses Real Dangers," *The Washington Post*, Febraury 20, 2016, accessed July 16, 2016, https://www.washingtonpost.com/world/middle_east/turkeys-increasingly-desperate-predicament-poses-real-dangers/2016/02/20/a3374030-d593-11e5-a65b-587e721fb231_story.html?tid=a_inl.

52. Neil MacFarquar, "Russia and Turkey Vow to Restore Frayed Ties," *The International New York Times*, August 11, 2016, 5.

53. As cited in Y. Güçlü, *Historical Archives and the Historians' Commission to Investigate the Armenian Events of 1915* (Lanham, MD: University Press of America, 2015), 273–4.

54. Ibid., 215; Also see: "No: 56, 22 April 2009, Joint Statement of The Ministries of Foreign Affairs of The Republic of Turkey, The Republic of Armenia and The Swiss Federal Department of Foreign Affairs," *Republic of Turkey Ministry*

of Foreign Affairs, accessed June 18, 2016, http://www.mfa.gov.tr/no_-56_-22-april-2009_-press-release-regarding-the-turkish-armenian-relations.en.mfa.

55. "Timeline: 2008–2009," *European Stability Initiative (ESI)*, accessed June 18, 2016, http://www.esiweb.org/index.php?lang=en&id=322&debate_ID=2&slide_ID=2. For a broader account on worsening of Turkey-Armenia process, see the section: *The Process under Attack* in T. De Waal, *Great Catastrophe: Armenians and Turks in the Shadow of Genocide* (Oxford: Oxford University Press, 2015).

56. L. Atamian, "The Nagorno-Karabakh Conflict," *The Huffington Post*, April 19, 2016, accessed June 10, 2016, http://www.huffingtonpost.com/luna-atamian-/the-nagornokarabakh-confl_b_9716858.html.

57. "Issues of Greek – Turkish Relations," *Hellenic Republic: Ministry of Foreign Affairs*, 2016, accessed July 3, 2016, http://www.mfa.gr/en/issues-of-greek-turkish-relations/.

58. Stephen Kinzer, "Earthquakes Help Warm Greek-Turkish Relations," September 13, 1999, *New York Times*, accessed July 3, 2016, http://www.nytimes.com/1999/09/13/world/earthquakes-help-warm-greek-turkish-relations.html?pagewanted=all.

59. "Relations between Turkey and Greece," *Republic of Turkey: Ministry of Foreign Affairs*, 2001, accessed July 3, 2016, http://www.mfa.gov.tr/relations-between-turkey-and-greece.en.mfa.

60. Ayla Jean Yackley, "Greece, in Trouble Elsewhere, Boosts Cooperation with Turkey," *Reuters*, March 4, 2013, accessed July 3, 2016, http://www.reuters.com/article/us-turkey-greece-idUSBRE9230V120130304.

61. Ibid.

62. Philip Chrysopoulos, "Refugee Crisis Puts Greece-Turkey Relations to the Test," *Greek Reporter*, February 22, 2016, accessed July 3, 2016, http://greece.greekreporter.com/2016/02/22/refugee-crisis-puts-greece-turkey-relations-to-the-test/#sthash.Rb8NQMZJ.idjWN8zM.dpuf.

63. "Erdogan-Olmert Spat May Raise Tensions between Turkey and Israel," *Hürriyet*, February 18, 2009, accessed June 3, 2016, http://www.hurriyet.com.tr/erdogan-olmert-spat-may-raise-tensions-between-turkey-and-israel-11031584.

64. K. Bennhold, "Leaders of Turkey and Israel Clash at Davos Panel," *The New York Times*, January 29, 2009, accessed June 3, 2016, http://www.nytimes.com/2009/01/30/world/europe/30clash.html?_r=0.

65. Y. Katz, "Nine Dead in Vicious Conflict Aboard 'Mavi Marmara,'" *The Jeruselam Post*, June 1, 2010, accessed June 3, 2016, http://www.jpost.com/Israel/Nine-dead-in-Vicious-conflict-aboard-Mavi-Marmara.

66. http://www.timesofisrael.com/israel-turkey-to-announce-detente-next-week-report/.

67. M. Akyol, "Is Ennahda Following in AKP Footsteps?," *AlMonitor:Turkey Pulse*, June 2, 2016, accessed June 11, 2016, http://www.al-monitor.com/pulse/originals/2016/06/turkey-tunisia-ennahda-emulating-akp.html#ixzz4BJuf6Rwi.

68. "Turkish Foreign Policy: Erdogan's Lament," *The Economist*, April 7, 2011, accessed June 11, 2016, http://www.economist.com/node/18530682.

69. S. A. Cook, "Arab Spring, Turkish Fall," *Foreign Policy*, May 5, 2011, accessed June 11, 2016, http://foreignpolicy.com/2011/05/05/arab-spring-turkish-fall-2/.

70. "Turkey's PM Erdogan Urges Col Muammar Gaddafi to Quit," *BBC News*, May 3, 2011, accessed June 12, 2016, http://www.bbc.com/news/world-europe-13265825.
71. H. J. Barkey, "Turkey and the Arab Spring," *Carnegie Endowment for International Peace*, April 26, 2011, accessed June 11, 2016, http://carnegieendowment.org/2011/04/26/turkey-and-arab-spring.
72. J. Burch, "Turkey's Erdogan Slams World's 'Double Standards' on Egypt," *Reuters*, July 19, 2013, accessed June 18, 2016, http://www.reuters.com/article/us-egypt-protests-turkey-idUSBRE96I0NJ20130719.
73. N. Ismail, "Turkey's Quagmire since the Arab Spring," *Open Democracy*, October 6, 2014, accessed June 11, 2016, https://www.opendemocracy.net/arab-awakening/nishaat-ismail/turkey's-quagmire-since-arab-spring.
74. Akyol, "Is Ennahda Following in AKP Footsteps?"
75. Ibid.

8

The Syrian Quagmire

*Despite the Secretary's efforts to deescalate the violence and forge
ahead with the political track, we believe that achieving our objectives
will continue to elude us if we do not include the use of military
force as an option to enforce the Cessation of Hostilities (CoH) and
compel the Syrian regime to abide by its terms as well as to
negotiate a political solution in good faith.[1]*

—Foreign Service Officers Dissent Channel

Hafez al-Assad, Syria's President from 1971 to 2000, provided strategic
support to the PKK to enhance his leverage over Ankara. Syria became
the hub of PKK activities in the 1980s. Abdullah Ocalan, the PKK chief,
lived in Syria from 1979 until 1998. The PKK's founding conference
was held in Syria in 1991. The PKK formalized its armed struggle at a
meeting in Syria in 1992, and moved its headquarters from Lebanon's
Beka'a Valley to Syria later that year.

The PKK was a pan-Kurdish liberation and human rights movement rooted in Turkey and Syria where clan groupings stretch across
the border. About two hundred and fifty thousand Kurds in Syria
were not able to become Syrian citizens because their male ances-
tors were refugees from Turkey. Though Assad denied the PKK's
presence on Syrian soil, the organization operated in plain sight.
Ocalan lived in a Damascus villa. The PKK had training facilities in
Sahnaya, Shebaa and Al-Nashabiya. About a third of PKK fighters
were actually ethnic Kurds from Syria. When Sheikh Said Pirran's
rebellion was put down by Ataturk in 1925, many survivors found
sanctuary in Syria, which was under French control at the time. More
Kurds went to Syria when Ataturk implemented his "Turkification"
policy in the 1930s. Another wave came to Syria in the 1980s and
1990s when Turkey's scorched-earth tactics rendered the southeast uninhabitable. According to Ocalan, "Most Syrian Kurds are

immigrants who fled to Syria from the oppression and violence of Turkish governments."[2]

Ataturk objected when Alexandretta Province was placed under French control after the First World War. He insisted on calling the province "Hatay" and demanded control. The border dispute between Turkey and Syria turned violent in 1937. In response to a guerilla insurgency, France rewarded Ataturk's coercion by ceding Alexandretta to Turkey. Syria maintained its claim to Hatay, which it calls Liwa al-Iskandaron.

In 1998, Turkey and Syria almost went to war again. Contentious issues included Syria's continuing claims over Hatay, as well as disputes over water from the Euphrates River. The core issue, however, was Syria's sanctuary for Ocalan and support of the PKK. As the PKK intensified its cross-border attacks, Ankara grew increasingly impatient with Assad and threatened reprisals. The Turkish army massed on the Turkey-Syria border in September 1998. The Turkish General Staff (TGS) issued an unequivocal warning. Either evict Ocalan or Turkey will invade. Assad acquiesced, signing the Adana Agreement on October 20, 1998. The accord required Syria to list the PKK as a terrorist organization, close PKK bases in Syria, and evict Ocalan.[3] After a global manhunt, Ocalan was captured in Nairobi and sentenced to death in 1999. He is currently serving a life sentence at a maximum-security prison on Imrali Island in the Aegean Sea.

The Syrian government went above and beyond requirements in the Adana Agreement. On its own and in concert with Turkey, it launched military operations against the PKK, arresting its members and sending them to Turkey. PKK members with Turkish citizenship who resided in Syria were rounded up and deported. Syria tightened its border with Turkey to prevent PKK infiltrations. It allowed hot pursuit operations by Turkish troops on Syrian soil. The Syrian government shut down the PKK's communications apparatus, closing publications and blocking radio transmissions. Statements and editorials against Turkey in official media were banned. Pro-PKK demonstrations were prohibited. PKK sympathizers were barred from running for office in local and national elections.

Assad's death in 2000 created new opportunities for cooperation between Turkey and Syria, especially in the security field. Nine meetings on police cooperation were held between October 1998 and January 2002.[4] Police agencies agreed to share intelligence and expedite cross-border operations. In July 2002, Huseyin Kivrikoglu and Hasan Turkmani, the Turkish and Syrian chiefs of their armed forces, met in

Ankara to sign an agreement on joint training. Kivrikoglu praised the deal: "This cooperation will spread to other fields and a new term will begin in Turkish-Syrian relations."[5]

The election of Erdogan's Justice and Development Party (AKP) in November 2002 infused bilateral relations with new dynamism. Syria was a high priority when Ahmet Davutoglu articulated his "zero problems with neighbors" concept. Turkey and Syria share a border of more than nine hundred kilometers. Erdogan made a concerted effort to establish cordial ties with Hafez's son, Bashar al-Assad. Rapprochement was limited by hard-liners around Assad who had advised his father and still influenced policy.

In a landmark visit, Assad traveled to Istanbul in 2004. His three-day trip was the first ever by a Syrian head of government. It was more than a working trip. Assad was accompanied by his wife, Asma. They dined and socialized with Erdogan and his wife, Emine. On matters of state, Assad met his Turkish counterpart, President Ahmet Necdet Sezer. The Syrian delegation included ministers with an economic portfolio. They negotiated agreements to reduce trade barriers, including an accord to eliminate double taxation. The two sides also discussed conditions in Iraq and the Israeli-Palestinian conflict. Israel's Prime Minister Ehud Olmert requested that Turkey use its influence with Syria to gain the release of Israeli soldiers abducted by Hezbollah. Ankara's mediation would encompass a more comprehensive effort to strike a peace accord between Syria and Israel, including thorny issues such as the Golan Heights and water rights.

US-Turkish relations were strained during this period, partly because of Turkey's rapprochement with Syria. Washington criticized Ankara for undermining US efforts to encourage Syria's withdrawal from Lebanon, calling it "unacceptable." The Bush administration was also troubled by Turkey's actions in Iraq, where Turkish and Syrian strategic interests overlapped. The independence aspirations of Iraqi Kurds presented a challenge to both Turkey and Syria. They developed a common front against Iraqi Kurdistan's independence. They also acted in parallel to suppress their respective Kurdish minorities.[6]

Assad accepted Turkish sovereignty over Hatay Province, abandoning historic claims to Alexandretta. Syria's concession set the stage for conciliation and greater collaboration. Turkish and Syrian officials—including heads of government—started meeting on a regular basis. Erdogan typically emphasized economic diplomacy. Whenever Erdogan traveled, he was accompanied by large delegations of Turkish businessmen. Erdogan saw economic interdependence between Turkey and Syria as a way of shaping Syria's regional policies. Beyond benefitting from each other's markets, Erdogan viewed Syria as Turkey's portal to markets in other Arab countries. Similarly, Turkey is the route for Syrian goods in Europe.

Turkey and Syria signed a Free Trade Agreement (FTA) on January 1, 2007. Customs duties were dramatically reduced and gradually phased out. As a result of the FTA, trade volume rose from $796 million in 2006 to $2.5 billion in 2010. Turkish officials projected that bilateral trade would reach $5 billion by 2012. The FTA also catalyzed investment, with Turkish companies investing $1 billion. Syria's second city, Aleppo, became an investment hub. By 2011, Turkey was Syria's largest trading partner. Many Syrians went to Gaziantep to buy consumer goods and foodstuffs.[7]

Assad was on a charm offensive. He and Asma made a four-day visit to Ankara starting on October 16, 2007. They attended an elaborate dinner hosted by President Abdullah Gul and his wife, Hayrunnisa. In the following days, Assad met Erdogan, Parliament Speaker Koksal Toptan, Foreign Minister Ali Babacan, and former President Ahmet Necdet Sezer.

Erdogan made a reciprocal visit to Damascus in April 2007. On the eve of Erdogan's arrival, seven PKK members, including a top commander, were handed over to Turkish authorities as a "goodwill gesture."[8] A die-hard fan of Fenerbahce, Erdogan attended the inauguration of a soccer stadium in Aleppo where he watched a match between Fenerbahce and Al-Ittihad. Beyond sport, bilateral talks focused on energy issues. Turkish Energy Minister Hilmi Guler explored building a dam and hydroelectric facility on the Orontes/Asi River. He and his Syrian counterpart also discussed transporting natural gas from Egypt to Turkey via Syria.

As a measure of their affinity for Turkey, Assad and Asma vacationed in Bodrum, an Aegean resort community, in August 2008. Erdogan greeted Assad at the airport. The gesture of hospitality was a sign of their growing amity. The two leaders had a working lunch on the veranda of Assad's seaside hotel. They discussed Turkey's mediation between Syria and Israel. Turkey had convened four rounds of indirect talks to discuss the Syria-Israel relationship. Its mediation was at a delicate stage, requiring close coordination with the Syrian government. Damascus was motivated to go along with Ankara's mediation, in part, to advance its bilateral relations with Turkey.[9]

Erdogan and Assad also discussed Iran's nuclear activities. Though Turkey and Iran are regional rivals, Erdogan was hoping to resolve the impasse between Iran and the UN Security Council. George W. Bush's second term as president was winding down; Erdogan feared that the "October surprise" could be a pre-emptive strike by the United States against Iran's nuclear facilities.

Turkey's Foreign Minister Ali Babacan and Syria's Foreign Minister Walid Muallem announced plans for visa free travel on September 7, 2009. Normal travel and trade was a milestone towards overall normalization of bilateral relations. The two sides also deepened their security cooperation vis-à-vis the PKK. Assad endorsed Turkey's incursion into Iraqi Kurdistan to attack PKK bases. On regional security issues, they strategized about Turkey's efforts to ease tensions between Damascus and Baghdad, as well as its mediation between Syria and Israel. Many Ba'athists relocated to Syria after Saddam was overthrown, making Syria a center of support for Iraq's insurgency. Saddam loyalists found common cause with Al-Qaeda in Mesopotamia, which became Al-Qaeda in Iraq, and later morphed into the Islamic State in Iraq and Syria (ISIS). Syria's Sunni rebellion was inspired by the transnational Salafist movement.

Over years of steady interaction, Erdogan and Assad developed a close personal relationship. Assad described Turkey as Syria's "best friend." Erdogan referred to Syrians as "brothers." Davutoglu undertook extensive diplomacy, visiting Damascus more than forty times. In slow, steady, and unspectacular fashion, Davutoglu explored areas where the national interests of Turkey and Syria overlapped. He negotiated the first-ever Turkish-Syrian joint military exercise, which was held in April 2009. Davutoglu declared: Turkey and Syria share a "common fate, history, and future."[10]

The personal chemistry between Erdogan and Assad, combined with Davutoglu's meticulous diplomacy, helped Turkey and Syria deepen and institutionalize their cooperation. Erdogan and Assad issued a Joint Political Declaration establishing High-Level Strategic Cooperation Council (HLSCC) during Assad's visit to Turkey on September 16, 2009. The following month, the HLSCC convened at the ministerial level with reciprocal meetings in Gaziantep and Aleppo. As a result of the Visa-Exemption Agreement, tourist traffic more than doubled between 2009 and 2010. Other agreements encompassed cooperation in various fields—political, security, commercial, cultural, health, agriculture, environment, transportation, education, and water. When the prime ministers from Turkey and Syria met in Damascus on December 23, 2009, they signed fifty agreements on bilateral cooperation. The HLSCC met again in October and December 2010, signing an additional thirteen agreements, including a historic counterterrorism agreement, followed by a counterinsurgency pact.[11] Davutoglu said, "When all of these mechanisms are brought together, we are sure that the environment of economic integration, welfare and peace will make great progress. We want this understanding to spread into our region and the region to turn into a very wide zone of welfare and strong stability."[12]

Washington watched warily as Turkey and Syria strengthened their bilateral relations. Turkey was pursuing an independent diplomacy, asserting itself regionally and on the world stage. Davutoglu never sought permission from the State Department. As a good diplomat, however, he kept US officials informed of his contact with Iran and mediation between Syria and Israel.

Rapprochement between Turkey and Syria ended abruptly with the onset of Syria's civil war. In March 2011, teenagers painted revolutionary slogans on a school wall in Dara. Syrian police arrested and tortured the youth. Dara residents protested, and police fired on the crowd. The heavy-handed security response fueled protests across the country. Violence engulfed Aleppo, and spread to the suburbs of Damascus. By June, hundreds of thousands of protesters were demanding Assad's resignation.

Violence assumed sectarian overtones. The Shia-Sunni schism in Islam dates back to the seventh century when Abu Bakr, Mohammed's companion, was elected the first caliph. Other followers of the Prophet favored Ali ibn Abi Talib, Mohammed's cousin, son-in-law, and blood relative. Shiite is an Arabic term describing "Ali partisans." The term Sunni means "the way." Ali's assassination and the defeat of Huseyin, Ali's son, at the Battle of Karbala in 680 AD initiated a struggle for control of the broader Muslim community. The rivalry continues to the present day with deadly sectarian conflict between Shiites and Sunnis in Iraq, Yemen, Lebanon, and other countries.

Syria's leadership cohort is dominated by Alawites, a sect of Islam that is doctrinally distinct from Shiism but in close association. Alawites only represent about 15 percent of Syria's population, but control the country's wealth, politics, and security structures. Sunnis represent about 70 percent of Syrians. Hafez al-Assad's Syrian Ba'ath Party prevented sectarian conflict through strictly secular governance and absolute authoritarian rule. However, his strongman tactics could not suppress sectarian and ethnic differences between Syrians.

Neither Hafez nor his son Bashar al-Assad allowed dissent or challenge to their hegemonic authority. Sunnis affiliated with the Muslim Brotherhood (MB) rebelled between 1976 and 1982. The Brotherhood took control of Hama, a city of about two hundred and fifty thousand people. Hafez al-Assad responded by carpet bombing the city, killing up to twenty-five thousand people. Many "Brothers" were killed in Hama, but the militant Islamic Movement survived. It was fueled by conditions of social, economic, and political inequality that existed under Assad's rule. Tensions, which surfaced in March 2011, represented another phase of Syria's struggle with the Muslim Brotherhood. "Hama rules" refer to overwhelming indiscriminate force to counter insurrection.

Erdogan tried to use his close personal relationship with Assad to dissuade him from further aggression. He called Assad on multiple occasions, urging him to stop attacks and adopt a "positive, reformist approach." Davutoglu went to Damascus with both warnings and offers of assistance. He too was rebuffed.

Erdogan grew increasingly exasperated. He was insulted that Assad, whom he had cultivated over many years, ignored his entreaties. After trying personal diplomacy, Erdogan warned, "We do not want to see another Hama massacre."[13] He declared, "[It is] impossible to remain silent." He signaled support for the protesters, praising their "fight for freedom."[14] Erdogan admonished Assad to avoid the "painful events" of Libya. On November 22, 2011, he likened Assad to Moammar al-Qhaddafi and called on him to resign.[15] "Just remove yourself from that seat before shedding more blood, before torturing more and for the welfare of your country, as well as the region."[16] Erdogan admonished, "It is not heroism to fight against your own people."[17] He warned, "While a nation—especially one that is our kin and relative—is being tormented, we have absolutely no intention to turn a blind eye, to turn our backs on Syria."[18]

Assad felt betrayed. He believed that if any country could empathize with Syria's fight against terrorism, it would be Turkey, which waged a decades-long struggle with the PKK. Erdogan's criticism of Syria was repeatedly broadcast on state-controlled media, riling Syrians. Eight years of confidence building unraveled quickly. Staged by the Syrian government, demonstrators stormed Turkish missions in Damascus, Aleppo, and Latakia, burning Turkish flags in angry protest.[19]

Conditions in Syria worsened, as government opponents took up arms to defend themselves. Militias were formed to provide security to local communities and expel government forces who were committing crimes against the people. The crackdown fueled further support for the rebels. Syria's conflict turned into a proxy war between Iran, which supported Alawites, and the Arab Gulf states, which backed Sunni militias. Turkey joined Qatar, Saudi Arabia, and members of the Gulf Cooperation Council (GCC) to support the rebels. Foreign fighters entered the fray; Hezbollah supported Assad and Sunnis from Chechnya and elsewhere sided with the insurgents.

Erdogan emerged as Assad's fiercest critic. Erdogan was especially sensitive to violations against the Muslim Brotherhood after Mohammed Morsi was removed by a military coup in Egypt. The AKP, a *de facto* branch of the Muslim Brotherhood, arranged exile for its leaders in Turkey. They set up offices in Istanbul and held public meetings to consider a strategy for supporting the MB movement. The Syrian National Council (SNC), a coalition of rebel forces in Syria, opened an office in Istanbul. Its leaders were living large, organizing conferences at five star hotels and jetting between capitals appealing for support. However, they lacked credibility with Syrians in Syria, who were suffering from barrel bombs and constant shelling.

By January 2013, the United Nations human rights office reported that more than sixty thousand had died[20] and more than two million people were displaced by Syria's civil war.[21] Erdogan became more and more vocal, calling on the United States to intervene and stop the carnage. Obama resisted demands to get involved militarily. He ran for president on a platform to disengage the United States from wars in the Middle East. Despite Syria's horrors, he did not believe that the United States had a compelling national security interest in the conflict. The United States was involved diplomatically, but Obama adamantly opposed military intervention.

A defining moment occurred in August 2013. Syrian government troops used aircraft, helicopters and heavy artillery against rebels hunkered down east of Damascus. Unable to dislodge them, Syrian chemical weapons (CW) specialists readied an attack against the northern suburb of Adra. US spy satellites recorded the events. On August 20, Obama sent a message to Assad in response to a question during a press conference at the White House. "We have been very clear to the Assad regime, but also to other players on the ground, that a red line for us is when we start seeing a whole bunch of chemical weapons moving around or being utilized. That would change my calculus. That would change my equation."[22]

The next day, US intelligence agencies observed Syrian forces loading rocket launchers with CW and donning gas masks. Surveillance recorded rocket and artillery flashes from government positions behind the front lines. Social media reported attacks using CW, including sarin and mustard gas. US monitors intercepted an after-action assessment between Syrian officials, followed by an order to the CW team to "cease operations." "We intercepted communications involving a senior official intimately familiar with the offensive who confirmed that chemical weapons were used by the regime," US officials reported. Though a barrage of conventional artillery tried to cover up the use of CW, the United States published communications intercepts and satellite imagery irrefutably documenting its use. CW caused the death of 1,429 civilians, including at least 426 children on August 21, 2013. The attack on Adra was not the first time Syria used CW. It had used CW tipped missiles throughout the year.

Obama's red line was more deterrent than threat. His advisers insisted that the comment was about the movement of CW, not its actual use. It was not a policy shift or a commitment to take military action. Obama's critics heaped scorn on him for not enforcing the red line. Former US Defense Secretary Robert Gates called it a "serious mistake" that hurt America's credibility in the world.[23] Senator John McCain said, "Unfortunately, the red line that the president of the United States has written was apparently written in disappearing ink."[24] He maintained that the shifting red line was a sign of weakness, which convinced Vladimir Putin he could invade Crimea without fear of retribution. Secretary of State Hillary Clinton reflected, "The failure to help build up a credible fighting force of the people who were the originators of the protests against Assad . . . left a big vacuum, which the jihadists have now filled."[25] She criticized Obama's flip remark about intervention—"Don't do stupid stuff." According to Clinton, "Great nations need organizing principles, and 'Don't do stupid stuff' is not an organizing principle."[26]

Under pressure, the White House sent a resolution to Congress that would sanction military action to "prevent or deter the use or proliferation" of chemical or biological weapons "within, to or from Syria" and to "protect the United States and its allies and partners against the threat posed by such weapons."[27] The administration made a half-hearted effort to promote the resolution. Congressional hawks said they would not support military strikes unless military action was a part of an overall diplomatic and security strategy, shaping the battlefield and catalyzing more effective diplomacy.

Kerry made a passing comment about the UN taking charge of Syria's disarmament. Russia's Foreign Minister Sergei Lavrov seized on Kerry's suggestion and proposed that the UN remove and destroy Syria's chemical weapons stockpile. US officials insisted that Obama's credible threat of military force was driving diplomacy. To Erdogan's dismay, Assad agreed to cooperate with the Organization for the Prohibition of Chemical Weapons (OPCW), thereby avoiding military action.

Sub-contracting Syria's disarmament to the United Nations gave Putin an opening to assert Russia's role in Syria. By requiring a UN Security Council resolution, the deal clearly put Russia in the driver's seat. It further undermined the perception of US leadership in Syria and the world. General Salim Idris, head of the US-backed Supreme Military Council, scorned the plan. "This initiative does not interest us. Russia is a partner with the regime in killing the Syrian people."[28] Disarmament of CW was ostensibly completed the following year. However, the OPCW found that chlorine was used "systematically and repeatedly" in artillery attacks between April and July 2014. More recent reports also suggest the use of chlorine-tipped artillery.

In response to demands "to do something," the US Congress authorized a train and equip program for the Syrian rebels on September 17, 2014. Training facilities were set up in Turkey, Jordan, and Qatar, costing $500 million. However, the program was ineffective. Turkey delayed setting up its facility. Vetting participants was problematic. After more than a year, General Lloyd Austin, commander of US Central Command, testified to Congress that the train and equip program had readied no more than four or five fighters, far short of the goal of five thousand anti-ISIS fighters by 2015. McCain called it a "debacle."[29] The fiasco radicalized fighters in the field. The Nusra Front and other jihadis turned on the US-backed Free Syrian Army. US-backed rebels joined the jihadis rather than fight them. Turkey and GCC countries wanted Washington to expand assistance to the rebels. But, as the rebels became more radicalized, US officials feared that Islamist extremists would fill the power vacuum created by Assad's fall.

The battle for Kobani was a turning point in the campaign against ISIS, and in US-Turkey relations. Kobani is a medium-sized city on the Turkey–Syria border. Kobani is inhabited by mostly Kurds who constitute about 10 percent of Syria's population.[30] Its defenders, the People's Protection Units (YPG) of the Democratic Union Party (PYD) fought bravely, but were no match for ISIS armor, artillery, and improvised vehicle borne explosive devices. As the battle unfolded in the autumn of 2014, Ankara turned a blind eye to the imminent slaughter. Moreover, it actively obstructed Kobani's rescue by blocking Kurds who tried to cross the border to help their brethren in Kobani. International media had a bird's eye view of the battlefield. Riots erupted across Turkey as angry Kurds protested the government's inaction. Erdogan aggravated the grief of Kurds, declaring, "Kobani fell or is about to fall."[31]

The United States had apparently forsaken the YPG. Many respected experts on the region, including former US Ambassador Ryan Crocker, believed that Kobani had no strategic value. The Obama administration delayed, but finally decided that Kobani's fall would be a major public relations victory for ISIS. Broadcasting beheadings on social media would be a recruitment tool. In an about face, Kerry called the Kurds "valiant" and said it would be "irresponsible" and "morally very difficult" not to support them.[32] ISIS had occupied about 80 percent of Kobani, when US war planes intervened to stop its advance. With YPG fighters about to run out of ammunition, US C-130 transport planes dropped twenty-four tons of small arms and ammunition and ten tons of medical supplies. The air-drop was deemed absolutely necessary in the "crisis moment." The equipment came from the Peshmerga in Iraqi Kurdistan. While Kurds welcomed assistance, they asked why it took so long. If aid was delivered sooner, ISIS would not have penetrated the city and fewer people would have been killed. Kurds blamed Turkey for delaying their rescue.[33]

Kurds from across the region rushed to join the fray. The YPG was joined by PKK members and PJAK fighters from Iran. Turkey relented so that the United States could facilitate travel for Peshmerga from Iraqi Kurdistan through Turkey to Kobani. Forty percent of Kurdish fighters in Kobani were female, belonging to the Women's Protection Units (YPJ). ISIS martyrs were assured virgins in heaven if they died at the hands of a man. However, being killed by a woman carried penalties in the hereafter. The tide turned. After weeks of fierce house-to-house fighting, ISIS was driven from the city.

Erdogan tried to dissuade Obama from supporting the YPG and YPJ. He views the Syrian Kurds with deep suspicion because of their historic and ideological ties to the PKK. US officials overruled Ankara's concerns. "Let me say very respectfully to our allies the Turks that we understand fully the fundamentals of their opposition and ours to any kind of terrorist group and particularly obviously the challenges they face with respect [to] the PKK," Kerry said. "But we have undertaken coalition effort to degrade and destroy ISIL." The YPG is "valiantly fighting ISIL and we cannot take our eye off the prize."[34] While the PKK is considered a foreign terrorist organization (FTO) by the State Department, the PYD is not.

Erdogan was incensed. He blasted the Obama administration, saying it was responsible for a "sea of blood" in Syria. Erdogan maintained, "The PYD is a terrorist organization like the PKK and they work together. We cannot speak of good terrorists versus bad terrorists. Daesh (ISIS) is a terrorist organization and so are the PYD and the PKK."[35] Erdogan asked rhetorically, "Are you with us or with this terrorist organization?"[36]

The YPG and YPJ with forty thousand fighters became an invaluable security partner of the United States. Over Erdogan's objections, the Pentagon expanded assistance to the YPG. With US air support, the YPG rolled up ISIS territory, seizing the strategic border gate at Tal Abyad. The crossing was a critical supply route for fighters and supplies transiting from Turkey to Raqqa, the ISIS capitol in eastern Syria. Erdogan was furious when Ambassador McGurk Special Presidential Envoy for the Global Coalition to Counter ISIL, the US Special Envoy for Syria, met PYD officials in Kobani and was given a plaque by the YPG. "How can we trust you?" Erdogan queried. "Is it me who is your partner or the terrorists in Kobani? Do you accept the PKK as a terrorist organization? Then why don't you list the PYD as a terrorist organization too?"[37]

In contrast to the YPG, Turkey was increasingly autocratic and a reluctant member of the multinational coalition. US Central Command (CENTCOM) Commander Lloyd Austin and US coordinator for the anti-ISIS coalition, General John Allen, repeatedly visited Ankara to negotiate use of Incirlik. Erdogan held out, insisting that Turkey would only agree if the United States committed to targeting Assad's forces. He also demanded that the United States allow Turkey to deploy troops as a security buffer inside Syria.

Given a choice between Turkey and the Kurds, it was understood that the United States would always choose Turkey. US coordination with the PYD was tactical, not political. Its cochair, Salih Muslim, was not issued a US visa. Washington allowed Turkey to prevent the United Nations from inviting PYD representatives to participate in the Geneva peace talks.

While keeping the PYD at arm's length, US officials admired the PYD's administration of a self-governing territory called Rojava, which spanned the cantons of Jazira, Kobani, and Afrin. Salih Muslim maintained that Rojava was a model of grass-roots democracy, women's empowerment, and environmental sustainability. Arabs and other non-Kurdish minorities were involved in local administration. Rojava was exemplary of how Syria could be governed as a federal state after Assad.

A Kobani solidarity rally of Kurds in Turkey planning cross-border humanitarian assistance was attacked on July 20, 2015. The suicide bombing in Suruc near the Syrian border killed thirty-three people. The Kurdistan Freedom Falcons (TAK) responded by killing two police officers whom they accused of complicity in the attack. Turkey agreed to make Incirlik available to the multinational coalition after months of wrangling. But instead of attacking ISIS, Turkey launched strikes against the PKK in Iraqi Kurdistan and along the Turkey-Iraq border.

With tensions on the rise, Ankara grew increasingly concerned about the YPG's battlefield victories in northern Syria. After taking control of Tal Abyad, the YPG secured the main road south to Raqqa in June 2015. It seized Azaz, a border town in northwestern Syria, and moved west across the Euphrates River, taking steps to connect Kurdish-controlled territory and create a security buffer close to Syria's border with Turkey. US warplanes supported YPG operations west of the Euphrates. In deference to Turkey's concerns about Kurdish-controlled territory along its border with Syria, however, the United States made it clear to the YPG that its fighters would pull back after defeating ISIS in Mambij. Ankara asked the United States to join a ground offensive to retake Azaz and launched heavy artillery attacks against the YPG. However, the United States refused. The YPG was its best ally in Syria.

Ambassador Robert S. Ford, former US Special Envoy to Syria, drew a clear link between military action and diplomacy. "Many people working on Syria for the State Department have long urged a tougher policy with the Assad government as a means of facilitating arrival at a negotiated political deal to set up a new Syrian government." Fifty-one US officials used the State Department's dissent channel to convey their concerns about Obama's Syria policy, or lack thereof. "It is time that the United States, guided by our strategic interests and moral convictions, lead a global effort to put an end to this conflict once and for all."[38] Diplomacy is less effective without the leverage that comes from a credible threat of force.

129

Assad was defiant, vowing to retake "every inch" of rebel-controlled territory. Assad's bellicose position had a negative effect on the negotiations between the United States and Russia as well as between Assad and the opposition. Turkey pledged to expand its assistance in the face of Assad's renewed commitment to a military solution, making the prospect of a negotiated solution even more remote. Turkey prevented the PYD from joining UN-mediated talks in Geneva, thereby excluding a major player from negotiations.

Turkish Special Forces, tanks, and fighters with the Free Syrian Army (FSA) launched "Operation Euphrates Shield" invading and occupying Syria on August 24, 2016. Erdogan said the cross-border action was against ISIS. It was really targeting the YPG. According to Erdogan, Euphrates Shield was aimed at the YPG and "terror groups that threaten our country." Foreign Minister Mevlut Cavusoglu pledged that Turkey would "do what is necessary" to keep Kurdish fighters east of the Euphrates River.[39] As Turkish troops pushed deeper into Syria, Turkey announced plans for a safe zone ninety kilometers long and forty kilometers wide, stretching from Jarablus to Marea, deep into Kurdish-controlled territory.

Jarablus was "liberated" from ISIS with barely a shot. Before crossing the border, Ankara made a deal with the Islamic State to rescue them from the YPG's advance on Jarablus. ISIS forces simply changed into FSA uniforms. Unlike Falluja and other battles where ISIS used civilians as human shields, civilians were evacuated so they could not identify newly clad FSA members as ISIS fighters.[40]

Biden arrived in Ankara the morning of August 24. His mission was to mend relations with Turkey, which were badly frayed by Erdogan's accusations of US involvement in the coup and the Justice Department's unwillingness to extradite Fethullah Gulen. Biden publicly endorsed Operation Euphrates Shield. He also claimed that the United States provided air power. However, eye witnesses said no bombs were actually dropped on Jarablus.

US officials were increasingly concerned as Turkey pressed its offensive. A senior Pentagon official told CNN, "The Turks never cared about Jarablus until the Kurds wanted to get there."[41] Opening another front in its war against the Kurds, Turkish forces crossed the border gate attacking civilians in Kobani on September 2, 2016.[42] US officials called on Turkey and the YPG to deconflict. McGurk said Turkey's targeting of the PYD was "unacceptable and a source of deep concern."[43]

Erdogan attended the G20 meeting in China on September 4, 2016. He called on Russia and the United States to allow a no-fly zone in Northern Syria. The no-fly zone was linked to a security buffer, which would be enforced by Turkish troops. The Obama administration quietly rejected Erdogan's plan. Supporting Turkey would make the United States complicit in Turkey's land grab. Operation Euphrates Shield violated Syria's sovereignty. Syria's mosaic of combatants was already chaotic. The presence of Turkish troops on the ground further complicated prospects for the Geneva peace process. Three Turkish troops were killed and ten wounded in an air strike by Syria on November 24, 2016. Turkey vowed to retaliate, risking escalation.

Turkey was involved in a multiplicity of conflicts in Syria, antagonist with all—friend to none. Erdogan and Assad had a falling out, which pitted Turkey against the Syrian regime. Turkey was opposed by Russia and Iran, which supported Assad. Turkey targeted the YPG because of its purported ties to the PKK. ISIS turned on Turkey after benefitting from its financing, supply of weapons, and logistical support.

Notes

1. M. Fisher, "The State Department's Dissent Memo on Syria: An Explanation," *New York Times*, June 22, 2016, accessed June 24, 2016, http://www.nytimes.com/2016/06/23/world/middleeast/syria-assad-obama-diplomats-memo.html.
2. H. Ose, "The PKK-Assad Regime Story: Harmony, Discord and OCALAN," *NowMmedia*, October 4, 2015, accessed June 14, 2016, https://now.mmedia.me/lb/en/commentary/565108-the-pkk-assad-regime-story-harmony-discord-and-ocalan.
3. D. Phillips, *From Bullets to Ballots: Violent Muslim Movements in Transition* (New Brunswick, NJ: Transaction, 2009), 130.
4. D. Aras, "Turkish-Syrian Relations Go Downhill: The Syrian Uprising," *Middle East Quarterly*, Spring 2012, 41–50, accessed June 6, 2016, http://www.meforum.org/3206/turkish-syrian-relations.
5. "Old Foes Turkey, Syria Sign Military Accord," *Hürriyet Daily News*, June 21, 2002, accessed June 16, 2016, http://www.hurriyetdailynews.com/old-foes-turkey-syria-sign-military-accord.aspx?pageID=438&n=old-foes-turkey-syria-sign-military-accord-2002-06-21.
6. "Assad Becomes First Head of Syria to Visit Turkey," *VoaNews*, October 30, 2009, accessed June 16, 2016, http://www.voanews.com/content/a-13-a-2004-01-06-4-assad/394126.html.
7. "Relations between Turkey–Syria," *Republic of Turkey Ministry of Foreign Affairs*, accessed June 14, 2016, http://www.mfa.gov.tr/relations-between-turkey%E2%80%93syria.en.mfa.
8. "Ankara Media Reaction Report Wednesday, April 4, 2007," *WikiLeaks*, accessed June 16, 2016, https://wikileaks.org/plusd/cables/07ANKARA774_a.html.

9. "Syria's Assad Meets Erdogan as Turkey Mediates for Mideast Peace," *Hürriyet*, August 5, 2008, accessed June 16, 2016, http://www.hurriyet.com.tr/syrias-assad-meets-erdogan-as-turkey-mediates-for-mideast-peace-9586510.

10. D. Schenker, "Turkey's Shift on Syria Gives West Room to Get Tougher on Assad," June 9, 2011, *The Washington Institute*, accessed June 14, 2016, http://www.washingtoninstitute.org/policy-analysis/view/turkeys-shift-on-syria-gives-west-room-to-get-tougher-on-assad.

11. "Relations between Turkey–Syria."

12. "Turkey, Syria: Nations Sign Historic Accord, End Visa Requirements," *Los Angeles Times*, September 17, 2009, accessed June 5, 2016, http://latimesblogs.latimes.com/babylonbeyond/2009/09/turkey-syria-two-nations-sign-historic-accord-end-visa-requirements.html.

13. Schenker, "Turkey's Shift on Syria Gives West Room to Get Tougher on Assad."

14. Ibid.

15. S. Arsu, "Turkish Premier Urges Assad to Quit in Syria," November 22, 2011, *New York Times*, accessed June 14, 2016, http://www.nytimes.com/2011/11/23/world/middleeast/turkish-leader-says-syrian-president-should-quit.html?_r=0.

16. Daily News Editorials, "Credit Turkey's Erdogan for Powerful Statement Demanding that Syria's Assad Stop his Brutal Crackdown, Leave Power," November 25, 2011, *NYDailyNews*, accessed June 26, 2016, http://www.nydailynews.com/opinion/credit-turkey-erdogan-powerful-statement-demanding-syria-assad-stop-brutal-crackdown-leave-power-article-1.982082.

17. Ibid.

18. "Turkish Official Urges Assad to Resign," *Boston Globe*, accessed June 15, 2016, https://www.bostonglobe.com/news/world/2011/11/23/prime-minister-turkey-calls-syrian-president-assad-resign/uYp95HKEJwDL3zUZyhyxTJ/story.html.

19. Arsu, "Turkish Premier Urges Assad to Quit in Syria."

20. "Data Suggests Syria Death Toll Could be More than 60,000, Says UN human Rights Office," *UN News Centre*, January 2, 2013, accessed June 20, 2016, http://www.un.org/apps/news/story.asp?NewsID=43866#.V3QdRLTid6k.

21. Press Release, "Syria Displacement Crisis Worsens as Protracted Humanitarian Emergency Looms," January 14, 2013, *International Rescue Committee*, accessed June 20, 2016, https://www.rescue.org/press-release/syria-displacement-crisis-worsens-protracted-humanitarian-emergency-looms.

22. C. Good, "President Obama's 'Red Line': What He Actually Said about Syria and Chemical Weapons," *abcNews*, August 26, 2013, accessed June 16, 2016, http://abcnews.go.com/blogs/politics/2013/08/president-obamas-red-line-what-he-actually-said-about-syria-and-chemical-weapons/.

23. R. Ballhaus, "Gates: Syria Red Line Was 'Serious Mistake,'" January 15, 2014, *The Wall Street Journal*, accessed June 18, 2016, http://blogs.wsj.com/washwire/2014/01/15/gates-syria-red-line-was-serious-mistake/.

24. M. Williams, "John McCain: Obama's 'Red Line' on Syria 'Written in Disappearing Ink,'" *The Guardian*, May 5, 2013, accessed June 17, 2016, https://www.theguardian.com/world/2013/may/05/john-mccain-obama-syria-red-line.

25. E. Durkin, "Hillary Clinton Criticizes Obama Foreign Policy in Interview: 'Failure' to Help Syrian Rebels Led to Strong ISIS," *NY Daily News*, August

11, 2014, accessed June 15, 2016, http://www.nydailynews.com/news/politics/hillary-clinton-criticizes-obama-foreign-policy-interview-failure-syrian-rebels-led-strong-isis-article-1.1899301.

26. Ibid.

27. P. Baker and J. Weisman, "Obama Seeks Approval by Congress for Strike in Syria," *New York Times*, August 31, 2013, accessed June 17, 2016, http://www.nytimes.com/2013/09/01/world/middleeast/syria.html.

28. M. R. Gordon, "U.S. and Russia Reach Deal to Destroy Syria's Chemical Arms," *New York Times*, September 14, 2013, accessed June 17, 2016, http://www.nytimes.com/2013/09/15/world/middleeast/syria-talks.html?module=ArrowsNav&contentCollection=Middle%20East&action=keypress&region=FixedLeft&pgtype=article.

29. S. Ackerman, "US Has Trained Only 'Four or Five' Syrian Fighters against Isis, top General Testifies," *The Guardian*, September 16, 2015, accessed June 20, 2016, https://www.theguardian.com/us-news/2015/sep/16/us-military-syrian-isis-fighters.

30. S. Lindemann, "Ethnic Exclusion and the Puzzle of Diverging Conflict Trajectories: A Paired Comparison of Kurds in Syria and Turkey," *MMG Working Paper*, (11-10), 2011, accessed June 20, 2016, http://www.mmg.mpg.de/de/publikationen/working-papers.

31. "Erdogan: Kobani düştü düşecek!," *Haber Türk*, October 7, 2014, accessed July 24, 2016, http://www.haberturk.com/gundem/haber/997321-erdogan-kobani-dustu-dusecek.

32. "'Irresponsible' not to Aid Kurds in Kobane against IS: Kerry," *Al Monitor*, accessed June 21, 2016, http://www.al-monitor.com/pulse/ar/contents/afp/2014/10/iraq-syria-conflict-us-kerry.html.

33. C. Letsch, "US Drops Weapons and Ammunition to Help Kurdish Fighters in Kobani," *The Guardian*, October 20, 2014, accessed June 20, 2016, https://www.theguardian.com/world/2014/oct/20/turkey-iraqi-kurds-kobani-isis-fighters-us-air-drops-arms.

34. "Turkey Enabling Iraqi Kurdish Forces to Cross Borders and Defend Kobane," *AlJazeera International*, October 20, 2014, accessed June 22, 2016, http://america.aljazeera.com/articles/2014/10/20/kobane-iraqi-kurds.html.

35. "Erdogan says PKK and PYD Both Terrorist Organisations," *TRTWorld*, October 5, 2015, accessed June 23, 2016, http://www.trtworld.com/turkey/erdogan-says-pkk-and-pyd-both-terrorist-organisations-8918.

36. G. Botelho, "Turkish Leader: U.S. Responsible for 'Sea of Blood' for Supporting Syrian Kurds," *CNN*, February 10, 2016, accessed June 20, 2016, http://edition.cnn.com/2016/02/10/middleeast/turkey-erdogan-criticizes-us/.

37. "Erdogan Irate Over US Envoy Meeting with YPG in Kobani," *Press TV*, February 8, 2016, accessed June 20, 2016, http://www.presstv.com/Detail/2016/02/08/449194/Turkey-Erdogan-US-Brett-McGurk.

38. M. Lander, "51 U.S. Diplomats Urge Strikes Against Assad in Syria," *New York Times*, June 16, 2016, accessed June 20, 2016, http://www.nytimes.com/2016/06/17/world/middleeast/syria-assad-obama-airstrikes-diplomats-memo.html?_r=0.

39. Tom Stevenson, "Turkey's Syria Offensive Aimed at Kurdish YPG," *DW*, August 24, 2016, accessed September 8, 2016, http://www.dw.com/en/turkeys-syria-offensive-aimed-at-kurdish-ypg/a-19497653.

40.   Anonymous interview by the author. August 31, 2016.
41.   Euan McKirdy, Jason Hanna, and Isil Sariyuce, "Turkey Sends Tanks into Syria Against ISIS; Rebels Reportedly Capture Town," *CNN*, August 24, 2016, accessed September 8, 2016, from http://www.cnn.com/2016/08/24/middleeast/turkish-troops-isis-syria-operation/.
42.   Statement issued by the Kobane Reconstruction Board-Europe on September 2, 2016.
43.   Reuters, "U.S. Calls Turkey's Syria Clashes 'Unacceptable', Urges Focus on ISIS," *NBC News*, August 29, 2016, accessed on September 8, 2016, http://www.nbcnews.com/storyline/isis-terror/u-s-calls-turkey-s-syria-clashes-unacceptable-urges-focus-n639266.

9

Terror Ties

Erdogan criticized "smear campaigns [and] attempts to distort perception about us." He decried, "A systematic attack on Turkey's international reputation", complaining that "Turkey has been subject to very unjust and ill-intentioned news items from media organizations. My request from our friends in the United States is to make your assessment about Turkey by basing your information on objective sources."[1]

—Recep Tayyip Erdogan (September 22, 2014)

Turkey stepped up its supply of weapons to Islamist insurgents when the US failed to intervene after Syria used chemical weapons in August 2013. The Turkish National Intelligence Agency (MIT) established an infrastructure for supporting jihadists, ranging from military cooperation and weapons transfers to logistical support, financial assistance, and the provision of medical services. In addition to Turkey's support to Islamist groups in Syria, it supported Al Qaeda in Libya and Hamas in Palestine.[2]

Turkey's involvement was confirmed by Vice President Joe Biden during remarks at Harvard University. Biden said, "Our allies in the region were our largest problem in Syria. The Turks . . . the Saudis, the Emiratis . . . were so determined to take down Assad and essentially have a proxy Sunni-Shia war . . . they poured hundreds of millions of dollars and tens, thousands of tons of weapons into anyone who would fight against Assad . . . the people who were being supplied were Al Nusra and Al Qaeda and the extremist elements of jihadis coming from other parts of the world."[3] Biden elaborated, "We could not convince our colleagues to stop supplying them . . . President Erdogan told me, he's an old friend, 'You were right. We let too many people through.'"[4]

Erdogan was furious at Biden's off-the-cuff remarks. He denied admitting that Turkey ever supported Islamist militants. "Biden has to apologize for his statements," said Erdogan, or Biden will become "history to me."[5] Erdogan's hubris towards the vice president was unprecedented. His surprise may stem from the fact that MIT's supply chain was organized with the knowledge and blessing of the CIA.

Biden's candor risked a major falling between the United States and Turkey at a time when the Obama administration was asking Ankara to do more in countering ISIS. The Office of the Vice President worked on damage control. Biden called Erdogan to reaffirm the shared commitment of the United States and Turkey to fighting ISIS. Biden's spokesperson described the conversation. "The Vice President apologized for any implication that Turkey or other Allies and partners in the region had intentionally supplied or facilitated the growth of ISIL or other violent extremists in Syria. The Vice President made clear that the United States greatly values the commitments and sacrifices made by our Allies and partners from around the world to combat the scourge of ISIL, including Turkey."[6]

Biden did not retract what he said. He was contrite about having said it. His *mea culpa* involved clever wordsmithing. Including the term "deliberately" allowed both sides some political cover. While his public statement mollified Erdogan, the exchange was symptomatic of a deeper discord in US-Turkey relations.

There is no way to determine the extent of Turkey's collaboration with ISIS. There is, however, vast circumstantial evidence of Turkey's involvement. PYD commanders in Syria collect the passports of deceased ISIS fighters. Almost all of them have been stamped in Turkey. ISIS fighters use SIM cards in cell phones that come from Turkey. There is a record of financial transactions involving ISIS fighters at Western Union offices in towns near Turkey's border with Syria. Turkey became the shopping bazaar for the Islamic State and the preferred destination for rest and recreation. ISIS fighters were warmly received.

Media reports suggest the allegations of complicity are correct. They include credible international sources such as *The New York Times*, *The Washington Post*, *The Guardian*, *The Daily Mail*, *BBC*, and *Sky News*, Turkish sources—*CNN Turk*, *Hurriyet Daily News*, *Taraf*, *Cumhuriyet*, and *Radikal* among others, as well as blogs and social media of Turkish and Kurdish eyewitnesses. Following are the allegations of Turkey's complicity with ISIS, and their sources.

Turkey Provided Weapons

Cengiz Candar, a well-respected Turkish journalist, maintained that MIT helped "midwife" the Islamic state in Iraq and Syria, as well as other jihadi groups.[7] According to an ISIS commander, "Most of the fighters who joined us in the beginning of the war came via Turkey, and so did our equipment and supplies."[8] Kemal Kilicdaroglu, head of the Republican People's Party (CHP), produced a statement from the Adana Office of the Prosecutor on October 14, 2014, maintaining that Turkey supplied weapons to terror groups.[9] He also produced interview transcripts from truck drivers who delivered weapons to combatants in Syria.[10] The Turkish government claimed the trucks were for humanitarian aid to the Turkmen, but the Turkmen said no humanitarian aid was delivered.[11]

CHP Vice President Bulent Tezcan asserted that three trucks were stopped in Adana for inspection on January 19, 2014.[12] The trucks were loaded with weapons at Esenboga Airport in Ankara. The drivers drove the trucks to the border, where an agent for MIT was supposed to take over and drive the trucks to Syria. This happened many times. When the trucks were stopped, MIT agents tried to keep the inspectors from looking inside the crates. The inspectors found rockets, arms, and ammunitions. There were also vaults of gold and money under the weapons.[13]

Fuat Avni, a prominent social media activist, released audio tapes on October 12, 2014, which confirmed that Turkey provided financial and military aid to terrorist groups associated with Al Qaeda. On the tapes, Erdogan pressured the Turkish Armed Forces to go to war with Syria. Erdogan demanded that Hakan Fidan, the head of MIT, come up with a justification. Fidan told Prime Minister Ahmet Davutoglu, Yasar Guler, a senior defense official, and Undersecretary for Foreign Affairs Feridun Sinirlioglu: "If need be, I'll send four men into Syria. I'll formulate a reason to go to war by shooting 8 rockets into Turkey; I'll have them attack the Tomb of Suleiman Shah."[14]

OdaTV reported on September 27, 2014 that Saudi Emir Bander Bin Sultan financed the transportation of arms to ISIS that were delivered through Turkey. A flight leaving Germany dropped off arms in the Etimesgut airport in Turkey, which were split into three containers, two for ISIS and one for Hamas in Gaza.[15] Turkey also sent weapons to Islamist fighters in Libya in a weapons-for-oil swap. In September 2014, the Greek coast guard intercepted a ship carrying ammunition to Libya. Turkey also allegedly sent weapons to Boko Harem in Nigeria, using Turkish Airlines.[16] In another case from 2013, Turkish police seized precursor materials to manufacture sarin gas. Al-Nusra was the intended recipient. MIT intervened to arrange the release of the detained suspects.[17]

Turkey Provided Transport and Logistical Assistance

On June 13, 2014, Interior Minister Muammar Guler signed a directive: "According to our regional gains, we will help al-Nusra militants against the branch of PKK terrorist organization, the PYD. Hatay is a strategic location for the mujahideen crossing from within our borders to Syria. Logistical support for Islamist groups will be increased, and their training, hospital care, and safe passage will mostly take place in Hatay." The directive also indicated, "MIT and the Religious Affairs Directorate will coordinate the placement of fighters in public accommodations."[18]

Hurriyet Daily News reported on September 26, 2014, "The feelings of the AKP's heavyweights are not limited to Ankara. I was shocked to hear words of admiration for ISIL from some high-level civil servants even in Sanliurfa. 'They are like us, fighting against seven great powers in the War of Independence,'" one said. "Rather than the PKK on the other side, I would rather have ISIL as a neighbor," said another. An AKP council member posted on his Facebook page: "Thankfully ISIS exists . . . May you never run out of ammunition."[19] A Turkish Social Security Institution supervisor used the ISIS logo in internal correspondences.[20]

An article in *The Daily Mail* on August 25, 2014, indicated that many foreign militants joined ISIS in Syria and Iraq after traveling through Turkey, and Turkey did not try to stop them. It described how foreign militants, especially from the United Kingdom, go to Syria and Iraq through the Turkish border. They call the border the "Gateway to Jihad." Turkish army soldiers either turn a blind eye and let them pass, or the jihadists pay the border guards as little as $10 to facilitate their crossing.[21]

Britain's *Sky News* obtained documents showing that the Turkish government has stamped passports of foreign militants seeking to cross the Turkish border into Syria to join ISIS.[22] *The BBC* interviewed villagers, who claim that buses travel at night, carrying jihadists to fight Kurdish forces in Syria and Iraq.[23] A senior Egyptian official indicated on October 9, 2014 that Turkish intelligence is passing satellite imagery and other data to ISIS.[24]

Turkey Provided Training

CNN Turk reported on July 29, 2014, that in the heart of Istanbul, places like Duzce and Adapazari, have become gathering spots for terrorists. Turks who joined an affiliate of ISIS were recorded at a public gathering in Istanbul, which took place on July 28, 2014.[25] Another video shows an ISIS affiliate holding a prayer gathering in Omerli, a district of Istanbul.[26] Training occurs with the knowledge of Turkish security forces. Training videos are posted on an ISIS propaganda website in Turkish.[27]

CHP Vice President Sezgin Tanrikulu submitted parliamentary questions to the minister of the interior, Efkan Ala, asking: "Is it true that a camp or camps have been allocated to an affiliate of ISIS in Istanbul? What is this affiliate? Who is it made up of? Is the rumor true that the same area allocated for the camp is also used for military exercises?"[28] The minister denied the existence of training facilities.

Kemal Kilicdaroglu warned the AKP government not to provide money and training to terror groups on October 14, 2014.[29] He said, "It isn't right for armed groups to be trained on Turkish soil. You bring foreign fighters to Turkey, put money in their pockets, guns in their hands, and you ask them to kill Muslims in Syria. We told them to stop helping ISIS. Ahmet Davutoglu asked us to show proof. Everyone knows that they're helping ISIS."[30]

Turkey Offered Medical Care

An ISIS commander told *The Washington Post* on August 12, 2014, "We used to have some fighters—even high-level members of the Islamic State—getting treated in Turkish hospitals."[31] *Taraf* reported on October 12, 2014, that Dengir Mir Mehmet Firat, a founder of the AKP, said that Turkey treats ISIS fighters in hospitals. "The government was helping the wounded. The minister of health said, "It is a human obligation to care for the ISIS wounded."[32]

According to *Taraf*, Ahmet El H., one of the top commanders at ISIS and Al Baghdadi's right-hand man, was treated at a hospital in Sanliurfa, Turkey, along with other ISIS militants. *Taraf* identified eight ISIS fighters who were transported through the Sanliurfa border crossing to receive medical care—Mustafa A., Yusuf El R., Mustafa H., Halil El M., Muhammet El H., Ahmet El S., Hasan H., and Salim El D. The Turkish government paid for their treatment.[33]

Turkey Assists Recruitment

Kemal Kilicdaroglu claimed on October 14, 2014, that ISIS offices in Istanbul and Gaziantep recruit fighters.[34] On October 10, 2014, the mufti of Konya said that a hundred people from Konya joined ISIS four days prior.[35] *OdaTV* released a video showing ISIS militants riding a bus in Istanbul.[36]

OdaTV reports that *Takva Haber,* an ISIS propaganda media outlet, recruited Turkish-speaking individuals in Germany.[37] The website is registered at the address of a school called Irfan Koleji, which was established by Ilim Yayma Vakfi, a foundation created by Erdogan and Davutoglu, among others. Minister of Sports Suat Kilic, an AKP member, visited Salafists who are ISIS supporters in Germany. The foundation is known for reaching out to supporters via free Qur'an distributions and financing of suicide attacks in Syria and Iraq.

Turkish Forces Join the Battle

In a statement on September 20, 2014, Demir Celik, a member of Parliament with the Peoples' Democratic Party (HDP) claimed that Turkish Special Forces fight alongside ISIS[38]

On October 7, 2014, IBDA-C, a militant Islamic organization in Turkey, pledged support to ISIS. A Turk who is a commander in ISIS indicated that, "[Turkey is] involved in all of this" and, after fighting in Syria, "10,000 ISIS members will come to Turkey." ISIS militants come from Syria to Turkey frequently for rest, taking a break from the front-line. The group claimed that Turkey will experience an Islamic revolution, and Turks should be ready for jihad.[39]

Seymour Hersh wrote in *The London Review of Books* that ISIS conducted sarin attacks in Syria, and that Turkish officials knew about the attacks. "'For months there had been acute concern among senior military leaders and the intelligence community about the role in the war of Syria's neighbors, especially Turkey. Prime Minister Recep Tayyip Erdogan was known to be supporting the al-Nusra Front, a jihadist faction among the rebel opposition, as well as other Islamist rebel groups. 'We knew there were some in the Turkish government,' a former senior US intelligence official who has access to current intelligence, told me, 'Who believed they could get Assad's nuts in a vice by dabbling with a sarin attack inside Syria—and forcing Obama to make good on his red line threat.'"[40]

Turkey Helped ISIS in Kobani

Anwar Moslem, Mayor of Kobani, said on September 19, 2014: "Based on the intelligence we got two days before the breakout of the current war, trains full of forces and ammunition, which were passing by north of Kobani, had an-hour-and-ten-to-twenty-minute-long stops in these villages: Salib Qaran, Gire Sor, Moshrefat Ezzo. There are evidences, witnesses, and videos about this. Why is ISIS strong only in Kobane's east? Why is it not strong either in its south or west? Since these trains stopped in villages located in the east of Kobane, we guess they had brought ammunition and additional force for ISIS." In the second article on September 30, 2014, a CHP delegation visited Kobani, where locals claimed that everything from the clothes ISIS militants wear to their guns come from Turkey.[41]

A *Nuhaber* video on September 25, 2014 showed Turkish military convoys carrying tanks and ammunition moving freely under ISIS flags in the Jarablus region of Syria and at the Karkamis border crossing. There was Turkish script on the trucks. Diken reported, "ISIS fighters crossed the border from Turkey into Syria, over the Turkish train tracks that delineate the border, in full view of Turkish soldiers. They were met there by PYD fighters and stopped."[42]

Saleh Muslim, PYD co-chair, claimed that 120 militants crossed into Syria from Turkey between October 20 and 24, 2014.[43] According to an op-ed written by a YPG commander in *The New York Times* on October 29, 2014, Turkey allows ISIS militants and their equipment to pass freely over the border.[44] A Kurdish commander in Kobani claims that almost all ISIS militants have Turkish entry stamps on their passports.[45] *OdaTV* released a photograph of a Turkish soldier befriending ISIS militants.[46]

Turkey's involvement with ISIS oil trade is also a great concern. Turkish smugglers facilitated ISIS oil exports, which generated up to $50 million each month for the Islamic State. Turkey-ISIS oil trade undermined US efforts to undermine the organization by depriving it of financial support. News reports implicated Erdogan's family in oil trade with ISIS. According to Claudia Roth, deputy speaker of the Bundestag and a Green Party MP, Erdogan's "dealings with the ISIS are unacceptable. Also that the ISIS has been able to sell its oil via Turkey is extraordinary."[47] Erdogan took these charges seriously. He promised "to vacate his post as Turkey's president if the claims are substantiated by concrete evidence."[48]

ISIS began taking over oil fields in late spring 2014. Since then, ISIS has expanded its operations by creating a loosely integrated and thriving underground economy, consisting of approximately sixty percent of Syria's oil assets and seven oil-producing facilities in Iraq. At its peak, ISIS extracted about thirty thousand barrels per day from Syria, smuggled to middlemen in Turkey who purchased ISIS oil for as little as $18 per barrel. In 2014, the ISIS "finance ministry" put at 253 the number of oil wells under ISIS control in Syria. Of these, 161 were operational, using production equipment from Turkey and other neighboring countries.

Upon extraction, oil was refined on site and then brought to market through an extensive supply chain in the Turkish municipalities of Sanliurfa, Urfa, Hakkari, Siirt, Batman, Osmaniya, Gaziantep, Sirnak, Adana, Kahramarmaras, Adiyaman and Mardin. Illegal pipelines transported oil from Syria to nearby border towns in Turkey where the oil was sold for as little as 1.25 Turkish liras per liter ($0.42).[49] The string of trading hubs for ISIS oil ended up in Adana, home to the major tanker shipping port of Ceyhan on the Eastern Mediterranean. The terminal is operated by Botas International Limited, a Turkish state company. [50]

Oil was also transported by truck across the border. The Russian Ministry of Defense provided satellite imagery of oil tankers crossing at Reyhanli.[51] Vladimir Putin detailed the scope of the operation in a meeting with his G-20 colleagues. "I've shown photos taken from space and from aircraft which clearly demonstrate the scale of the illegal trade in oil and petroleum products," he told journalists on the sidelines of the G-20 summit in Antalya on November 15, 2015. That day, US war planes destroyed more than hundred ISIS oil trucks, an effort that was widely reported in Western media. In the second half of November 2015 after Russia's revelations, Moscow and Washington destroyed thirteen hundred ISIS oil transport vehicles.[52]

Russia's Defense Ministry accused Erdogan's family members of being involved in oil trade with ISIS. Deputy Defense Minister Anatoly Antonov indicated, "According to available information, the highest level of the political leadership of the country, President Erdogan and his family, are involved in this criminal business."[53] CHP MP Aykut Erdogdu alleged that Berat Albayrak, Erdogan's son-in-law, and Ziya Ilgen, his brother-in-law, were directly involved. Albayrak was elected as AKP deputy in June 2015 and then appointed minister of energy and natural resources in November 2015. A court case was brought against Erdogdu for "insulting the President."[54]

Erdogan's son, Bilal, is also allegedly benefitting. He has a marine transport company, BMZ group, which owns a Maltese shipping company involved in oil transport. According to Gursel Tekin, CHP vice president, BMZ is "a family business and president Erdogan's close relatives hold shares in BMZ and they misused public funds and took illicit loans from Turkish banks." Bilal Erdogan arrived in Bologna with $1 billion in October 2015. The Bologna prosecutor opened an investigation into Bilal's money laundering.[55]

Oil sales initially provided the majority of ISIS revenue, but it gradually declined due to an extensive campaign of US-led air strikes in

2015.[56]According to the US Government, revenues also decreased due to Turkey's crackdown on oil smuggling. The State Department dismissed Moscow's charge that Erdogan and his family were involved with ISIS oil trade. According to Amos Hochstein, US special envoy and coordinator for international energy affairs, "The amount of oil being smuggled is extremely low and has decreased over time and is of no significance from a volume perspective—both volume of oil and volume of revenue."[57] This claim was refuted by an ISIS commander who maintained: "I know of a lot of cooperation. I don't see how Turkey can attack the organization too hard. There are shared interests."[58]

Russia's UN Ambassador Vitaly Churkin wrote the UN Security Council in March 2016, accusing Turkey of acting as the main supplier of weapons and ammunition to ISIS. Churkin accused MIT of overseeing the operation.[59] Despite evidence provided by Churkin, Russia lacks credibility as a claimant. It had grievance with Turkey for shooting down its air force plane.

There is no "smoking gun" linking the Government of Turkey or Erdogan and his family directly to ISIS oil sales. It is apparent, however, that Turkey turned a blind eye to the ISIS oil trade in 2014 and 2015. Turkey failed to seal its border, facilitating ISIS oil exports. Turks profited at stages of the supply chain.

Turkey's support for Islamic extremism in Syria was part of a broader effort to support jihadists. The German federal government issued a confidential intelligence assessment in response to a query from a member of the Bundestag. The report was published by ARD, one of Germany's leading news broadcasters on August 16, 2016. According to the report, the federal government sees Turkey as a "centralized action platform for Islamist groups." It sites Erdogan's deliberate policy of cooperation with Islamist and terrorist organizations in the Middle East, noting: "Many expressions of solidarity and support for the Egyptian Muslim Brotherhood, Hamas, and armed Islamist opposition in Syria." The report also emphasizes the "ideological affinity" between the AKP and the Muslim Brotherhood. According to ARD, Chancellor Angela Merkel and Foreign Minister Frank-Walter Steinmeier deliberately refrained from criticizing Turkey, although they were informed of the confidential report.[60]

Foreign intelligence agencies did not publicly implicate Turkey for assisting terror groups, but they discreetly raised concerns. Under mounting international pressure, Turkey finally took steps to seal its border beginning in the second half of 2015. It also started to arrest and deport militants. By turning on its former friends in the Islamist insurgent network, Erdogan incurred their wrath. CIA Director John O. Brennan said, "Turkey has been cracking down on some of the transit of foreign fighters who are flowing into as well as out of Turkey, and they [Turkey] are part of the coalition providing support, allowing their territory to be used by coalition aircraft. So there are a lot of reasons why Daesh would want to strike back."[61]

Beginning in October 2015, the United States based a squadron of A-10 attack planes, KC-135 refueling tankers, as well as surveillance and armed drones at Incirlik. The KC-135s handled one-third of all refueling activities for planes flying in the skies above Iraq and Syria. Because of Incirlik's proximity, planes using Incirlik could stay aloft much longer than planes taking off from aircraft carriers or from bases in Persian Gulf countries. The agreement to use Incirlik also paved the way for the Pentagon to base the high mobility artillery rocket system (HIMARS) in Turkey for use against militants in Syria.

ISIS media grew increasingly critical of Erdogan. ISIS called Turkey an "apostate regime" aligned with the "crusaders." *Dabiq*, the ISIS on-line magazine, published several critical stories about Erdogan, including a front-page photo of Erdogan and Obama together.[62] To punish Turkey for allowing use of Incirlik by US war planes, ISIS stepped up attacks on targets in Turkey. ISIS was allegedly responsible for a bombing in Suruc, which killed thirty-three people in July 2015. A bombing in Ankara killed 106 people in October. Two ISIS suicide bombings in 2016 targeted tourists in Istanbul's Sultanahmet Square and Beyoglu district.

In response, Turkey increased surveillance and tracking of ISIS and its network of jihadi affiliates. It deported four thousand suspects from Turkey. It banned forty-nine thousand people from one hundred countries from entering Turkey. More resources were provided to the Interior Ministry's Migration Management Directorate, which tracks foreigners who rent apartments that are used as ISIS dormitories. It is also monitoring surface transport, requiring full and accurate names on passenger manifests and then cross-referencing the manifests with lists of known or suspected terrorists.

An anonymous Turkish security official casts doubt on Turkey's counter-terrorism efforts. He asks, "Why is ISIS attacking Turkey even though Turkey provides logistics and weapons? Whenever Erdogan is criticized by the West, ISIS attacks. It mostly attacks Kurds and tourists. For example, Turkish MIT coordinated attacks with ISIS before the Nuclear Summit in Washington, which occurred right after Brussels attacks. The government always uses the same scenario. First, it creates a crisis environment using ISIS attacks and then it acts. Whenever there is an attack in Turkey, the government blames ISIS or the PKK to deflect international pressure on Erdogan." Turkey's cross-border military action on August 24, 2016, occurred right after the bombing of a Kurdish wedding in Gaziantep where fifty-five people were killed.[63] The anonymous security official insists these are not conspiracy theories. He claims to have first-hand knowledge. The veracity of his claims cannot be confirmed.

We do know, however, that Turkey's attempts to crackdown on ISIS were too few and too late. For every terrorist who is killed, arrested, or deported, a new one takes his place. Under increasing pressure from coalition air strikes, foreign fighters are leaving Syria and Iraq to resettle in Turkey. Putting the genie back in the bottle is easier said than done.[64]

Turkey used the ISIS threat to justify a national security and crackdown on Turkish media. Reporting on Turkey's links to ISIS by journalists in Turkey has almost stopped entirely, as journalists were arrested and media outlets shut down. Can Dundar, editor of *Cumhuriyet,* received a sentence of five years and ten months, and Erdem Gul, the paper's Ankara bureau chief, was sentenced to five years, for reporting on MIT's shipments of weapons to Islamists fighting the Syrian government. Dundar said the sentence was "not given only to suppress and silence us" but to "intimidate the Turkish media and make us scared of writing."[65] During the post-coup crackdown, Candar noted: "The civilian dictatorship has already begun."[66]

Notes

1. Recep Tayyip Edogan. Council on Foreign Relations. September 22, 2014.
2. Anonymous source within the Turkish Anti-Smuggling and Organized Crime Department. Information provided on August 24, 2016.
3. "Biden: Turks, Saudis, UAE funded and Armed Al Nusra and Al Qaeda," October 4, 2014, accessed June 25, 2016, https://mideastshuffle.com/2014/10/04/biden-turks-saudis-uae-funded-and-armed-al-nusra-and-al-qaeda/.
4. "Vice President Joe Biden Apologizes to Turkey, UAE," October 6, 2014, accessed June 25, 2016, http://edition.cnn.com/2014/10/05/politics/isis-biden-erdogan-apology/.
5. Ibid.
6. Ibid.
7. "Will Turkey Midwife Independent Kurdistan?," July 17, 2014, accessed June 25, 2016, http://www.realclearworld.com/2014/07/17/will_turkey_midwife_independent_kurdistan_160143.html.

8. Faiola, Anthony and Souad Mekhennet (August 12, 2014). "In Turkey, a late crackdown on Islamist fighters." *The Washington Post.* Accessed on September 8, 2016 from https://www.washingtonpost.com/world/how-turkey-became-the-shopping-mall-for-the-islamic-state/2014/08/12/5ef-f70bf-a38a-4334-9aa9-ae3fc1714c4b_story.html

9. Kılıçdaroğlu: 'Davutoğlu belge istiyordun, al sana belge', October 14, 2014, accessed June 25, 2016, http://www.cumhuriyet.com.tr/video/video/130347/Kilicdaroglu___Davutoglu_belge_istiyordun__al_sana_belge_.html.

10. Kılıçdaroğlu IŞİD'e giden silahların belgesini gösterdi, October 14, 2014, accessed June 25, 2016, http://www.samanyoluhaber.com/gundem/Kilic-daroglu-ISIDe-giden-silahlarin-belgesini-gosterdi/1064168/.

11. Kılıçdaroğlu: IŞİD'e silah yardımına ilişkin belge mi istiyordun, işte belgeler!, October 14, 2014, accessed June 25, 2016, http://t24.com.tr/haber/kilicdaro-glu-bizim-tezkere-onerimiz-millidir-yabanci-asker-de-isgal-de-yok-ice-risinde,273829.

12. CHP tutanakları açıkladı: O tırlardan onlarca füze çıktı, July 21, 2014, accessed June 25, 2016, http://www.cumhuriyet.com.tr/haber/turkiye/97017/CHP_tutanaklari_acikladi__O_tirlardan_onlarca_fuze_cikti.html.

13. Anonymous source within the Turkish Anti-Smuggling and Organized Crime Department. Information provided on August 24, 2016.

14. Başçalanın Seçim Güdümlü Savaş Planı 1-1, May 26, 2014, accessed June 25, 2016, https://www.youtube.com/watch?feature=youtu.be&v=c-1GooSDwJ8.

15. "IŞİD'e Türkiye'den böyle yardım edildi," September 27, 2014, *OdaTV*, accessed August 10, 2016, http://odatv.com/n.php?n=iside-turkiyeden-boyle-yardim-edildi-2709141200.

16. http://www.ibtimes.co.uk/haddad-1-ship-loaded-turkish-weapons-isla-mists-libya-suspected-oil-gunds-deal-1520295.

17. http://www.cumhurriyet.com.tr/haber/turkiye/455713/Sarin_Gazi-Davasi_nda_karar_verildi_Eren_Erdem-hakli-cikti.html.

18. "MİT, IŞİD'i Muammer Güler'in emriyle ağırladı," *Radical*, June 13, 2014, accessed August 10, 2016, http://www.radikal.com.tr/politika/mit-isi-di-muammer-gulerin-emriyle-agirladi-1196924/.

19. IŞİD iyi ki varsın, Allah kurşununu azaltmasın, October 4, 2014, accessed June 25, 2016, http://odatv.com/n.php?n=isid-iyi-ki-varsin-allah-kur-sununu-azaltmasin-0410141200.

20. "Devlet yazışmalarını IŞİD logosuyla yapıyoruz," *Oda TV*, February 10, 2014, accessed September 8, 2016, http://odatv.com/n.php?n=devlet-yazismalar-ini-isid-logosuyla-yapiyoruz-0210141200.

21. Sam Greenhill, "How Seven Radicalised Young Britons a Week Are Taking the Gateway to Jihad," *Daily Mail*, August 25, 2014, accessed August 10, 2016, http://www.dailymail.co.uk/news/article-2734239/How-seven-rad-icalised-young-Britons-week-taking-Gateway-Jihad.html.

22. New report shows Turkey-ISIL links, October 21, 2014, accessed June 25, 2016, http://edition.presstv.ir/detail/383033.html.

23. Turkey help Jihadists ISIS-BBC VIDEO, September 19, 2014, accessed June 25, 2016, https://www.youtube.com/watch?v=qARNhiyHvZA.

24. "Turkey 'Providing Direct Support' to Isis," October 9, 2014, accessed June 25, 2016, http://www.wnd.com/2014/10/turkey-providing-direct-sup-port-to-isis/#!

25. İstanbul'da piknik yapıp cihat çağrısında bulundular, July 29, 2014, accessed June 25, 2016, http://www.cnnturk.com/video/turkiye/istanbulda-piknik-yapip-cihat-cagrisinda-bulundular.

26. Tanrıkulu: Hükümet IŞİD'e İstanbul'da kamp yeri mi verdi?, July 30, 2014, accessed June 25, 2016, http://www.radikal.com.tr/turkiye/tanrikulu-hukumet-iside-istanbulda-kamp-yeri-mi-verdi-1204375/.

27. See takvahaber.net.

28. İstanbul'da IŞİD kampı iddiası Meclis gündeminde, July 31, 2014, accessed June 25, 2016, http://arsiv.taraf.com.tr/haber-istanbulda-isid-kampi-iddiasi-meclis-gundeminde-160456/.

29. Kılıçdaroğlu: 'Davutoğlu belge istiyordun, al sana belge', October 14, 2014, accessed June 25, 2016, http://www.cumhuriyet.com.tr/video/video/130347/Kilicdaroglu___Davutoglu_belge_istiyordun__al_sana_belge_.html.

30. "İŞİD İle Türkiye Ortak"(November 12, 2014). *Kurdistan Aktuel*, accessed September 8, 2016, http://www.kurdistan-aktuel.org/dunya/i-id-ile-turkiye-ortak-h1487.html.

31. "In Turkey, a Late Crackdown on Islamist Fighters," August 12, 2014, accessed June 28, 2016, https://www.washingtonpost.com/world/how-turkey-became-the-shopping-mall-for-the-islamic-state/2014/08/12/5eff70bf-a38a-4334-9aa9-ae3fc1714c4b_story.html.

32. AKP kurucularından Fırat: Hükümet, aşırı dinci grupları silahlandırdı; AKP'li Kürtler de Kobanê için ayaklandı, October 12, 2014, accessed June 28, 2016, http://t24.com.tr/haber/akpnin-kurucularindan-firat-hukumet-asiri-dinci-gruplari-silahlandirdi-akpli-kurtler-de-kobane-icin-ayaklandi,273589.

33. IŞİD militanları devlet kesesinden tedavi oldu, September 11, 2014, accessed June 28, 2016, http://arsiv.taraf.com.tr/haber-isid-militanlari-devlet-kesesinden-tedavi-oldu-163522/.

34. Kılıçdaroğlu: 'Davutoğlu belge istiyordun, al sana belge', October 12, 2014, accessed June 25, 2016, http://www.cumhuriyet.com.tr/video/video/130347/Kilicdaroglu___Davutoglu_belge_istiyordun__al_sana_belge_.html.

35. For more information, see Kılıçdaroğlu IŞİD'e giden silahların belgesini gösterdi, October 14, 2014, from http://www.samanyoluhaber.com/gundem/Kilicdaroglu-ISIDe-giden-silahlarin-belgesini-gosterdi/1064168/ and Kılıçdaroğlu: IŞİD'e silah yardımına ilişkin belge mi istiyordun, işte belgeler!, October 14, 2014, from http://t24.com.tr/haber/kilicdaroglu-bizim-tezkere-onerimiz-millidir-yabanci-asker-de-isgal-de-yok-icerisinde,273829.

36. Gundem, accessed June 25, 2016, http://odatv.com/vid_video.php?id=8D3C0.

37. ISID in Adresi Erdogan ve Davutoglunun Cikti, accessed June 28, 2016, http://odatv.com/n.php?n=isidin-adresi-erdogan-ve-davutoglunun-cikti-2710141200.

38. Two Thousand Turkish Special Forces in ISIS, September 20, 2014, accessed June 25, 2016, http://kurdishquestion.com/kurdistan/west-kurdistan/two-thousand-turkish-special-forces-in-isis.html.

39. "İstanbul'da Işid'cilerden 'İç Savaş' Toplantisi," *Ileri Haber*, November 30, 2016, accessed August 10, 2016, http://ilerihaber.org/istanbulda-isidcilerden-ic-savas-toplantisi/3807/.

40. The Red Line and the Rat Line, April 17, 2014, accessed July 14, 2016, http://www.lrb.co.uk/v36/n08/seymour-m-hersh/the-red-line-and-the-rat-line.

41. "IŞİD saflarında savaşan Türkiye'li resmi görevliler var," September 30, 2014, accessed July 15, 2016, http://odatv.com/n.php?n=isid-saflarinda-sav-asan-turkiyeli-resmi-gorevliler-var--3009141200.

42. IŞİD militanları sıfır noktasında görüntülendi, October 1, 2014, accessed June 28, 2016, http://www.diken.com.tr/isid-militanlari-sifir-noktasinda-go-runtulendi/.

43. PYD lideri Müslim: Türkiye'nin IŞİD'e desteği sürüyor, daha bu hafta sınırı 120 militan geçti, October 24, 2014, accessed July 14, 2016, http://www.diken.com.tr/pyd-lideri-salih-muslim-turkiyenin-iside-destegi-suruyor-daha-bu-hafta-siniri-120-militan-gecti/.

44. Türkiye'nin IŞİD'i desteklediğinin kanıtları var, October 29, 2014, accessed July 1, 2016, http://www.odatv.com/n.php?n=turkiyenin-isidi-destekledig-inin-kanitlari-var-2910141200.

45. IŞİD teröristlerinin pasaportunda T.C. damgası var, October 21, 2014, accessed July 15, 2016, http://www.odatv.com/n.php?n=isid-teroristleri-nin-pasaportunda-t.c.-damgasi-var--2110141200.

46. Türk askeri IŞİD'le hatıra fotoğrafı mı çektirdi, October 11, 2014, accessed July 15, 2016, http://www.odatv.com/n.php?n=turk-askeri-isidle-hatira-fo-tografi-mi-cektirdi--1110141200.

47. "German Deputy Speaker: NATO Must Stop Turkey Support for ISIS," *Rudaw*, October 12, 2014, accessed July 15, 2016, http://rudaw.net/english/middleeast/12102014.

48. Cengiz Candar, "Turkey Takes a Hit from the Russian Hammer," *Al-Monitor*, December 4, 2015, accessed August 10, 2016, http://www.al-monitor.com/pulse/originals/2015/12/turkey-syria-russia-downing-of-russian-jet-west-ern-anvil.html#ixzz4H9OyM7KI.

49. Taştekin, Fehim, "Sınırsız sınır . . . ," *Radikal*, September 13, 2014, accessed September 8, 2016, http://www.radikal.com.tr/yazarlar/fehim-tastekin/sinirsiz-sinir-1212462/.

50. "ISIS Export Gateway to Global Crude Oil Markets," *London Shipping Law Centre, Maritime Business Forum*, March 12, 2015, accessed June 15, 2016, http://www.marsecreview.com/wp-content/uploads/2015/03/PAPER-on-CRUDE-OIL-and-ISIS.pdf.

51. Mevzuattan çıktı . . . Erdogan zorda! İşte IŞİD petrolüne belge, *Gazeteciler*, December 4, 2015, accessed July 1, 2016, http://www.gazetecileronline.com/newsdetails/18904-/GazetecilerOnline/mevzuattan-cikti-erdogan-zor-da-iste-isid-petrolune.

52. "ISIS Oil Trade Full Frontal: 'Raqqa's Rockefellers', Bilal Erdogan, KRG Crude, And The Israel Connection," *Zero Hedge*, November 29, 2015, accessed July 14, 2016, http://www.zerohedge.com/news/2015-11-28/isis-oil-trade-full-frontal-raqqas-rockefellers-bilal-erdogan-krg-crude-and-israel-c.

53. "Syria Conflict: Russia Accuses Erdogan of Trading Oil with IS," *BBC News*, December 2, 2015, accessed July 15, 2016, http://www.bbc.com/news/world-middle-east-34982951.

54. Aykut Erdoğdu yolsuzluk bağlantılarını belgeleriyle anlattı, *Çağdaş Ses*, October 21, 2015, accessed July 15, 2016, http://siyasihaber1.org/chpli-altiok-ve-hdpli-kurkcu-isidten-petrol-alimini-4-ay-once-meclise-tasimisti.

55.   İtalya savcılığına Bilal Erdogan şikayeti, *Rota Haber*, December 4, 2015, accessed July 14, 2016, http://www.rotahaber.com/dunya/italya-savciligi-na-bilal-erdogan-sikayeti-h572139.html.

56.   "Islamic State Financing and US Policy Approaches," *Congressional Research Service*, April 10, 2015, accessed July 15, 2016, https://www.fas.org/sgp/crs/terror/R43980.pdf.

57.   "ISIS Oil Smuggling to Turkey Insignificant: US Official," *The Daily Star*, December 4, 2015, accessed June 26, 2016, http://www.dailystar.com.lb/News/Middle-East/2015/Dec-04/325974-isis-oil-smuggling-to-turkey-in-significant-us-official.ashx#.VmI2SVCLf7E.facebook.

58.   "Turkey Sends in Jets as Syria's Agony Spills over Every Border," *The Guardian*, July 25, 2015, accessed July 15, 2016, https://www.theguardian.com/world/2015/jul/26/isis-syria-turkey-us.

59.   "Russia Accuses Turkey of Smuggling Weapons to ISIS," April 1, 2016, accessed June 26, 2016, http://www.ctvnews.ca/world/russia-accuses-tur-key-of-smuggling-weapons-to-isis-1.2842385.

60.   Arnd Henze. "Turkey 'Platform for Action' for Islamists," ARD Studio Broadcast, August 16, 2016.

61.   Rukmini Callimachi, "Turkey, a Conduit for Fighters Joining ISIS, Begins to Feel Its Wrath," *New York Times*, June 29, 2016, accessed August 10, 2016, http://www.nytimes.com/2016/06/30/world/middleeast/turkey-a-conduit-for-fighters-joining-isis-begins-to-feel-its-wrath.html.

62.   Ibid., , accessed July 1, 2016, http://www.nytimes.com/2016/06/30/world/middleeast/turkey-a-conduit-for-fighters-joining-isis-begins-to-feel-its-wrath.html?emc=edit_th_20160630&nl=todaysheadlines&n-lid=59698281&_r=0.

63.   Anonymous source within the Turkish Anti-Smuggling and Organized Crime Department. Information provided on August 24, 2016.

64.   "Are Turkey's Efforts to Combat Foreign Fighters Too Late?," July 12, 2016, accessed July 14, 2016, http://www.al-monitor.com/pulse/originals/2016/07/turkey-too-late-dealing-foreign-terrorist-fighters.html#ixzz4ENDXhhtO.

65.   Turkey jails *Cumhuriyet* journalists Can Dundar and Erdem Gul, May 6, 2016, accessed June 26, 2016, http://www.bbc.com/news/world-eu-rope-36233282.

66.   ARD Studio Interview with Can Dundar, July 24, 2016.

Part III

Crackdown

10

Consolidation

Let's make this period a time of reforms, prioritizing a new constitution. The Turkish republic has enjoyed its best period in the last thirteen years. Now, we shouldn't be worried about changing the nature of the regime.[1]

—Recep Tayyip Erdogan

Erdogan systematically consolidated his political power by marginalizing potential rivals within the Justice and Development Party (AKP). Friends and allies were abandoned. Political parties that opposed constitutional reform, such as the Peoples' Democratic Party (HDP), were threatened with legal action. The Turkish Grand National Assembly (TGNA) removed parliamentary immunity of HDP deputies leading to the arrest of 11 party leaders including Co-Chairman Selahattin Demirtas. Erdogan's consolidation of power and mandatory observance of his ideology had its own name—"Erdoganism."

Erdogan became the first directly elected president, winning 52 percent of the vote on August 10, 2014. It was widely assumed that when he became president, Abdullah Gul would become prime minister. A similar arrangement occurred in Russia where Vladimir Putin and Dmitry Medvedev made the swap. But Erdogan was not interested in power sharing. He wanted to direct both party and policy. A power struggle might impede the creation of a strong presidential system— Erdogan's ultimate objective.

Gul was on record opposing a presidential system for Turkey, preferring to upgrade the current parliamentary system to European standards. "I favor the parliamentary system," said Gul. "A presidential system is also a democratic one, but only if there are checks and balances."[2] Erdogan and Gul are very different yet complementary. Levent Gultekin, a prominent intellectual, commented on their early political careers. "Abdullah Gul has the wisdom, a calm style,

153

and progressive policies; Erdogan had the charisma and political magnetism."[3] Over the years, however, their styles and world views would increasingly diverge.

Gul was more liberal and pro-European than Erdogan. Gul understood that Turkey's EU candidacy required strict adherence to the Copenhagen criteria on human rights. According to Gul, "A safer world can only be secured through the rule of law. States are the guardians of the rule of law, which they themselves should observe, adhere and promote."[4] In 2013, he and Bulent Arinc favored dialogue with the Gezi Park protesters.[5] They criticized the police for excessive force.[6] He spoke out in support of press freedom and freedom of expression.

Gul also favored dialogue with the PKK. Gul adopted a conciliatory tone during a visit to Hakkari soon after being elected president. He stressed that resolution of the Kurdish question lay in the further democratization of the country. "I understand what you think and what the Kurdish people have gone through. A solution will take some time, and all interested parties should contribute to dialog for a possible solution."[7] According to Gul: "The biggest problem of Turkey is the Kurdish problem. It has to be solved." He added, "[Turkey has a] historic possibility to solve it through discussions."[8]

He disapproved of the foreign policy pursued by Erdogan and Ahmet Davutoglu, which alienated Turkey in the region and from the West. For example, Gul's personal diplomacy put Turkey and Armenia on track to normalization. However, Erdogan scuttled the deal in fealty to Azerbaijan. Gul is pious but does not blindly support the Muslim Brotherhood. He wants to help Sunni victims in Syria, but opposes Turkey's cooperation with the Islamic State.

Though Gul is a man of convictions, he was too passive. Gul condoned actions by Erdogan of which he disapproved. After the Gezi Park crackdown, the government initiated laws restricting Internet, Facebook, and Twitter. Gul disagreed with these measures, but he signed the legislation into law. Gul's acquiescence tainted his reputation on human rights and credibility as a reformer. He lacked the backbone to contest Erdogan's decisions publicly.

He was also politically naïve. Gul was popular with the AKP rank-and-file. He could have run and won the chairmanship of the AKP at the end of his term as president. Gul would have become head of the party, led the party in general elections, and become prime minister. However, he did not want to act against Erdogan's wishes. He was loyal to Erdogan and trusted his good intentions. Gul was also cautious to avoid the appearance of advocating Islamist rule in Turkey, which risked fueling dissent within the AKP and between the AKP and the military.

Toward the end of Gul's term as president, he was excluded from the AKP's inner circle. Erdogan's operatives sidelined him from the party's affairs. Erdogan wanted an obedient prime minister who would do his bidding until an executive presidency could be legally established. Erdogan pronounced the importance of party unity, then dumped Gul. He selected Davutoglu as his puppet prime minister. Erdogan spitefully removed Gul, Bulent Arinc, and some other AKP stalwarts from the party's honorary list of founding members.[9]

During his farewell reception at the presidential palace on August 19, 2014, Gul spoke about "great disrespect from within his own camp." Gul was not consulted on Davutoglu's appointment. Davutoglu was Gul's protégé. He groomed him to become foreign minister. Gul's wife, Hayrunnisa, threatened to reveal the AKP's sordid inner workings and "start the real intifada."[10]

Gul sent a written message to the AKP congress on August 22, congratulating Davutoglu. "Turkey does not have the patience to waste any more time facing difficulties like economic, political, social issues and security problems like terror. I believe this congress will enable our people to focus on its real problems and find solutions once again".[11] Despite his positive approach, Gul was smeared by Erdogan's agents in the media. Ankara Deputy Yalcin Akdogan wrote in *Yeni Safak*, "This party does not owe a debt to anyone. All the posts gained by the AKP are Erdogan's achievements. He therefore has the right to decide who will take over which post."

Erdogan pushed through a decision to limit AKP officials to three terms in government. On the surface, it looked like an effort to promote new leadership. Actually, Erdogan wanted to eliminate the old guard, which tended to be more independent. The new generation was more beholden to Erdogan.

Bulent Arinc, who served five years as TGNA speaker and seven years as deputy prime minister, was another member of the AKP inner circle who was pushed out of power. Arinc was a prominent member of the old guard. He led the "reformist movement" during the late 1990s, which advocated a more progressive Islamism than Erbakan's. Gul and Arinc went way back. Gul took over as head of the reformist movement with Arinc's support.

After years in AKP politics, Arinc retired in November 2015. Upon formally leaving his political posts, Arinc had nothing to lose from speaking his mind. "We were a party of 'us,'" said Arinc. "But now we have turned into a party of 'me.'"[12] Arinc disputed Erdogan's policies across the board. On CNN Turk, Arinc criticized the failed peace process with the PKK. Arinc spoke about the Dolmabahce Consensus between the government and the pro-Kurdish HDP, which was announced in February 2015. Erdogan condemned the agreement, insisting that it was negotiated without his knowledge. However, Arinc asserted that Erdogan authorized negotiations and knew every detail. The revelation questioned both Erdogan's honesty, as well as his commitment to peace with the Kurds.

Arinc lamented Erdogan's targeting of former generals and security officials. He asserted that "Ergenekon" and "Operation Sledgehammer" were not about national security. They were artifices used to justify a crackdown on the secular elite, which upheld Kemalist principles, and could potentially oppose Erdogan's executive presidency. Arinc also objected to Erdogan's targeting independent media, which Erdogan saw as a challenge to his supremacy.

In addition, Arinc scoffed at Erdogan's allegations of a powerful "parallel state" organized by Fethullah Gulen to overthrow the government. According to Arinc, Gulen posed no real danger to the government. The witch hunt, which followed revelations of corruption in December 2013, was a device to accelerate the consolidation of power by Erdogan. The crackdown sought to silence dissent and root out opposition. It was also a ploy to eliminate adversaries in the judicial and police bureaucracy who might implicate Erdogan in their investigation of official corruption.

Arinc also criticized Erdogan's public relations hit men who demonized anyone opposing their boss. When Arinc spoke out, Erdogan's defamation machine went into high gear. Pro-Erdogan newspapers such as *Star*, *Aksam*, and *Gunes* accused Arinc of "treason." Because he supported the peace process with Kurds, they condemned him for "speaking in the language of the terrorists." Erdogan would not mention Arinc by name, calling him "this person," and accusing him of "dishonesty."

Ahmet Davutoglu was elected the AKP's new leader on August 27, 2014. Being elected AKP chair set the stage for him to become prime minister. In silent protest, neither Gul nor Arinc attended the AKP congress. The CHP's Kemal Kilicdaroglu said of Davutoglu: "You are not the prime minister. You are a kid seated on the prime minister's chair [for a photo-op]."[13] Davutoglu was often called Erdogan's lap dog for his ironclad obedience. Erdogan and Davutoglu appeared in lock step. But beneath the veneer of unity, they differed over important issues—the Kurdish peace process, the refugee and migrant crisis, as well as constitutional reform enhancing presidential powers.

Tactical mistakes by Davutoglu deepened differences with Erdogan. He publicly proposed a trial for some of the ministers ensnared in the corruption probe of 2013. Davutoglu thought they would be acquitted, vindicating Erdogan's approach to the investigation. However, Erdogan opposed the move. He squashed the vote by a parliamentary commission that would have referred the case to Turkey's Supreme Court.

Davutoglu believed that clean government would appeal to voters and drafted a bill called "The Transparency Package." The legislation required the president, senior judicial officials, party officials, provincial and district-level party executives, and executives of radio and television channels to declare their assets. Erdogan met with AKP leaders behind Davutoglu's back and killed the bill. Davutoglu put on a brave face, but was deeply unhappy about Erdogan's actions.

Davutoglu proved to be an energetic but uninspiring campaigner. Erdogan lost his voice during a critical phase of the campaign for local elections in 2014. Davutoglu took the lead campaigning, but lacked Erdogan's appeal. The AKP won, but the margin was narrower than expected. Davutoglu was blamed for the party's lackluster showing.

Erdogan also disapproved of Davutoglu's cabinet appointments. Davutoglu convinced Hakan Fidan, MIT's head, to run for parliament so he could assume a cabinet position in Davutoglu's government. Erdogan did not approve and sent Fidan back to his post at MIT. Erdogan reproached Fidan for acting independently. "He should have taken my consent before leaving the job."[14]

The AKP won only 40.7 percent of the vote in national elections on June 7, 2015.[15] Though the AKP was still by far Turkey's most popular party, it performed much worse than expected. For the first time in thirteen years, the AKP lost a majority in the parliament. Davutoglu campaigned tirelessly, but simply did not connect with voters.

Erdogan lost faith in Davutoglu's leadership. He blocked the formation of a coalition government and pushed for new elections. Erdogan took matters into his own hands, escalating conflict with the PKK. In July 2015, he launched intense air strikes against PKK positions in Iraqi

Kurdistan. Turkish war planes also bombed villages and small cities in southeast Turkey, which Erdogan accused of harboring "terrorists."

The AKP announced elections for November 1, 2015. This time, Erdogan vigorously participated in the campaign. The electorate was swayed by his message of stability and promises of economic growth. The AKP gained 49.5 percent of the vote. The outcome was a dramatic reversal of the results in June. The AKP won 341 seats, more than the 276 seats needed to avoid a coalition and form a government alone. With sixty more seats, the government would have been able to change the constitution without calling a referendum. Davutoglu addressed supporters on election night, "You saw the dirty games played in our country, and you have changed the game."[16] However, it was Erdogan not Davutoglu who was the game changer.

The EU insisted on negotiating an arrangement to address the refugee and migrant crisis with Davutoglu, sidelining Erdogan. In March 2016, Davutoglu reached a provisional agreement with the EU. The deal included a financial aid package, the promise of visa free travel for Turkish citizens to EU Member States, and accelerated negotiations of Turkey's EU candidacy. Davutoglu was acclaimed by the international press. Erdogan thought that Davutoglu had become too big for his britches. He interpreted Davutoglu's prominence as a challenge to his authority. The EU imposed seventy-two criteria, which stalled implementation. The European Commission issued a nonbinding recommendation, punting the final decision to member states and the European Parliament. When implementation of the EU-Turkey deal was delayed, Erdogan blamed Davutoglu.

Davutoglu resigned in May 2016. Pro-AKP media emphasized party unity. However, Davutoglu's remarks at the AKP congress on May 22 raised doubts. "After a short period of time since the latest elections, it was not my intention or desire to hold a congress. The main reason behind holding a congress, and surrendering the post, after we received 49.5 percent of the vote, is because I value the unity and the solidarity of our party and worry that AK Party movement could be damaged."[17] He continued, "We might bid farewell to our positions and offices, but we would never say goodbye to our principles and ideals. No one is indispensable to this [AKP] movement. But this movement has indispensable values." Visibly shaken, Davutoglu whitewashed differences with Erdogan, describing their relationship as "brotherly." Davutoglu affirmed, "You will never hear me say negative things about our president. My loyalty to him will last until the end."[18]

Erdogan wanted the AKP to nominate Berat Albayrak, his thirty-seven-year old son-in-law and energy minister, as prime minister. Other than his loyalty to Erdogan, Albayrak's primary qualification for the job was organizing smear campaigns against Gul and Davutoglu. Erdogan's nepotism was even too much for die-hard AKP loyalists, who feared a public backlash. Erdogan was dissuaded from putting Albayrak's name in nomination. Transport Minister Binali Yildirim was nominated instead. He was the sole candidate, unanimously elected by 1,405 delegates at the extraordinary AKP congress on May 22, 2016. Davutoglu sat sheepishly next to Yildirim during the proceedings. According to Gul, "President Erdogan is responsible for our successes and failures from now on."[19]

The HDP was another rival to be eliminated. The HDP was a big winner in elections on June 7. It received 13.12 percent of the vote, giving it eighty seats in the TGNA. Selahattin Demirtas, the HDP's charismatic co-chair, appealed beyond the party's Kurdish base. In addition to Kurdish voters, the HDP was supported by progressives who opposed Erdogan's authoritarianism and some secular elite who thought the HDP could help prevent the rise of Erdogan's Islamism.

Erdogan went on the offensive. After restarting the war with the PKK, he sought to discredit the HDP by portraying it as the political wing of the PKK. He blamed Demirtas for endorsing democratic autonomy, calling him a terrorist. Demirtas responded, "Hopefully the authorities will read this declaration one more time with calmness, and see that self-rule [and] autonomy offer a very significant opportunity for all of us in terms of living together."[20] He questioned, "What will you solve by bombing all provinces, just because a few youth took up arms?"[21] Erdogan's attack dogs accused him of excusing "PKK terror." Demirtas was investigated for "making terrorism propaganda," "inciting a crime," and "encouraging sedition."[22] The investigation included the alleged violation of Article 302 of the Turkish Penal Code, "disrupting the unity and territorial integrity of the state."[23]

In addition to attacks from government propagandists, Demirtas was blamed by many Kurds for failing to reject violent extremism more clearly. He was also blamed for failing to negotiate a *modus vivendi* with the government. The people were scared and held the HDP responsible for the escalation of deadly violence. The Kurdish Communities Union (KCK) took a maximalist position, opposing the HDP. It rejected the authority of all state agencies. Local politicians declared self-government in many towns and provinces. Kurds under siege dug trenches and erected barricades intended to keep the armed forces from entering their communities. Conflict and curfew ruined the local economy. Scores of civilians were affected. At least 338 civilians died and over 355,000 people were displaced between July 2015 and 2016.[24]

The HDP won only 10.7 percent of the vote on November 1, 2015. It was barely enough to cross the 10 percent barrier and be seated in the parliament. Its fifty-nine parliamentary seats were twenty-one fewer than it gained in June's election. Meral Danis Bestas, the HDP's deputy co-chair, explained the HDP's poor performance. "This was not a normal election. In an atmosphere of oppression and killing, we were facing an all-out assault with detentions and illegal measures. We entered the elections in that atmosphere. We couldn't run a proper election campaign. We couldn't hold rallies and reach out to the people. We were practically made invisible. Ninety-five percent of national television channels were off-limits to us. When all other political parties were always on screen, our news, activities and the statements of our leaders were not reported. This severely affected the outcome." According to Bestas, "We were not facing only the government. The Turkish armed forces, security services, bureaucracy and judiciary were all arrayed against us as one. We didn't run for elections in a just, free and equal democratic atmosphere."[25]

The government's campaign to discredit the HDP continued after elections. The Justice Ministry presented files to the prosecutor, detailing terrorism related charges against HDP deputies. Charges included "establishing an organization to commit crimes," "belonging to an armed terrorist organization," and "committing crimes on behalf of a terror organization." Charges brought against Demirtas included "publicly insulting the Republic of Turkey, making propaganda for a terrorist organization and aiding a terrorist organization willingly and intentionally." Demirtas rejected the allegations, declaring that he and other HDP deputies would ignore court subpoenas.[26]

Led by the AKP caucus, 367 MPs voted to lift parliamentary immunity for 50 HDP legislators, including Demirtas.[27] According to *Sabah*, "With the passing of the bill, the pro-Kurdish Peoples' Democratic Party (HDP), which is accused of siding with the PKK through remarks and actions, will come to justice." [28] Sure enough, Demirtas and HDP Co-Chair Figen Yuksekdag, were dragged from their homes in the middle of the night on November 2, 2016 and charged with terrorism. Raids were conducted at the HDP offices in Ankara where 9 members of parliament were detained.

Demirtas and his HDP colleagues expected the government to target them. In April, he warned Members of the European Parliament (MEPs) and the US Congress that such action was imminent. He asked them to organize a campaign on behalf of HDP deputies when their parliamentary immunity was revoked and they were arrested. MEPs issued a statement linking visa-free travel for Turkish citizens to the rule of law in Turkey, specifically criticizing measures against the HDP.

The Gulen movement represented another challenge to Erdogan's authority. Gulenists were accused of terrorism and plotting to overthrow the democratically elected government. To Erdogan, they were a state within the state, insidiously plotting a coup. The police and judiciary were especially threatening. Erdogan wanted to dismantle the network of Hizmet schools before their graduates assumed too much prominence. He compiled a list of Gulenists to be purged at the slightest provocation.

Erdogan established a de facto executive presidency by ignoring checks and balances and acting with impunity. Erdogan successfully eradicated potential rivals in the AKP. He undermined other political parties and groups that might stand in his way. As a result of Erdogan's measures to consolidate power, Turkey became more deeply divided. Democracy was undermined and society deeply polarized. Disquiet and crisis loomed.

Notes

1. Ece Toksabay and Melih Aslan, "Turkey's Erdogan Calls for New Constitution as EU Frets about Rights," *Reuters*, November 2, 2015, accessed July 5, 2016, http://www.reuters.com/article/us-turkey-erdogan-constitution-idUSKCN0SZ0WL20151110.

2. Semih Idiz, "What Does the Future Hold for Abdullah Gul?," *Al-Monitor*, August 22, 2014, accessed July 3, 2016, http://www.al-monitor.com/pulse/ru/contents/articles/originals/2014/08/turkey-gul-erdogan-davutoglu-president-akp.html.

3. Cengiz Candar, "No Room for Gul in Erdogan's Turkey," *Al-Monitor*, August 15, 2014, accessed July 6, 2016, http://www.al-monitor.com/pulse/originals/2014/08/candar-erdogan-honorable-exit-gul-akp-prime-minister.html#ixzz4DKdUTAPK.

4. Accessed July 6, 2016, www.mfa.gov.tr/data/BAKANLIK/ . . . /Abdullah-Gul_Speecheskisaltilmis versiyon.pdf.

5. Sebnem Arsu, "Turkish Official Apologizes for Force Used at Start of Riots," *New York Times*, June 4, 2013, accessed July 6, 2016, http://www.nytimes.com/2013/06/05/world/europe/turkey-riots.html?_r=0.

6. "Unrest in Turkey: MEPs Call for Reconciliation and Warn Against Harsh Measures," *Hurriyet Daily News*, June 13, 2013, accessed July 6, 2016 http://www.hurriyetdailynews.com/unrest-in-turkey-meps-

call-for-reconciliation-and-warn-against-harsh-measures.aspx?page-ID=238&nID=48772&NewsCatID=351.

7. Emrullah Uslu, "President Abdullah Gul Takes an Active Role in Easing Kurdish Unrest," *Eurasia Daily Monitor*, December 4, 2008, accessed July 8, 2016, http://www.jamestown.org/programs/edm/single/?tx_ttnews%5Btt_news%5D=34220&tx_ttnews%5BbackPid%5D=166&no_cache=1#.V3_UezV5y_4.

8. Alexander Christie-Miller, "The PKK and the Closure of Turkey's Kurdish Opening," *Middle East Research and Information Project*, August 4, 2010, accessed July 6, 2016 http://www.merip.org/mero/mero080410.

9. "Gül ve Arınç AKP'nin kurucuları arasında neden yok, kimler listeden çıkarıldı?," February 23, 2016, accessed July 16, 2016, http://t24.com.tr/haber/gul-ve-arinc-akpnin-kuruculari-arasinda-neden-yok-kimler-listeden-cikarildi,329227.

10. Idiz, "What Does the Future Hold for Abdullah Gul?"

11. "Davutoğlu and AKP Founders Imply The Party Has Departed From Its Values," *The Turkish Sun*, May 23, 2016, accessed July 5, 2016, http://theturkishsun.com/davutoglu-and-akp-founders-imply-the-party-has-departed-from-its-values-19328/.

12. Mustafa Akyol, "AKP Moderate Declared 'Traitor'," *Al-Monitor*, October 31, 2013, accessed July 5, 2016, http://www.al-monitor.com/pulse/originals/2016/02/turkey-moderate-akp-pillar-declared-traitor.html#ixzz4DX-JLdlSZ.

13. Burak Bekdil, "Turkey: Davutoglu vs. Davutoglu," *Gatestone Institute*, March 26, 2015, accessed July 7, 2016, http://www.gatestoneinstitute.org/5446/turkey-davutoglu.

14. Ibid.

15. Kevin A. Lees, "Can Abdullah Gül Save Turkish Democracy?," *Huffington Post*, August 27, 2014, accessed July 3, 2016, http://www.huffingtonpost.com/kevin-a-lees/can-abdullah-guel-save-turkey_b_5719609.html.

16. "Turkey Election: Ruling AKP Regains Majority," *BBC*, November 2, 2015, accessed July 7, 2016, http://www.bbc.com/news/world-europe-34694420.

17. Tim Arango and Ceylan Yeginsu, "How Erdogan Moved to Solidify Power by Ousting a Pivotal Ally," *New York Times*, May 5, 2016, accessed July 8, 2016, http://www.nytimes.com/2016/05/06/world/europe/ahmet-davutoglu-turkey-prime-minister.html?_r=0.

18. Ibid.

19. "Davutoğlu And AKP Founders Imply The Party Has Departed From Its Values."

20. "HDP, the PKK and Parliamentary Immunity," *Daily Sabah*, May 21, 2016, accessed July 8, 2016, http://www.dailysabah.com/legislation/2016/05/21/hdp-the-pkk-and-parliamentary-immunity.

21. Ibid.

22. Ibid.

23. Ibid.

24. "Turkey: State Blocks Probes of Southeast Killings Allow UN to Investigate Cizre Abuses; Repeal New Law to Block Prosecutions," *Human Rights Watch*, July 11, 2016, accessed August 8, 2016, https://www.hrw.org/news/2016/07/11/turkey-state-blocks-probes-southeast-killings.

25. Mahmut Bozarslan, "After Big Win in June, Why Did HDP Lose this Time?," *Al-Monitor*, November 5, 2015, accessed July 8, 2016, from http://www.al-monitor.com/pulse/originals/2015/11/turkey-elections-hdp-lose-kurds-face-tough-choices-pkk.html#ixzz4DnJOL0UK.

26. Merve Aydogan, "Recent Report Cites HDP Deputies' Close Affiliation with, Aiding, Abetting PKK," *Daily Sabah*, June 26, 2016, accessed July 8, 2016, http://www.dailysabah.com/war-on-terror/2016/06/27/recent-report-cites-hdp-deputies-close-affiliation-with-aiding-abetting-pkk.

27. Members of Parliament from other parties were also affected by the bill to lift parliamentary immunity.

28. "HDP, the PKK and Parliamentary Immunity."

11

Under Siege

The Turkish Armed Forces, in accordance with the constitution, have seized management of the country to reinstate democracy, human rights, and freedom, and to ensure public order, which has deteriorated.

—Coup plotters (July 15, 2016)

The Ataturk Airport in Istanbul was bombed on June 29, 2016. Forty-five people were killed and more than two hundred injured in the carnage. Turks were badly shaken by the incident that struck one of the country's most secure and iconic targets.

No organization took responsibility for the bombing; but, the attack had all the hallmarks of ISIS. It occurred during Ramadan and on the second anniversary of ISIS declaring a caliphate in Syria and Iraq. The attackers, who used automatic weapons and suicide vests were from Dagestan, Uzbekistan, and Kyrgyzstan.

Obama expressed support: "Let me just publicly extend my deepest condolences to the people of Turkey for the terrible attack that took place in Istanbul."[1] Other world leaders echoed his expression of sympathy. Despite rhetorical solidarity, Turkey found itself isolated and with few friends. Its relations with the United States were strained by Erdogan's Islamist and antidemocratic rule. Its cooperation with the EU imperiled by halting implementation of the deal to address the refugee and migrant crisis. Many Turks felt an extraordinary sense of vulnerability as a result of the attacks.

Erdogan's confrontational style did not reassure. His pugilistic approach also polarized members of Turkey's Armed Forces (TSK). Turkey has a history of military coups in 1960, 1971, 1980, and 1997. As the guardian of secular democratic rule, the military did not try to hold onto power. It engineered a political transition, often involving elections. As a protégé of Erbakan and a leading figure in the Refah

165

Party, Erdogan was directly affected by the 1997 coup. He was profoundly wary of challenges from the military.

Moreover, Egypt's coup in 2013 made a deep impression on Erdogan. The parallels are striking. Just as Egyptians were rallying for greater freedoms in Tahrir Square, Turks were gathering in Gezi Park demanding human rights. Erdogan identified with Mohammed Morsi as a kindred spirit and fraternal political ally. The AKP and the Muslim Brotherhood are cut from the same cloth. Erdogan denounced General Abdel Fattah el-Sisi for seizing control of the government, arresting Morsi, and cracking down on the Muslim Brotherhood.

Events in Egypt heightened Erdogan's concern about the TSK. Turkey's bumbling and erratic support for Islamic extremists in Syria invited blow-back from ISIS, riling the military. The unprovoked and unwinnable war against Kurds also frustrated members of the military, some of whom were accused of war crimes for killing Kurdish civilians. As the protector of Kemalism, the military objected to the AKP's Islamist government. They resented the Ergenekon and Sledgehammer affairs, which culminated in show trials of respected officers. Erdogan planned a Supreme Military Council for August 1–4, 2016, at which senior officers would be removed in a reshuffle.

Erdogan may be paranoid but, as shown by events, even paranoid people have enemies. A TSK faction tried to seize control of the government on July 15, 2016. They issued a statement: "The Turkish Armed Forces, in accordance with the constitution, have seized management of the country to reinstate democracy, human rights, and freedom, and to ensure public order, which has deteriorated." In support of Ataturk's mantra—"peace at home and peace abroad"—they announced creation of a "Peace at Home Council" to "restore democracy."[2]

Erdogan was vacationing in Marmaris on July 15. Mutinous soldiers arrived at his hotel to arrest him, but he had checked out and was on his way to the Dalaman Airport by the time they arrived. The first public inkling of the event was early evening when mechanized units of the land forces used tanks to block the Bosphorus Bridge and the Fatih Sultan Mehmet Bridge, crossing from the Asian side to the European side of Istanbul. The land forces on the bridge were joined by members of the gendarmerie, a branch of the military police. Because the tanks were blocking traffic in only one direction, Istanbulites assumed it was a counterterrorism operation. People realized there was a coup underway when helicopters and fighter jets started to streak across the skies. Their sonic boom sounded like explosions.

The coup plotters moved simultaneously to seize government build-ings in Ankara. Supported by F-16 fighter jets, they occupied the army headquarters, bombed and seized the Turkish Grand National Assem-bly (TGNA). Prominent TSK members were arrested. Chairman of the General Staff, General Hulusi Akar, and Deputy Chief of Staff General Yasar Guler were imprisoned at Akincilar air base on the outskirts of Ankara. Commander of the Land Forces General Salih Zeki Colak, Gendarmerie Commander General Galip Mendi, Commander of the Air Force General Abidin Unal, and Commander of the Turkish Naval Forces Bulent Bostanoglu were also taken into custody.[3] Hakan Fidan was rushed to a secure location during a pitched battle for control of the National Intelligence Agency (MIT) headquarters. Media was also tar-geted. *TRT*, one of the least watched national television channels, went dark, taken off the air. A helicopter landed at *CNN Turk* with soldiers storming the building during a live broadcast.[4] The coup plotters had apparently demonstrated their ability to plan and execute a rebellion, using air and ground forces, without MIT being aware.

The White House did not react immediately, calibrating its response to events on the ground. Hours after the coup, the White House issued a statement: President Obama and Secretary of State John F. Kerry "agreed that all parties in Turkey should support the democratically elected government . . . show restraint, and avoid any violence or bloodshed."[5] Kerry issued a statement of his own, indicating that he had spoken with Foreign Minister Mevlut Cavusoglu to emphasize America's "absolute support" for civilian government and democratic institutions."[6] German Chancellor Angela Merkel also weighed in. "It's tragic that so many people died during this attempted coup. The bloodshed in Turkey must stop now." She emphasized that credible political change can only be achieved via elections and through political institutions. "Tanks on the streets and air strikes against its own people are injustice," Merkel added.[7]

Erdogan disappeared during the first hours of the coup. Finally, at three in the morning, Erdogan spoke to the nation using FaceTime from the phone of a Turkish television anchor on his official plane. He called on people to take to the streets in defense of Turkey's democracy. It was ironic that Erdogan's lifeline to the Turkish public was a social media application that he had sought to silence. Communicating with supporters was a turning point.

Imams echoed Erdogan's appeal, rallying the faithful from microphones atop minarets. The chant "Allahu akbar"—"God is Great"—reverberated from the muezzins of mosques. Many thousands responded, with AKP supporters gathering at the Ataturk Airport and in Istanbul's Taksim Square. Throngs assembled outside the presidential palace in Ankara chanting, "There is no God but God." People power was a call to prayer and protest.

Erdogan made a dramatic appearance at half past three in the morning at the Istanbul airport. He stood on top of a bus and addressed an adoring crowd of supporters wrapped in Turkish flags and chanting his name. "This government, brought to power by the people, is in charge. I am here; I am with you." He declared, "Turkey is proud of you."[8]

The coup started to unravel with Erdogan's return. According to John Kerry, "It does not appear to be a very brilliantly planned or executed event."[9] The botched coup plotters made some serious mistakes. They did not kill or arrest Erdogan and Binali Yildirim. They failed to close all media, including social media. Events were broadcast in real time during the first hours of the putsch despite restricted access to Twitter, Facebook and YouTube. Both supporters and opponents of the coup broadcast images and live videos on social networks. Television news networks around the world showed confusing and contradictory images, as producers tried to make sense of the events. The coup plotters lacked support within the military to accomplish what they set out to do. They did not present someone as the face of the rebellion with assurance that order was being restored. Nor did they have domestic political or popular support. Even opposition parties, the CHP and HDP, issued statements opposing the coup. While Erdogan was calling his supporters to the streets, the coup plotters issued statements instructing people to stay indoors.

For sure, Erdogan is a polarizing figure; Turkey is deeply divided between his backers and detractors. Throughout it all, Erdogan remained hugely popular among his core constituents. Even Turks who oppose Erdogan are fundamentally against military rule. Turks do not believed that military intervention is the path to democracy. They appreciate the process of democracy even when they disagree with the results.

The blame game started immediately. Upon his return to Istanbul, Erdogan accused Fethullah Gulen of masterminding the coup. Erdogan has such disdain for Gulen that he does not refer to him by name, simply calling him "Pennsylvania." Erdogan issued a chilling threat: "This latest action is an action of treason, and they will have to pay heavily for that." He proclaimed, "This attempt, this move, is a great favor from

God for us. Why? Because this move will allow us to clean up the armed forces, which needs to be completely clean."[10] He vowed to purge "all state institutions of the virus" spread by Gulen's supporters.[11]

Erdogan blamed the insurgency on disgruntled military officers operating outside the chain of command. General Akin Ozturk, the former commander of the air force; General Adem Huduti, commander of the second army responsible for counter-terrorism in the southeast; and Lieutenant General Erdal Ozturk, commander of the third army corps in Istanbul were arrested. Commander of the Incirlik Air Force base General Bekir Ercan Van, was also arrested. General Van approached US officials to request asylum, but Washington denied his appeal.

General Umit Dundar was in close contact with Erdogan during the early hours of the coup. At a time when Erdogan did not know who to trust, Dundar was at his side, a steady hand. Sycophants and loyalists were promoted. Dundar was appointed acting military chief. He proclaimed, "[Turkey] displayed a historic cooperation between the government and the people. The nation will never forget this betrayal."[12]

Conspiracy theories are always prevalent in Turkey. The coup plotters were so inept that many saw the coup as a hoax. They believed it was staged by Erdogan so he could appear as the people's hero, rescuing democracy and using the coup to justify a crackdown on his opponents. On July 19, a *Financial Times* tweet indicated that one-third of Turks surveyed believe that Erdogan was behind the coup.[13]

However, it is difficult to imagine a hoax of such magnitude. More likely, the coup was uncovered; Erdogan let it proceed just far enough so it seemed credible, then shut it down, riding to the rescue on his white and red TK private plane. Defeating the coup was not a victory for democracy. It was a victory for Erdogan who took steps to neutralize the opposition and justify measures consolidating his dictatorship.

The coup caused considerable economic turmoil. As a result of economic uncertainty, Turkey faced the prospect of waning economic growth, a struggle to attract international investors, and financial market volatility. Undermining the rule of law also eroded investor confidence. The Borsa Istanbul 100 index closed down 7.1 percent during the first full day of trading after the coup attempt. The iShares MSCI/Turkey exchange-traded hedge fund tumbled more than 6 percent in after-hours trading. It was down 2.5 percent and the Turkish lira weakened by 4.4 percent against the dollar on the first day of trading after the coup.[14] Turkey was already facing a sizeable current account deficit, which stood at around 4.5 percent of the country's annual Gross Domestic Product (GDP) in 2015. The coup imperiled foreign direct investment and credit markets. Tourism was hit by boycotts, instability, and terror attacks. Moody's Investor Service downgraded Turkey's sovereign credit rating to non-investment grade. The junk rating resulted from concerns about external financing and prospects of Turkey's slowing economy.

More important than money lost, there was considerable loss of life. It is estimated that 312 people died during the coup attempt, including 145 civilians. At least 1,440 people were wounded.[15] Some disturbing footage surfaced of soldiers on the Bosphorus Bridge being beaten by the mob of Erdogan supporters. A ghastly ISIS-style beheading was broadcast on social media. Officers were paraded on television beaten and badly bruised.

Erdogan demanded that the United States arrest and extradite Fethullah Gulen. Kerry responded by offering US help investigating the coup. He requested that Erdogan present evidence against Gulen that "withstands scrutiny." The US Government would not apply its extradition treaty with Turkey based on allegations. The US Department of Justice would require concrete evidence linking Gulen to the coup. Kerry said, "What we need is genuine evidence that withstands the standard of scrutiny that exists in many countries. And if it meets that standard, there's no interest we have of standing in the way of appropriately honoring the treaty we have with Turkey with respect to extradition."[16] When Erdogan personally pressed Obama to extradite Gulen, Obama explained that the Justice Department processes extradition requests and it was not his decision to make.

Beyond their anger over Gulen's residency in the United States, Turkish officials accused the US of directly supporting the coup. Suleyman Soylu, the labor minister, brazenly accused the United States of plotting the coup and helping to carry it out. Despite denials from John Bass, US ambassador to Turkey, the situation became incendiary. The drumbeat of criticism fueled anti-Americanism, potentially risking the safety of US citizens in Turkey and damaging US-Turkey relations. On October 30, 2016, the families of US consulate staff in Istanbul were ordered to leave Turkey amidst mounting security concerns.

The bellicose rhetoric was so intense that Obama called Erdogan to assure him that the United States was not involved. When accusations continued, Obama issued a public denial: "Any reports that we had any previous knowledge of a coup attempt, that there was any US involvement in it, that we were anything other than entirely supportive of Turkish democracy are completely false."[17] Obama affirmed his support for Turkish "democracy," yet the United States and the EU grew increasingly concerned about extra-judicial actions that targeted coup plotters and opponents of the regime.

Turkey declared a three-month state of emergency, giving the government extraordinary powers, bypassing parliament and ruling by decree. The state of emergency was extended for a second three-month period, as the crackdown intensified.

As of November 2016, more than 40,000 people were detained or arrested since the coup. More than 100,000 people were dismissed from state institutions including the judiciary, military, and security forces.

Roughly one-third of the 220 brigadier generals and 10 major generals were detained. One third of all admirals were arrested. Many majors and lieutenant colonels were taken into custody. About six thousand soldiers of various ranks, mostly conscript privates, were imprisoned and about nine thousand police officers dismissed.

The education sector was decimated. About 21,000 teachers were suspended or fired. An additional 11,000 Kurdish educators were suspended for suspected links to the PKK. 1,577 university deans were forced to resign. The state of emergency undermined meritocracy; Erdogan was given authority to appoint university heads.

The rule of law was undermined. 2,754 judges were dismissed, including members of the High Council of Judges and Prosecutors. A member of the Constitutional Court was arrested and charged with collusion. Ten members of Turkey's highest administrative court were detained. At least thirty governors were fired. Under new state of emergency provisions, prosecutors were given permission to record lawyer-client conversations, and judges were empowered to deny the accused access to a lawyer for up to 3 months." The World Justice Index placed Turkey 99th out of 113 countries in its rule of law ranking, behind Iran and Myanmar."

Freedom of expression was a major victim. Arrest warrants were issued for 120 journalists. A total of 160 news sources were closed during 3 months following the coup, including 15 Kurdish news outlets. The only Kurdish- language daily newspaper was shut down. Turkey gained the dubious distinction as the largest jailer of journalists of any country in the world."

Additionally, civil society was targeted. The Ministry of Interior revoked the passports of 49,211 Turkish citizens.[18] Private property was confiscated and retirement benefits canceled.

Washington pressed Turkey to follow the rule of law and maintain democratic principles. Kerry warned, "There must be no arbitrary purges, no criminal sanctions outside the framework of the rule of law and the justice system."[19] Kerry was in regular contact with Cavusoglu who repeatedly assured him that the government would respect democracy and the rule of law. Nonetheless, Kerry warned that NATO would "measure" Turkey's actions. He also raised the possibility of reviewing Turkey's NATO membership. Kerry said, "NATO also has a requirement with respect to democracy." He warned that the North Atlantic Council would be scrutinizing Turkey to make sure it adheres to the Alliance's standard of democratic governance. "Obviously, a lot of people have been arrested and arrested very quickly. The level of vigilance and scrutiny is obviously going to be significant in the days ahead. Hopefully we can work in a constructive way that prevents a backsliding." State Department Spokesman John Kirby backtracked, "It's too soon to say that their membership is at risk."[20]

Erdogan further roiled relations with the international community by suggesting that Turkey might reinstate the death penalty, which it abolished in 2004. At a huge "Democracy and Martyrs Rally," Erdogan said he would support capital punishment if the country's parliament voted to bring it back. The prospect of executions was abhorrent to the European Commission, which denies EU membership to any country that allows capital punishment. To the EU, a country's position on the death penalty is a litmus test of its commitment to human rights and rule of law.

Virtually every EU member state expressed grave concern. At a meeting of the European Council attended by twenty-eight foreign ministers on July 18, EU foreign policy chief Federica Mogherini affirmed, "No country can become a partner state if it introduces the death penalty." She added, "We call for the full observance of Turkey's constitutional order and we, as the EU, stress the importance of the rule of law. We need to have Turkey respect democracy, human rights and fundamental freedoms." Johannes Hahn, Austria's EU commissioner, regretted Erdogan's crackdown. "[It] is absolutely unacceptable. It is exactly what we feared." The mass arrests of judges looked "like something that had been prepared." French Foreign Minister Jean-Marc Ayrault reproached Erdogan from becoming more "authoritarian." He indicated, "We must be vigilant that Turkish authorities don't put in place a political system which turns against democracy." Luxembourg's Foreign Minister Jean Asselborn warned that relations between Turkey and the EU could be "destroyed" if Erdogan launches a witch hunt and indiscriminate crackdown against opponents.[21]

The possibility of a more intense crackdown loomed. A police intelligence official privately warned that Erdogan was plotting a second coup to "further consolidate his power." A second coup would demonstrate to Turkish public opinion that "we still have this threat." It would be used by Erdogan to complete his "transformation of Turkey.[22]

The "EU Turkey Progress Report" was issued on November 9, 2016. The report expressed grave concern about the rule of law and backsliding of fundamental freedoms. It highlighted "legislative amendments introduced by decree." It discussed the "derogation from [Turkey's] obligation to serve a number of fundamental rights protected by the European Convention on Human Rights." The report noted, "very extensive and surprising dismissals, arrests, and detentions" after the coup attempt. The crackdown "affected the whole spectrum of society with particular respect to the judiciary, police, gendarmerie, military, civil service, local authorities, academia, teachers, lawyers, the media and business community." It noted that "private companies were shut down, their assets seized or transferred to public institutions." Turkey was criticized for lifting the "law on the immunity of deputies leading to the arrest and detention of HDP co-chairs," as well as "human rights violations and the disproportionate use of force in the southeast" targeting civilians.[23] On November 24, 2016, the European Parliament voted to suspend talks with Turkey on EU membership.

Beyond their principled commitment to the rule of law, Europeans had practical concerns. They feared that Erdogan's crackdown would unleash a new wave of refugees fleeing inhospitable conditions in Turkey. The EU-Turkey deal on the return of Syrian refugees from Greece to Turkey would be cancelled if Turkey reinstated the death penalty. Refugees could refuse their deportation to Turkey, arguing that it would be unsafe and in violation of international humanitarian law. Turkey was already labeled an "unsafe country" by Amnesty International for its treatment of refugees and migrants. Post-coup conditions exacerbated security concerns. If the deal unraveled, a new wave of refugees crossing the Mediterranean to Greece could result.

The coup caused concern for the US–led multinational coalition fighting ISIS. Washington worried that Erdogan's witch hunt could undermine Turkey's participation in military operations. Right after the coup, Turkey arrested the commander of Incirlik Air Force Base, suspended all air operations out of Incirlik, and closed its airspace to military aircraft. It cut off electricity supplies to Incirlik for a week, forcing US personnel to use emergency generators. Though these measures were short-lived, Washington feared a more systemic problem. Would Erdogan be more focused on hunting down the coup plotters than targeting ISIS? Would Erdogan target the kurds, US allies in Syria under the guise of fighting terrorism? Would Turkey's military, fractured by forced retirements and arrests, have the will or capacity to engage jihadists?

The groundswell of Islamist fervor exacerbated Washington's security concerns. In the past, Erdogan tried to veil his support for Islamism in order to appear in conformity with secular standards. The coup pushed Erdogan's Islamism to the fore. And he made no effort to hide it. Erdogan summoned his pious followers to confront the coup while it was unfolding. In the days after the coup, eighty-five thousand mosques across Turkey blared a Muslim prayer for martyrs and called on the people to stay in the streets to guard against resurgent coup plotters. There are usually five calls to prayer at set times each day. The muezzins were constantly invoking civic action, reminding devotees that it was their political duty to support Erdogan.[24] Soner Cagaptay queried in *The Wall Street Journal*: "This is Turkey's Iran 1979 moment—will a brewing Islamic revolution overwhelm the forces of secularism?"[25]

Notes

1. R. Shabad, "Obama: 'We Stand with the People of Turkey' after Terror Attack," *CBSNews*, June 29, 2016, accessed July 9, 2016, http://www.cbsnews.com/news/obama-phones-turkish-president-after-istanbul-terror-attack/.
2. E. Cunningham, L. Sly, and Z. Karatas, "Erdogan Says His Government Is in Control after Bloody Coup Attempt in Turkey," *Washington Post*, July 16, 2016, accessed July 18, 2016, https://www.washingtonpost.com/world/turkeys-prime-minister-says-military-attempted-coup-against-government/2016/07/15/1709b04a-4ac6-11e6-8dac-0c6e4accc5b1_story.html.
3. M. Gurcan, "Why Turkey's Coup Didn't Stand a Chance," *Al Monitor: Turkey Pulse*, July 17, 2016, accessed July 18, 2016, http://www.al-monitor.com/pulse/originals/2016/07/turkey-kamikaze-coup-attempt-fails.html#ixzz4EmbcznrD.

4. Z. Bar'el, "Deep Rifts in Turkey Military Brass Boil Over Into Coup Attempt," *Haaretz*, July 16, 2016, accessed July 16, 2016, http://www.haaretz.com/middle-east-news/turkey/1.731265.

5. K. DeYoung, "The Coup in Turkey, Even if it Fails, Could Lead to Uncertainty in Anti-ISIS Fight," *The Washington Post*, July 15, 2016, accessed July 16, 2016, https://www.washingtonpost.com/world/national-security/the-coup-in-turkey-even-if-it-fails-could-lead-to-uncertainty-in-anti-isis-fight/2016/07/15/d5d181b4-4ae0-11e6-acbc-4d4870a079da_story.html.

6. Ibid.

7. A. Yuhas, J. Grierson, C. Phipps, S. Levin, and K. Rawlinson, "Turkey Coup Attempt: Erdogan Demands US Arrest Exiled Cleric Gülen Amid Crackdown on Army – As it Happened," *The Guardian*, July 16, 2016, accessed July 16, 2016, ttps://www.theguardian.com/world/live/2016/jul/15/turkey-coup-attempt-military-gunfire-ankara?CMP=Share_AndroidApp_Email.

8. Cunningham, Sly, and Karatas, "Erdogan Says His Government Is in Control after Bloody Coup Attempt in Turkey."

9. M. Fisher and A. Taub, "Turkey Was an Unlikely Victim of an Equally Unlikely Coup," *The New York Times*, July 16, 2016, accessed July 17, 2016, http://www.nytimes.com/2016/07/17/world/europe/turkey-was-an-unlikely-victim-of-an-equally-unlikely-coup.html?_r=0.

10. T. Arango and C. Yeginsu, "Turkey Cracks Down as Coup Unravels," July 17, 2016, *The New York Times*, A1.

11. T. Arango and C. Yeginsu, "Erdogan Triumphs but Turkey's Fate is Unclear," July 18, 2016, *The New York Times*, A1.

12. W. Worley and H. Cockburn, "Prime Minister Says 265 People Killed in Attempted Military Coup, Including at Least 100 'Plotters'," *Independent*, July 16, 2016, accessed July 17, 2016, http://www.independent.co.uk/news/world/europe/turkey-coup-dead-erdogan-military-chief-ankara-istanbul-death-toll-plotters-how-many-killed-wounded-a7140376.html.

13. Financial Times, twitter post, July 19, 2016, accessed August 1, 2016, https://twitter.com/ft/status/755505003985530880.

14. S. Fraser and P. Pylas, "Turkey Economy Facing Fresh Problems after Coup Attempt," *USNews*, July 18, 2016, accessed July 19, 2016, from http://www.usnews.com/news/business/articles/2016-07-18/turkey-economy-facing-fresh-problems-after-coup-attempt.

15. Worley and Cockburn, "Prime Minister Says 265 People Killed in Attempted Military Coup."

16. K. Morello, "Kerry Urges Turkey to Maintain Democratic Principles after Coup Attempt," *The Washington Post*, July 18, 2016, accessed July 18, 206, https://www.washingtonpost.com/world/kerry-warns-turkey-nato-membership-potentially-at-stake-in-crackdown/2016/07/18/f427ba8a-4850-11e6-8dac-0c6e4accc5b1_story.html.

17. Mark Landler, "Obama Denies U.S. Involvement in Coup Attempt in Turkey," *The New York Times*, July 23, 2016, A8.

18. Ceylan Yeginsu. The New York Times. "Turkey Detains Prominent Opposition Journalists. October 31,2016. http://www.cnn.com/20 16/09 /08/wo rld/tu rkey- teache rs-su spe nded/ (accessed November 7, 2016).

19. Morello, "Kerry Urges Turkey to Maintain Democratic Principles after Coup Attempt."

20. E. Cunningham and H. Naylor, "Turkish Authorities Expand Massive Purge of Opponents Following Coup Attempt," *The Washington Post*, July 18, 2016, accessed July 18, 2016, https://www.washingtonpost.com/world/turkish-purges-spread-to-police-forces-in-the-wake-of-quashed-coup/2016/07/18/b31b37de-4cb9-11e6-aa14-e0c1087f7583_story.html?tid=a_inl.

21. Ibid.

22. Anonymous interview by the author with a police intelligence official, October 14, 2016.

23. ec.europa.eu/enlargement/pdf/key.../2016/2:"0161109_report_turkey.pdf (accessed November 25, 2016).

24. T. Arango and C. Yeginsu, "Erdogan Triumphs but Turkey's Fate Is Unclear," *The New York Times*, July 18, 2016, A1.

25. S. Cagaptay, "Turkey Faces Its Iran 1979 Moment," July 17, 2016, *The Wall Street Journal*, accessed June 17, 2016, http://www.wsj.com/articles/turkey-faces-its-iran-1979-moment-1468797632.

12

Ending Exceptionalism

An Erdogan government restored to power will be even more prickly and paranoid than before. The man is going to be more autocratic than ever" (July 15). God seems to be on their side. They pray more and praise him more" (July 16). "I can't find my way out of this country. We are not allowed to travel outside (July 17). I am under risk and face unemployment. There are massive purges and I may be arrested if my name is on the list" (July 18). "The state of emergency makes it easy to purge those who do not support the government" (July 19). "There has never been such uncertainty. We will eventually move out and make a clean break. Thank you for your precious comradery. You cannot know how much it is appreciated" (July 20).

—E-mail messages from a well-known Turkish scholar scheduled to visit Columbia University for the fall semester of 2016

Erdogan had a choice after the failed coup attempt. He could either use the incident to reconcile with opponents, uniting Turks in common cause and service to the country, or he could crack down. Erdogan previously became more autocratic when under pressure. He was dismissive of the Gezi Park protests and the 2013 corruption investigation. Predictably, Erdogan doubled own after the failed coup attempt, unleashing his "inner Stalin."

Erdogan transformed Turkey into a giant gulag. The state of emergency further undermined the rule of law. Legitimate forms of dissent were denied. International travel was restricted. Background checks identified purported oppositionists and sought to link them with the Gulen movement. The post-coup period was manipulated by Erdogan to boost his cult of personality and foster a shallow national unity. Deputies with the National Action Party (MHP) vowed to support the executive presidency.

US policy cannot be based on wishful thinking. It must consider Turkey as it is, not as it was or how we wish it to be. US administrations have coddled Turkey for decades. Post-coup, US officials groveled to appease Erdogan in a fruitless effort to silence his spurious claims of Washington's complicity. Their actions were taken by Erdogan as a green light to intensify his crack down.

US-Turkey relations are at a crossroads. Washington can handle Turkey with kid gloves or, end Turkish exceptionalism. The 2016 presidential election provides an opportunity for a reset in US-Turkey relations. A reset does not mean ignoring Erdogan's cries.

A High Level Cooperation Council (HLCC) could be established to institutionalize and deepen collaboration in critical bilateral fields such as trade, energy, counterterrorism, and human rights. The council would meet twice each year, once in Ankara and once in Washington. Launched at a summit attended by the Turkish and US presidents, the council would be co-chaired by the US secretary of state and Turkey's foreign minister. It would complement day-to-day interaction, serving as a platform for discussing issues of mutual concern:

Counterterrorism

The United States needs a "Plan B" for fighting ISIS, given volatility in Turkey and the mass arrests of Turkish military officers. Plan B would involve diversified air combat operations using British bases in Cyprus—Akrotiri and Dhekelia. Bombing raids against ISIS targets in Iraq and Syria could also be launched from the Erbil base in Iraqi Kurdistan, which is currently limited to surveillance. The need to diversify air operations beyond Incirlik became apparent after the coup when Turkey effectively closed the base. Rumors that Ankara and Moscow were negotiating Incirlik as a staging ground for Russian warplanes exacerbated concerns about Turkey's reliability as a NATO member, especially in light of Russia's illegal annexation of Crimea and potential threats to NATO members who, under Article 5, the Alliance is obligated to protect.

In 2016, Turkey took steps to limit border crossings between Gaziantep and Kilis in Turkey and Jarablus and al-Rai areas in Syria. Turkey built a wall to limit the travel of jihadis. As of September 2016, the wall still had a major gap, and the border was still porous. Under the guise of assisting the Free Syrian Army, Turkey continued to support jihadists with artillery weapons, and logistics. Sealing the border is not a technical problem. It is a strategic choice and a matter of political will. The international community can verify Erdogan's assurances by working with Turkey to post monitors on the Turkish side of the border, verifying that the border is sealed.

Syria's Civil War

As of November 2016, there was no end in sight to Syria's grinding civil war. Pouring weapons and fighters into Syria only sustains and complicates the conflict, which so far has killed more than four hundred thousand people and displaced at least eleven million. Conditions in Aleppo during the fall of 2016 dramatized the urgent humanitarian needs of all sides. The United States, Turkey, and many countries want Assad to go. Realistically, his overthrow or departure is unlikely with Russia and Iran providing a lifeline. The inevitable result will be a political transition, preserving a role for Assad's Alawite circle. It will also involve a plan and timetable for Assad to step down and hold elections. Syria's future constitution would enshrine decentralization, enabling local control over government, economy, and resources. Though Syria's regions are not homogeneous, the governing group will control Damascus and territories North and West including Latakia. Kurds will consolidate self-rule in Rojava and Sunni Arabs will control the rest of Syria's territory. Allowing Assad to stay in power for the short term will be a bitter pill for Assad's opponents, but it is the only way forward.

Syrian Kurds

A power-sharing agreement for Syria must involve Syrian Kurds who represent at least 10 percent of Syria's population. To this end, Erdogan should end efforts to isolate the Democratic Union Party (PYD) diplomatically by preventing its participation in UN-sponsored talks in Geneva. The United States should intensify its security, economic, humanitarian, and political cooperation with Syrian Kurds. Acquiescing to Turkey's demands circumscribes Washington's influence over the course of events in Syria. The United States has no friends in Syria, except the PYD.

The Istanbul airport attack underlined that ISIS is the greatest threat to Turkey—not the Kurds. Instead of vilifying the People's Protection Units (YPG), Erdogan should make them partners in Turkey's regional security strategy. Operation Euphrates Shield was more aimed at limiting ambitions of the Syrian Kurds than attacking ISIS. By targeting the YPG, Erdogan tried to make the United States choose between Turkey and the PYD. However, the YPG is America's best ally in Syria. Erdogan's attempt to drive a wedge between the United States and the YPG raises a real question: Is Turkey or the PYG more reliable in the fight against ISIS?

Kurdistan Workers' Party

Erdogan is quick to blame the PKK for attacks against civilians in Turkey. However, Kurdish militants almost never kill foreigners or civilians. They typically target security forces and regime symbols. All sides must accept that there is no military solution to Turkey's Kurdish issue. Negotiations represent the only way forward. A mutual ceasefire existed until July 2015. The parties should return to the negotiating table with talks aimed at a cessation of hostilities, which would create conditions for realizing sustainable peace.

Turkey can build confidence in the peace process by investigating war crimes committed against civilians in Cizre and other municipalities in the Southeast, and prosecuting the perpetrators. If Turkey is unable or unwilling, then the UN High Commissioner for Human Rights should establish a commission of inquiry. Given the likelihood that Russia would obstruct the ICC or block the establishment of a special tribunal by the UN Security Council, the EU could take the lead by establishing.

The United States can also advance the cause of peace by initiating a review of the PKK's classification as a foreign terrorist organization (FTO). Delisting the PKK would marginalize more extremist groups like the Kurdistan Freedom Falcons. Delisting could be an impetus for negotiations. In other situations, more heinous groups than the PKK have been declassified as part of their reintegration into society and transformation into nonviolent political movements. Erdogan will strongly object if the United States delists the PKK, but vilifying the PKK is a disincentive to peace talks and a political agreement.

Human Rights

Turkey's human rights record was abysmal before the coup. Its extrajudicial activities since have undermined all pretense of democracy or by the rule of law. Torture violates the Geneva Conventions. Dismissing civil servants and educators betrays standards of decency. Turkey's EU candidacy will be canceled if it adopts the death penalty. In the context of Turkey's EU accession process and annual progress report, the European Commission should publish a report on gross violations of human rights and international humanitarian law in Turkey. The assessment should systematically assess items in the Turkish Penal Code and Constitution that are out of step with European norms and international standards. Article 301 of the Penal Code and Article 8 of the Anti-Terror Act should be withdrawn. Restrictions on Facebook and Twitter should end. The prosecutor should drop cases against HDP parliamentarians and the TGNA should restore the parliamentary immunity of HDP members and other deputies who are innocent of capital crimes. If Turkey continues its aggression against Kurdish regions in the Southeast, it will lose its right to govern. Then the discussion will go beyond human rights to include self-determination, raising the possibility of separating North Kurdistan from the clutches of Turkey's dictatorship.

Corruption

Corruption has a corrosive effect on democracy, while undermining faith of the electorate in the integrity of politicians. Erdogan can distinguish his presidency for clean government by giving a major public address vowing transparency and the rule of law. He would announce financial disclosure requirements for the president, his cabinet, senior officials from all the major parties, as well as media owners. In addition, Erdogan's family members would be required to place their assets in a blind trust. They would be prevented from business transactions during the term of Erdogan's presidency and for a period of one year after he steps down as president.

Reza Zarrab, a dual Turkish-Iranian national with close ties to Erdogan, was arrested at the Miami International Airport in May 2016. The US attorney in charge of prosecuting the case, Preet Bharara, has promised to expose Zarrab's money laundering and gold sales, which sought to evade sanctions on Iran. Zarrab may testify against Erdogan, his son Bilal, and Erdogan's inner circle. Erdogan's allegations about Washington's support for the coup and his attacks on the Department of Justice (DoJ) for refusing to extradite Fethullah Gulen are preemptive measures to discredit the DoJ in case Zarrab cooperats with the US attorney. The US Attorney should issue a superseding indictment that names Zarrab, Turkish officials, Erdogan family members, and friends who have broken US law, laundered money, or evaded Iran sanctions. Turkey's compliance with the superseding indictment would be required before acting on its request that the United States extradite Gulen.

Regional Reconciliation

The Istanbul airport attack came days after Erdogan sent a letter of apology to the family of the dead Russian Pilot, with the hope of putting Turkish-Russian relations back on track. Erdogan's meeting with

Vladimir Putin in St. Petersburg on August 9, 2016, ended a nine-month chill in Turkish-Russian relations. However, the rapprochement is transactional. It may be a tactic for Erdogan to gain leverage over the United States or to ensure that Turkey has a seat at the table for negotiations on Syria's future. Russia and Turkey still support different sides in Syria's civil war. Downing of the Russian plane won't be easily forgotten.

The same day that Erdogan wrote the pilot's family, Ankara announced normalization of relations with Israel, which apologized and paid restitution for the *Mavi Marmara* incident. Though these arrangements mark a new chapter in Turkey-Israel relations, Israelis are still aggrieved by Turkey's support for Hamas and Erdogan's hostility towards Israeli leaders.

Other reconciliation opportunities exist with Greece and Armenia. Turkey should intensify its support to resurrect negotiations on Cyprus. The deal terms are clear. Reopening the Halki seminary, improving working conditions for the Holy Patriarch in Istanbul, and restitution for properties seized from minorities would be important confidence-building measures.

Erdogan should apologize for the Armenian Genocide and end Turkey's denial campaign. The US president should also do as President Reagan did in 1982 and unequivocally characterize the events as "genocide." Despite the fact that Turkish and Armenian civil society are talking about the Armenian Genocide, Erdogan is unlikely to utter the "G-word." He has stonewalled ratification of the Protocol on Normalization and the Protocol on Diplomatic Relations between the Republic of Turkey and the Republic of Armenia. Opening the border to normal travel and trade would be a first step with practical benefits for both sides, advancing reconciliation at a people-to-people level.

The "Zero Problems with Neighbors" policy is a worthy goal, which can be achieved with sincere, sympathetic, and skillful diplomacy. Erdogan engaged in a blame game, accusing Ahmet Davutoglu of bungling diplomacy, which has led to Turkey's deteriorating relations in the region. Tensions are not Davutoglu's fault. Erdogan makes the decisions and should bear the responsibility.

It is unlikely that Erdogan will accept constructive advice. He is not known for humility and contrition. He does not admit fault or take counsel. Some suggest a more confrontational approach. They propose that Turkey be evicted from NATO. But this is too drastic under current circumstances. Anyhow, there is no mechanism in the North Atlantic Charter to evict a member. NATO's founders never envisioned a day when a member state would turn against the Alliance, either violating its security commitments or embracing dictatorship.

Erdogan is feigning rapprochement with Russia as leverage over NATO. False pretenses are a dangerous game. Nuclear weapons are based in Turkey. Turkey-Russia cooperation raises profound doubt about Turkey's reliability as a NATO member. How will Turkey respond if Russia invades the Baltic States or Poland? Will it act with its NATO allies or try to undermine unity in the Alliance? Ukraine is another flash point. NATO has been unanimous condemning Russia's seizure of Crimea and aggression against Eastern Ukraine. If conflict escalates in Ukraine, will Turkey act with NATO or against it?

John Kerry underscored the democracy commitment of NATO members. He rightly affirmed that NATO is more than a security alliance. It is a coalition of countries with shared values. There is a way to systematize concerns, short of evicting Turkey. The North Atlantic Alliance could establish a criteria-compliance review process. Verifiers would use Charter commitments as benchmarks and develop a scorecard evaluating performance. Turkey would not be the only country under review. Other Member States, such as Hungary, warrant scrutiny. NATO membership would be suspended if a country received a failing grade for consecutive years.

Critics also propose suspending Turkey's EU accession talks. Mogherini stated clearly that Turkey would be excluded from membership if it implemented the death penalty. Unless Turkey crosses clear red lines, like adopting the death penalty or committing summary executions, it would be better to keep Turkey as a candidate. Excluding it would be manipulated by ultranationalists to galvanize anti-Europe sentiment. Moreover, the EU accession process is known as a motivator of reform. Aspirant countries align with European values and adjust their policies to meet the terms of the "acquis communautaire." Excluding Turkey from either NATO or denying its European prospective would limit the West's leverage. The West's relationship with Turkey should be based on policies not personalities. Erdogan is not Turkey. He will not be in power forever. The European Parliament's vote to suspend accession negotiations is a shot across the bow.

The United States wants Turkey in the tent. Engagement is critical to overcoming differences. The United States and Turkey have a long track record of working together. It is undeniable, however, that the relationship is changing. Erdogan accused the United States of playing a role in the coup and blames Washington for failing to extradite Fethullah

Gulen. However, Turkey did not provide any actionable evidence to justify Gulen's extradition. Erdogan's accusations are inflammatory and reckless. Erdogan says one thing to the Turkish public, whipping them into a fervor of anti-Americanism, while Turkish officials are more conciliatory during private discussions with US counterparts. Duplicitous diplomacy among allies is tantamount to betrayal.

What will be Erdogan's legacy? Erdogan warned Egypt's President Hosni Mubarak during protests in Tahrir Square; "No government can survive against the will of its people. We are all passing, and we will be judged by what we left behind."[1]

Erdogan has presided over an economic boom since the AKP's election in 2002. He wants to be remembered for Turkey's national economic recovery and expansion, making Turkey a force in the G-20. Erdogan wants to be remembered for engineering an end to Syria's civil war, preserving Syria's sovereignty, ending the bloodshed, and removing Assad via democratic elections. He wants to be remembered for making peace with the Kurds, bringing to an end Turkey's civil war that has cost forty thousand lives since the 1980s.

Turkey is a deeply divided country. Turks have to decide what they want. Do Turks choose dictatorship or freedom? Do they prefer war without end waged against minorities and neighbors, or to live in peace? Do Turks prefer intolerance or pluralism where diversity is a strength? Do they want free markets or cleptocracy? Do Turks prefer Islamist governance or a country that tolerates differences?

William Shakespeare wrote in *Julius Caesar*, "The evil that men do lives after them; the good is oft interred with their bones." Erdogan can hold on to power through coercion and conflict. He can stoke the flames of violent conflict in Syria. Or he can pursue reforms and peace. The latter is probably wishful thinking. There is nothing in Erdogan's character or recent conduct to suggest he will take the high road of conciliation.

I have visited Turkey more than forty times. I have many Turkish friends whom I admire and respect. Turks are hospitable and kind. The Turks I know are modern and progressive. Kurds in Turkey are dignified and noble, even in their suffering. They believe the peaceful path to a brighter future goes through Europe.

Turks are lately afflicted by *huzun*. It is a Turkish term, which means melancholy, loss, and sadness. In its extreme, *huzun* implies a deep spiritual anguish.[2] Erdogan's crackdown after the coup reinforced a sense of powerlessness. Melancholy and despair have become pervasive. Demonstrations of unity are shallow and transitory.

I, too, am afflicted with *huzun*. Having spent decades of my career as a scholar, activist, and US official working on Turkey, I am deeply saddened by current trends. WikiLeaks published a collection of internal AKP email messages. It seems the Turkish government was monitoring my writings. I was identified in fourteen emails as a "prominent individual shaping American foreign policy" who "betrayed" Turkey by offering prescriptions for peace with the PKK. A Turkish friend wrote me, "Don't go to Turkey. You may be arrested or beaten up by pro-government gangs." She added, "After your book comes out, you can't even connect through Istanbul. Be careful, be safe." A member of the police intelligence division warned, "They will find some way of keeping you there."

Recep Tayyip Erdogan was initially a breath of fresh air. His appearance on the political scene marked a new chapter for Turkey, an opportunity for renewal, peace, and prosperity. His domestic supporters and admirers around the world, myself included, heralded his rise. But like any politician who stays in power too long, Erdogan was corrupted by his authority. Few Turks supported the coup. They know from experience that a military junta does not strengthen democracy. Erdogan's crackdown after the coup instilled fear and despair among Turks. Erdogan, the street kid from Kasimpasa betrayed their hopes for "peace at home and peace abroad."

Notes

1. David L. Phillips, "Why Are Turks so Angry?," *The World Policy*, June 11, 2013, accessed August 3, 2016, http://www.worldpolicy.org/blog/2013/06/11/why-are-turks-so-angry?page=1.
2. Tim Arango, "In Istanbul, Optimism Fades to Melancholy," *The New York Times*, July 19, 2016, p. A9.

Acronyms

ANAP	Motherland Party
AKP	Justice and Development Party
BDP	Peace and Democracy Party
CENTCOM	US Central Command
CHP	Republican People's Party
CPI	Corruption Perceptions Index
CW	Chemical Weapons
DOJ	Department of Justice
DTP	Democratic Society Party
DYP	True Path Party
EP	European Parliament
EU	European Union
FTA	Free Trade Agreement
FTO	Foreign Terrorist Organization
FSA	Free Syrian Army
GCC	Gulf Cooperation Council
GDP	Gross Domestic Product
GWOT	Global War on Terror
HADEP	People's Democracy Party
HDP	Peoples' Democratic Party
HEP	Kurdish People's Labor Party
HIMARS	High Mobility Artillery Rocket System
HLCC	High-Level Cooperation Council
HLSCC	High-Level Strategic Cooperation Council
IBDA-C	Great Eastern Islamic Raiders' Front
IHH	Humanitarian Relief Foundation
IDF	Israeli Defense Forces
IMF	International Monetary Fund
ITF	Iraqi Turkmen Front
ISAF	International Security Assistance Force
ISF	Iraqi Security Forces

ISIS	Islamic State in Iraq and Syria
ISIL	Islamic State in Iraq and the Levant
JCS	Joint Chiefs of Staff
KADEK	Kurdistan Freedom and Democracy Congress
KCK	Kurdish Communities Union
KONGRA-GEL	Kurdistan People's Congress
KRG	Kurdistan Regional Government
MB	Muslim Brotherhood
MEPs	Members of the European Parliament
MoU	Memorandum of Understanding
MIT	National Intelligence Agency
MHP	National Action Party
MSP	National Salvation Party
NATO	North Atlantic Treaty Organization
NSC	National Security Council
OPCW	Organization for the Prohibition of Chemical Weapons
PJAK	Free Life Party of Kurdistan
PKK	Kurdistan Workers' Party
PYD	Democratic Union Party in Syria
RTUK	Supreme Council of Radio and Television
SNC	Syrian National Council
SOFA	Status of Forces Agreement
TAK	Kurdistan Freedom Falcons
TGNA	Turkish Grand National Assembly
TIB	Telecommunications Directorate
TSK	Turkish Armed Forces
TGS	Turkish General Staff
UN	United Nations
UNSC	United Nations Security Council
YPG	People's Protection Units
YPJ	Women's Protection Units
YPG-H	Patriotic Revolutionary Youth Movement
YDG-H	The Patriotic Revolutionary Youth Movement

Glossary of Individuals
(as of September 01, 2016)

Abden Fattah el-Sissi is a general who removed Mohamed Morsi from power and became the president of Egypt in 2014.

Abdullah Gul was the pioneer of the Reformist Movement in the Virtue Party and was one of the founders of AKP. He was prime minister in 2002–2003, foreign minister from 2003 to 2007, and served as the eleventh president of the Turkish Republic from 2007 to 2014.

Abdullah Ocalan founded the Kurdistan Workers' Party (PKK) in 1978. He was arrested in 1999 and jailed at Imrali Prison. His followers referred to him as "Apo," which means uncle.

Abu Bakr was Prophet Mohammed's companion, who was elected the first caliph.

Ahmet Davutoglu is an academic who served as foreign minister of Turkey from 2009 to 2014. He became the prime minister in August 2014 and was removed in May 2016.

Ahmet Erdogan is Recep Tayyip Erdogan's father and a member of Turkey's coast guard.

Ahmet Necdet Sezer served as the president of Turkey from 2002 to 2007 and president of the Constitutional Court from 1998 to 2000.

Ahmet Turk was a member of the Turkish Grand National Assembly who chaired the former center-left, pro-Kurdish Democratic Society Party (DTP) in Turkey, and was stripped of his parliamentary immunity.

Ali Babacan is the former deputy prime minister in charge of the economy in Turkey. From 2007 to 2009, he served as the minister of foreign affairs.

Ali ibn Abi Talib was the fourth caliph. He was Prophet Mohammed's cousin, son-in-law, and blood relative.

Asma Assad is the wife of Syrian President Bashar al-Assad.

Avigdor Lieberman is Israel's defense minister who served as Israel's minister of foreign affairs from 2009 to 2015.

Aydin Dogan is a Turkish billionaire who owns properties and media outlets such as *Hurriyet, Posta*, and *CNN Turk*.

Aysel Tugluk was co-chair of the Democratic Society Party (DTP), who was stripped of her parliamentary immunity in 2009 when the party was banned.

Barack Obama was the forty-fourth president of the United States.

Bashar al-Assad has been president of Syria and commander-in-chief of the Syrian armed forces since 2000. He is also the general secretary of the ruling Ba'ath Party. He is the son of former Syrian President Hafez al-Assad.

Bekir Ercam Van was the commander of the Incirlik Air Base. He at the base were arrested after the coup attempt in July 2016.

Benyamin Netanyahu is the prime minister of Israel.

Berat Albayrak is Erdogan's son-in-law and the energy and natural resources minister since November 2015. He is the former CEO of Calik Holding.

Besir Atalay was Turkey's deputy prime minister between 2011 and 2014 and interior minister between 2007 and 2011.

Bilal Erdogan is a Turkish businessman and second son of Recep Tayyip Erdogan.

Binali Yildirim is a founding member of the AKP and close ally of Erdogan. He served as prime minister of Turkey beginning 2015.

Brett McGurk is the Special US Presidential Envoy for the Global Coalition to Counter ISIL.

Bulent Arinc served five years as speaker of the Turkish Grand National Assembly and seven years as deputy prime minister. Arinc was a prominent member of the old guard who led the "reformist movement" during the late 1990s. He retired from public office in November 2015.

Bulent Tezcan serves as the vice president of the Republican People's Party (CHP) since 2012.

Can Dundar was editor-in-chief of *Cumhurriyet*. He was prosecuted for reporting on Turkey's transfer of weapons to ISIS in Syria.

Cengiz Candar is a well-respected Turkish journalist, senior columnist, and a Middle East expert.

Colin Powell served in several senior military and civilian positions, including US secretary of state from 2001 to 2005.

Condolleeza Rice served as national security adviser from 2001 to 2005 before becoming US secretary of state.

David Petraeus is a retired US general who served in Iraq and went on to become director of the Central Intelligence Agency between September 2011 and November 2012.

Dick Cheney served as the forty-sixth vice president of United States. from 2001 to 2009. He was secretary of defense during the Gulf War.

Dmitry Medvedev is Russia's current prime minister, who was president from 2008 to 2014.

Efkan Ala is the minister of the interior in Turkey since November 2015.

Egemen Bagis is a member of the TGNA since 2002. As the former European Union affairs minister, he was the chief negotiator of Turkey in accession talks with the European Union.

Ehud Olmert was Israel's premier who worked with Recep Tayyip Erdogan to facilitate negotiations with Syria's Bashar al-Assad.

Emine Erdogan is the wife of Recep Tayyip Erdogan.

Erdogan Bayraktar is the former environment and urban planning minister, whom Erdogan dismissed in 2013.

Faisal I bin Hussein bin Ali al-Hashim was a member of the Hashemite dynasty and the king of Iraq from 1921 to 1933.

Federica Mogherini is an Italian politician and the current high representative of the European Union for foreign affairs and security policy and vice-president of the European Commission in the Juncker Commission since November 2014.

Fethullah Gulen is a Turkish Muslim preacher residing in Pennsylvania. He is leader of a movement called "Hizmet", which founded thousands of schools in Turkey and around the world. Erdogan accused Gulen of masterminding the coup of July 2015 and demanded his extradition.

Francis J. Ricciardone is a career foreign service officer who was US ambassador to Turkey from 2011 to 2014.

Fuat Avni is a prominent social-media activist, blogger, and whistleblower.

George H. W. Bush served as the forty-first president of the United States from 1989 to 1993. Prior to that, he served as the vice president of the United States from 1981 to 1989 and as director of the Central Intelligence Agency.

George W. Bush is the eldest son of President George H. W. Bush who was US president from 2001 to 2009. He served as the governor of Texas between 1995 and 2000.

Gilad Shalit is one of the three Israeli soldiers held hostage in Gaza. He was held for more than five years.

Hafez al-Assad served as the president of Syria from 1971 to 2000.

Hakan Fidan is the head of Turkey's National Intelligence Organization (MIT).

Hayrunnisa Gul is Abdullah Gul's wife.

Heider al-Abadi has been the prime minister of Iraq since 2014. Upon returning to Iraq from exile in 2003, he became the minister of communications and served as a member of Parliament representing the Dawa Party beginning in 2006.

Hillary Rodham Clinton was US secretary of state from 2009 to 2013, US senator from New York from 2001 to 2009, and first lady of the United States from 1993 to 2001.

Hilmi Ozkok was the twenty-fourth chief of the general staff of the Turkish Armed Forces, serving from 2002 to 2006.

Ibrahim Kalin is the press secretary, spokesman, and confidant of Recep Tayyip Erdogan.

Ihsan Hoca was Recep Tayyip Erdogan's mentor and elementary school teacher. He convinced Erdogan's father to allow him to attend Prayer Leader and Preacher School.

Ilker Basbug was the twenty-sixth chief of the general staff in the Republic of Turkey. He was charged during the Ergenekon trials, but released in 2014 when his conviction was overturned.

Ismail Kahraman is speaker of the Turkish Grand National Assembly since November 2015, and a close ally of Erdogan.

Jan Boehmermann is a German satirist and comedian. The German prosecutor brought charges against him for publicly reading a defamatory poem about Erdogan.

Javad Zarif is Iran's minister of foreign affairs.

John Allen is a four-star general who served as US coordinator for the anti-ISIS coalition.

John Bass is currently the US ambassador to Turkey.

John Kerry is a former US senator and Democratic presidential candidate who served as US secretary of state from 2013 to 2017.

John Kirby is a former rear admiral in the US Navy who currently serves as the US state department spokesman.

John McCain is the senior US senator from Arizona and was the Republican presidential nominee for the 2008 United States presidential election.

John O. Brennan is currently director of the US Central Intelligence Agency.

Joseph P. Biden was vice president of the United States from 2009 to 2017.

Kemal Kilicdaroglu is the main opposition leader in Turkey who served as chairman of the Republican People's Party (CHP) from 2010 to the present.

Kenan Evren was the seventh president of Turkey, serving from 1980 to 1989. He led the 1980 military coup in Turkey.

Leyla Zana is a Kurdish politician who spent ten years in Ankara's maximum-security prison for saying her parliamentary oath of office in Kurdish.

Lloyd Austin is a four-star general who heads the US Central Command (CENTCOM).

Mahmoud Ahmadinejad was the sixth president of the Islamic Republic of Iran, serving from 2005 to 2013.

Mahmut Kar is the Hizb-ut Tahrir (Liberation Party) Turkish media bureau president.

Marc Grossman is a former US ambassador to Turkey who also served as undersecretary of state for political affairs.

Masoud Barzani is the president of Iraqi Kurdistan.

Mehmet Ali Birand was a respected Turkish journalist, political commentator, and writer.

Mehmet Cavusoglu is the Turkish foreign minister.

Moammar Qhaddafi was leader of Libya, overthrown in 2012.

Mohammed Morsi is a Muslim Brotherhood leader who was the president of Egypt from June 2012 to July 2013.

Moncef Marzouki was the president of Tunisia from 2011 to 2014

Muhammad Hosni El Sayed Mubarak is a former Egyptian military leader who became the president of Egypt, serving from1981 to 2011.

Murat Karayilan is a Kurdistan Workers' Party (PKK) commander and co-founder.

Mustafa Akinci is the current president of the "Turkish Republic of Northern Cyprus".

Mustafa Kemal Ataturk led the Turkish war of independence and founded the Republic of Turkey in 1923. He was the first president of Turkey and founder of the Republican People's Party (CHP).

Necmettin Erbakan founded the Felicity Party in 2001. He served as prime minister for six months before being removed from office by the military.

Nicos Anastasiodrs is a founding member of the Youth of the Democratic Rally (NEDISY) and a member of the Cyprus National Council since 1995. He is the current president of the Republic of Cyprus, elected in 2013.

Nuri al-Maliki served as the prime minister of Iraq from 2006 to 2014.

Orhan Pamuk is a Turkish academic, screenwriter, and novelist who received the Nobel Prize in Literature in 2009.

Osman Baydemir is the former Peoples' Democratic Party (HDP) member of Parliament and long-serving mayor of Diyarbakir.

Paul D. Wolfowitz was president of the World Bank from 2005 to 2007. He served as the US undersecretary of defense from 2001 to 2005, in the administration of George W. Bush.

Preet Bharara is the US attorney for the Southern District of New York nominated by President Obama in 2009.

Qasim Suleimani heads the Iranian Revolutionary Guard's Quds force. He directs Iraqi Shiite militias called Popular Mobilization Forces.

Rashid al-Ganouchi is a respected Muslim scholar who was in exile in London between 1989 and 2011 before heading Tunisia's Ennahda movement.

Recep Tayyip Erdogan served as prime minister of Turkey from 2003 to 2014 and as president from 2014 to the present. He is the twelfth president of the Turkish Republic.

Reza Zarrab is a dual Iranian-Turkish national who has been charged with gold smuggling and violating US sanctions on Iran.

Richard Meyers is a four-star general who was the fifteenth chairman of the US joint chiefs of staff.

Richard Perle was assistant secretary of defense during the administration of President George H. W. Bush.

Robert Gates served as the US secretary of defense from 2006 to 2011.

Robert Kocharian was prime minister of Armenia from 1997 to 1998 who served as president of Armenia until 2008. Formerly, he was the president of Nagorno-Karabakh from 1994 to 1997.

Robert S. Ford is a former US special envoy to Syria. He has served as the US ambassador to Algeria from 2006 to 2008 and to Syria from 2010 to 2014.

Sakip Sabanci is a prominent Turkish philanthropist and businessman. His charity, "Vaska", supports over a hundred health, education, and cultural centers across Turkey.

Salih Muslim is a co-chair of the Democratic Union Party (PYD) in Syria.

Selahattin Demirtas is the co-chair of Peoples' Democratic Party (HDP), which gained more than 13 percent of the vote on June 7, 2015 elections. His parliamentary immunity was lifted in May 20, 2016, and he was arrested.

Sergey Lavrov is the foreign minister of Russia since 2004. From 1994 to 2004, he served as the permanent representative of Russia to the United Nations.

Sergh Sarkissian is the third president of Armenia who participated in normalization efforts between Armenia and Turkey.

Sheikh Said Pirran was a Zaza sheikh of the Sunni order who led the Sheikh Said Rebellion in 1925.

Shimon Perez was the president of Israel from 2007 to 2016.

Sirri Sureyya Onder is a member of the Turkish Parliament from the Peoples' Democratic Party (HDP). He was a negotiator in the peace talks between the Turkish state and Ocalan.

Sivan Perver is a famous Kurdish singer from Sanliurfa who lived in exile for thirty-seven years.

Stefan Fuele is a Czech diplomat who served as the European Union commissioner for enlargement between 2010 and 2014.

Suleyman Aslan is the former CEO of the state-owned Halkbank. He was accused of bribery, corruption, fraud, and money laundering in the 2013 corruption scandal.

Suleyman Soylu is the deputy chairman of the AKP. He is the minister of labor and social security since 2015.

Sultan Mehmet II was an Ottoman sultan. At the age of twenty one, he conquered Constantinople.

Tansu Ciller served as prime minister of Turkey from 1993 to 1996.

Tenzile Erdogan is the mother of President Recep Tayyip Erdogan.

Turgut Ozal was the founder of Motherland Party (ANAP). He served as the prime minister from 1983 to 1989 and became the eighth president of Turkey in 1989. His term ended with his death in 1993.

Umit Dundar is Turkey's first army commander, who was temporarily appointed chief of staff of the Turkish Armed Forces to replace Hulusi Akar upon the coup attempt in 2016.

Vitaly Churkin is Russia's permanent representative to the United Nations.

Vladimir Putin served as president of the Russian Federation between 2000 and 2008. He served as prime minister from 2008 to 2012 before being re-elected president.

Volkan Bozkir is Turkey's European Union minister.

Walid Muallem is a member of Syria's Ba'ath Party serving as foreign minister since 2006.

Yalcin Akdogan served as the deputy prime minister in Turkey from 2014 and 2016. He was a close ally to Erdogan and member of the AKP inner circle before being pushed out of power.

Yasar Buyukanit is the twenty-fifth chief of the Turkish general staff of the Turkish Armed Forces. In April 2007, he posted an "e-memorandum" referred to as an "e-coup."

Zalmay Zhalilzad is a former American diplomat. Under George W. Bush, he served as US ambassador to Iraq, Afghanistan, and as permanent representative to the United Nations.

Zeid Raad al-Hussein has served as the UN high commissioner for human rights since 2014.

Zbigniew Brzezinski served as US President Carter's national security adviser from 1977 to 1981.

Zine al-Abidine Ben Ali is the former president of Tunisia who served from 1989 to 2011, when he was forced to step down amid street protests.

About the Author

 David L. Phillips is currently director of the Program on Peace-Building and Rights at Columbia University's Institute for the Study of Human Rights. Phillips has served as foreign affairs expert and as senior adviser to the US Department of State during the administrations of Presidents Clinton, Bush, and Obama. He was also senior adviser to the United Nations Office for the Coordination of Humanitarian Affairs. Phillips has worked at academic institutions as executive director of Columbia University's International Conflict Resolution Program, director of American University's Program on Conflict Prevention and Peace-building, fellow at Harvard University's Future of Diplomacy Project, visiting scholar at Harvard University's Center for Middle East Studies, and professor of Preventive Diplomacy at the Diplomatic Academy of Vienna. He held senior positions at think tanks, such as deputy director of the Center for Preventive Action at the Council on Foreign Relations, senior fellow at the Preventive Diplomacy Program of the Center for Strategic and International Studies, senior fellow at the Atlantic Council, and project director at the International Peace Research Institute of Oslo. Phillips has also been a foundation executive, serving as president of the Congressional Human Rights Foundation and executive director of the Elie Wiesel Foundation for Humanity. Phillips has worked in media as an analyst and commentator for NBC News, CNBC, and the British Broadcasting Company. He is author of *The Kurdish Spring: A New Map for the Middle East* (Transaction Publishers); *Liberating Kosovo: Coercive Diplomacy and U.S. Intervention*; *From Bullets to Ballots: Violent Muslim Movements in Transition* (Transaction Publishers); *Losing Iraq: Inside the Post-War Reconstruction Fiasco*; and

Unsilencing the Past: Track Two Diplomacy and Turkish-Armenian Reconciliation. Phillips has authored dozens of policy reports and hundreds of articles in leading publications such as the *New York Times, Wall Street Journal, Financial Times, International Herald Tribune,* and *Foreign Affairs.*

Index